National Policies for Developing
High Technology Industries

D0162329

About the Book and Editors

Over the past three decades there has been a growing interest in policies designed to stimulate growth and development through the development of high technology industries. Often these industrial policies encourage development of the high technology informatics industry. Technological advances and the expansion of productive capabilities are viewed as a driving force in national economic strategies for increasingly larger stakes in a highly competitive and interconnected global market.

The authors of this volume look at the informatics industry in eight countries, Brazil, France, India, Japan, Korea, Mexico, Taiwan, and the U.S., as models for examining the role of governments in promoting advanced technology. The extent to which national policies succeed or fail in the implementation of general agendas for new industrial programs is seen in the widely varying approaches found in these countries. The authors consider the appropriate supporting infrastructure and long-range policy analysis and evaluation necessary for fostering competitive industry.

Francis W. Rushing is Chairman of the Department of Economics and Director of the International Center for Entrepreneurship, Georgia State University, and Senior Economic Consultant, Science Policy Program, International Policy Center, SRI International. Carole Ganz Brown is Senior Program Manager for Studies and Assessments at the Division of International Programs, National Science Foundation.

National Policies for Developing High Technology Industries

International Comparisons

**edited by Francis W. Rushing
and Carole Ganz Brown**

Westview Press / Boulder and London

Westview Special Studies in Science, Technology, and Public Policy

----

This Westview softcover edition was manufactured on our own premises using
equipment and methods that allow us to keep even specialized books in stock.
It is printed on acid-free paper and bound in softcovers that carry the
highest rating of the National Association of State Textbook Administrators,
in consultation with the Association of American Publishers and the Book
Manufacturers' Institute.

Published in 1986 in the United States of America by Westview Press, Inc.;
Frederick A. Praeger, Publisher; 5500 Central Avenue, Boulder, Colorado 80301

Library of Congress Catalog Card Number: 86-50530
ISBN: 0-8133-7280-1

Composition for this book was provided by the editors.
This book was produced without formal editing by the publisher.

Printed and bound in the United States of America

 The paper used in this publication meets the minimum requirements of
the American National Standard for Permanence of Paper for Printed
Library Materials Z39.48-1984.

10 9 8 7 6 5 4 3 2

Contents

Acknowledgments

The project from which this book has emerged was funded by grants from the International Division of the National Science Foundation and the U. S. Section, Brazil–U.S. Business Council. The Editors extend a special thanks to these organizations. However, the cases and the findings of the book are solely the responsibility of the authors and should not be attributed to the project sponsors.

The editors would like to express their appreciation to Keith Miceli and Sandi Beretta of the U. S. Section, Brazil–U.S. Business Council and to Catherine P. Ailes of SRI International who have provided helpful suggestions and support at all stages of this project. Betty R. Hutchins, Marilyn H. King, Marian M. Mealing and Mark W. Rider of Georgia State University have diligently and professionally prepared this manuscript for publication. We are indebted to each of them.

Kellie Masterson of Westview Press has assisted us in innumerable ways to ensure timely publication of this book. Finally, we would like to express our appreciation to the authors, whose scholarship and cooperation have made each stage of the project not only productive but also enjoyable.

Francis W. Rushing
Carole Ganz Brown

Foreword

International trade has grown dramatically since World War II as the world economy has become more integrated and interdependent. In this period, the United States has led the call for a reduction in trade barriers erected during the 1930's. While the General Agreement on Tariffs and Trade has provided a framework for negotiating the reduction of barriers, it has not accomplished their elimination. Nontariff barriers have emerged over the last two decades as the not-so-visible but ever-present obstructions to flows of goods and investments. These barriers, like tariffs and quotas, reflect attempts by governments to achieve their goals by tilting the outcomes of economic interaction toward their national interests.

The U.S. Section of the Brazil-U.S. Business Council cosponsored with the National Science Foundation the investigation of national policies for the development of the informatics industry in eight countries. Each case is different, and yet patterns emerge which recommend or discourage some of the policy options. The objectives of this project were to enhance the understanding of the role of governments in economic development and international trade, to identify costs and benefits to the domestic and world economy of national policies, and to provide a basis for developing trade policies for the United States. The publishing of National Policies for Developing High Technology Industries: International Comparisons is the culmination of the project and shares with policy makers, academics and business persons the findings of this distinguished group of scholars.

> Paul F. Oreffice
> Chairman, U.S. Section
> Brazil-U.S. Business Council
> and
> President and Chief Executive
> Officer
> The Dow Chemical Company

Foreword

High-technology has become so important worldwide that all nations seek to understand its benefits and to formulate policies to achieve them. All nations also fall short of possessing the policies required either to provide the most favorable environment for private sector initiatives to advance technology or for a thoroughly effective government role.

This volume makes an important contribution to this worldwide need to identify the goals, priorities, and strategies of nations when technological advance is at stake. For the United States, the results of this project come at a particularly opportune time as the benefits of technical advance—international competitiveness, productivity, national security—are high on the country's agenda. Comparisons between U.S. technology policies and those of other nations are helpful for several reasons.

In the United States, a great deal of what happens on the technology front is dependent on U.S. government decisions and practices as well as private sector activities. Government support for research, defense procurement, curbing of monopolies, patents and numerous other conditions set "industrial policy" in the United States. In particular, foreign experiences in government-industry teaming are playing a significant role in changing U.S. antitrust legislation which generally banned joint efforts among American companies.

Comparisons with other countries are also helping to identify critical deficiencies in U.S. national policy. On the educational front, statistics show that for every thousand college graduates America turns out, only seven are engineers. For Japan, the figure is forty. This kind of comparison is now a major force in current debate about the need to strengthen the U.S. research system.

A third consideration is that in the future a majority of technology advances will happen outside the United States. This country can clearly learn from others about how government policy can appropriately balance national innovation performance and acquisition of technology abroad.

These examples--and many others could be cited--
illustrate the ways the technology policies of other
countries can enrich U.S. strategies. In this competitive
world, it becomes imperative that attention be paid to
international developments.

For U.S. technology policy to be formulated in an international context, better understanding and more comprehensive information about the technology policies of other
countries becomes essential. In making a significant
contribution to this knowledge-base, this volume deserves
high-priority attention from leaders in government, science,
engineering and industry in the United States and worldwide.

Bodo Bartocha
Director
Division of International Programs
National Science Foundation

1

Introduction: Past Successes, Present Directions, and Future Issues

Carole Ganz Brown
National Science Foundation

Francis W. Rushing
Georgia State University and SRI International

PROLOGUE

Over the past three decades, there has been a growing interest in the nature and scope of government policies to stimulate growth and development through more rapid technological advances and expansion of productive capabilities for both domestic and foreign markets. An early major study in this arena--Technology, Economic Growth, and Public Policy,[1] written by R. R. Nelson, M. J. Peck, and E. D. Kalachek--focused on U.S. governmental policies to influence technological advance and economic growth; the book was published about two decades ago to address the concerns of public policy makers and scholars about these issues. More recently, the policies and programs of the United States and other major industrial nations supporting technological advancement in different industries have been studied by these scholars as well as others. Roy Rothwell and Walter Zegveld provide an excellent critical review of this literature in Reindustrialization and Technology.[2]

Today, interest in government policies supporting technological advance is worldwide and an important part of the current discussion is concerned with "high-technology" industries. In countries throughout the world, technological change in these industries is seen as a driving force in economic development and growth. Government policy is prescribed to explicitly facilitate the progress of these industries.

The stakes are no longer purely economic and domestic and certainly not small. Debate over the viability and desirability of a national industrial policy is often

politically and socially charged. High-technology
industries are seen as providing the cutting edge for
competitiveness and trade performance in the international
arena. These industries require global markets to recover
costs and create efficiencies, while manufacturing
production is increasingly transnational. Yet economic and
industrial relationships that are global in character
sometimes conflict with national policies which seek to
diminish dependency on other countries.

THE PROJECT

     Responding to the changing environment for developing
technology policies, the U.S. Section of the Brazil-U.S.
Trade Council, as part of its overall efforts to advance
U.S.-Brazil economic and industrial relations, initiated a
project to study the roles government can effectively play
in furthering high-technology industries.   The National
Science Foundation's Division of International Programs,
which has a long-standing interest in international
comparisons of science and technology policies, was a
co-sponsor. The project had two major components: (1) the
commissioning of eight case studies to serve as the basis
for drawing international comparisons and (2) the holding of
a two-day symposium for U.S. and foreign government,
industry, and academic representatives to discuss the
findings of the case studies and to draw international
comparisons.
     This volume includes a general overview framework for
analysis of the issues, the findings of the case studies,
and the major ideas presented at the symposium. The
objective of this publication is to contribute to the
ongoing debate about the roles governments have played and
can play in designing and implementing high technology
policies and provide some assessment of the various levels
of "success" various strategies have achieved. The authors
examine developments in a single high-technology
industry--informatics--and focus specifically on the
government policies of eight diverse countries--Brazil,
France, India, Japan, Korea, Mexico, Taiwan, and the United
States. For the purpose of these studies, the informatics
industry was interpreted to mean semiconductors, integrated
circuits, and computers, including mainframes, minis, and
micros, and word processors, and was chosen not only as an
illustration but because it merits a great deal of attention
in its own right.

As a point of departure for the inquiries, three
questions were posed: What do economic and technological
indicators show about the development of the informatics
industry in these countries? How have government policies
been designed to further the informatics industry? What
types of government programs and policies have been successful, and what types have been failures, and why? Not unex-
pectedly, countries varied widely with respect to the
availability of data, the scope and clarity of their policies, and the depth of experience and understanding of the
factors influencing policy effectiveness. The diversity of
focus and approach of the papers in this volume reflect
these differences. The comparisons and conclusions of the
overview paper illuminate many of the complexities underlying current worldwide debate over these government policies.

The symposium, National Policies for Developing High
Technology Industries: International Comparisons was
held 12-13 September 1985 at SRI International in
Washington, D.C. (The agenda and participants are included
in this volume in Appendixes A and B.) From the
presentations and discussions at the symposium some of the
major ideas have been compiled. They are presented here not
as summaries of the findings of the individual papers but
rather as reflections on all the cases and what, in
aggregate, has been learned from this project.

The major ideas discussed at the symposium can be
briefly summarized as follows:

1.   A strong case was made at the symposium that
government policies have played a critical role in the
development of national informatics industries both in
success stories (Japan and Taiwan), and in the less
successful case of France, which failed to establish a
strong national industry. In all the cases, promotion of
the industry by the government was by design and supported
with resources. Important differences of opinion emerged
about whether the United States was an exception to this
generalization. What was clear, however, was that with the
exception of Japan, national policies had been shaped by the
dual objectives of promoting national security and
industrial development.

2.   In contrasting the country studies, it became clear
that the policies and institutions used to successfully
advance the development of high-technology industries were
extremely diverse. There was agreement, however, that a
strong national informatics industry, whether, for example,
developed strictly indigenously or with foreign technology,

requires a cadre of science and engineering manpower. National policies must take into consideration how this infrastructure requirement of high-technology industries is to be met.

3. Competition, internal or with foreign firms, was also seen as critical to the development of strong high-technology industries. Competition was seen as promoting both technological advancement and production efficiency. Therefore, government policies need to be designed to take advantage of these benefits of competition.

4. Several important differences and similarities among national policies were then identified. Some of the government industrial development strategies were considered "forward building." That is, these policies had focused on existing capabilities in, say, consumer electronics, and had built forward into semiconductors, and subsequently, the range of informatics products. The Japanese government efforts were one example. Another strategy, "backward building," began with incentives for computer production and worked backward through semiconductor suppliers toward producers of advanced integrated circuit technology. Brazil and India, some participants thought, were emerging as examples of this approach. A third strategy, uniquely French, was the efforts of that government to establish national champion companies for computers and for semiconductors.

5. Protective policies of large domestic markets have been successful for some countries, notably Japan. But a focus on export markets also contributed to the development potential of that country. It was suggested that achieving appropriate scale of production and its associated efficiencies are needed to penetrate international markets. (This was the intent of the Japanese policies.) Others thought product quality was an equally important consideration. In all cases protection alone would not have been sufficient to meet international competitive standards.

6. There was general agreement that one proven strategy for public policy was to target an international market niche and develop policies to capture it. It was pointed out that countries--Japan, Taiwan, India--differing widely in size and capabilities have had success with this strategy.

7. Import barriers to foreign technology have always been controversial aspects of national policies to advance industrial development. Symposium participants pointed out that this is not likely to change in today's world. The independence from technological world leaders sought by some

countries had meant high opportunity costs in terms of the
level and rate of technical advance achieved by these
countries. Experience shows that competitiveness in world
markets suffers without acquisition of some foreign
technology to strengthen national industries at critical
stages in their development and to achieve manpower
training and production efficiency advantages.

8.   What is critical to the formulation of effective
national policies is analysis of the benefits and costs of
import barriers (and other strategies) in a broader
perspective than, say, hard currency saved from the purchase
of foreign technology or domestic jobs created. It was
recommended that policy analysis and evaluation should be
broad-gauged enough to consider such factors as reduced
competitiveness in world markets and lost efficiencies in
all domestic industries.

9.   Clearly, however, "rational" policy analysis has
not always ruled. For example, national pride, as an
important non-quantifiable variable, can enter into the
process of developing government policies. Here, even when
economic costs exceed economic benefits, potentially harmful
policies may be implemented.

10.   Strategies to develop a strong national science and
engineering workforce, incentives to encourage domestic
competition, and use of broad-gauged analysis to develop
national policies surfaced as some common elements of
effective government action to advance national capabilities
in high-technology industries.

11.   Symposium participants further observed that more
traditional national policies with reliance on government
subsidization of domestic industry and market reserved to
these companies were less likely to work in the future.
Past national success stories, such as that of Japan, relied
heavily on the willingness of the United States to leave
major markets open to foreign competitors while accepting
restrictions imposed by other nations on U.S. participation
in their domestic markets. This is less likely to happen in
the future especially in light of the increasing tendency of
U.S. high-technology companies to request action against
foreign firms when "unfair" practices are sighted. It was
also noted that U.S. willingness to consider trade
restraints to offset foreign government industrial subsidies
and other non-tariff barriers discussed under GATT, has
already destabilized the world trading order. Questions
were already being raised in several countries about the
viability of subsidized or protected markets as government
strategies in view of more aggressive U.S. economic
behavior.

12.   Participants predicted increasing conflict between
countries in the future if trade barriers, both tariff and
nontariff, are not controlled or modified. It was pointed
out that some countries had already changed their
approaches. Japan is opening up its markets to some extent.
India and Mexico are liberalizing constrictive technology
import policies. On the other hand, Brazil has become more
restrictive.

13.   The discussants agreed that the demonstrated benefits to all parties from transfers of technology and the
growing cost-sharing advantages of international joint-
ventures are also likely to undermine national efforts which
rely on direct subsidy and market reserve policies.

Finally, the symposium participants discussed the
importance of each nation's attempting to understand the
circumstances and objectives of the national policies of
other nations. All trading parties should seek ways of
reducing areas of conflict by proposing alternative paths to
the same objectives, while exhibiting patience as the
domestic environment gradually changes or alternative policies are being designed and implemented. Each country,
however, will have to adhere to the premise that international economic interaction can work toward the mutual
benefit of all parties. Confrontation, they said, and
direct action by countries to open up the markets of other
nations could make political acceptance of change in
national policies more difficult, and could, in the longer-
run, raise the level of conflict and thereby threaten loss
of, or failure to capture, the economic benefits each party
seeks. Efforts toward cooperation seem a rational course
for each nation to pursue its own interests and those of the
world economy. The conference ended on this theme.

EPILOGUE

The important policy issues raised by the papers in this
volume and discussed at the symposium appear to be major
forces that are going to be around for a long time.
Observations made at other recent policy forums tend to con-
firm that a protracted period of tensions--between technological self-sufficiency and interdependence, between
nationalism and global development of technology, between
strategies seeking political acceptance and strategies
emphasizing economic realities--can be expected.

A February 1986 U.S. National Academy of Engineering
symposium--World Technologies and National Sovereignty--

emphasized the conflicts resulting from today's high level
of international technological interdependence and the
diverse political concerns of nations trading in world
markets.

Arranged by the Center for Science and Technology Policy
of New York University, a two-day international
conference—Technical Cooperation and International
Competitiveness—was held near Pisa, Italy on April 2-4, 1986
to discuss the boundaries of international technical
cooperation under today's conditions of worldwide competition. Most recently, the 1986 National Science
Foundation Conference on Industrial Science and
Technological Innovation took as a major theme the tensions
between cooperation and competition in the global economy.

Current trends in the United States and other industrial
countries also portend a future in which advancing national
policies that are effective and not conflictive will continue to be difficult. For instance, in the United States
heated debate is going on about the problems concerning U.S.
collaboration in high-technology with other countries.
Harvard University's Robert Reich recently observed that
Boeing is giving away its aerospace technology in a proposed
joint venture with Japan; and he advised that these sorts of
joint ventures should be barred.[3]

In April of 1986, the Reagan administration announced
plans to intensify pressure on U.S. trading partners to protect American copyrights, patents and trademarks. Among
other things, the special tariff preferences now given to
developing countries would be limited, in cases where these
governments do not take steps to safeguard U.S. intellectual
property.

There are also signs that U.S. corporations and those of
Japan and Europe may be rethinking their global corporate
strategy. Kenichi Ohmae, the managing director of McKinsy &
Company's Tokyo office, recently concluded that multinational corporations are increasingly retreating from developing regions in response to barriers such as tariffs,
local content laws and ownership requirements on foreign
companies. The new global enterprise will be involved in
fewer countries, he concludes.[4]

Other forces are emerging which have the potential to
positively affect the future of national policies in technology and economics. Some of the major ones are:

a) New foundations will emerge for high-technology
leadership primarily through the important changes now going
on in how to view competitiveness. Traditionally, competitiveness was seen to depend primarily on effective marketing
strategies. But this has been changing dramatically as a

result of recent major technological advances in manufacturing. Consequently, competitiveness in production technologies will gain as an essential basis for high-technology advantage.

   b. New players will have to be considered in the international game. The most interesting is the People's Republic of China with its intensive programs of rehabilitation of university professors and industrial engineers. The PRC has instituted programs in large industrial plants and small enterprises in which profit motivation plays an important role. This country will probably gain rapidly in technological capabilities and competitiveness in the next decade.

   c. New approaches to estimating the benefits of national policies will be adopted in response to the accelerating worldwide diffusion, transfer, and adoption of technologies. These approaches will recognize the global nature of technological change. The effects of these changes will no longer be independent of one another and certainly not locally restricted in their impacts.

   The dissemination of this volume will extend the discussion of the issues surrounding the formulation of national policies to a broader constituency, and the time is right to rethink the whole process of formulating national policies. Certainly countries will continue to choose policies that have been tried by other countries and have shown promise. But the future needs more attention in the policy-setting process. In today's environment, what is needed is a strong shift in emphasis from the successes of the past to the realities of the future.

NOTES

   1. R. R. Nelson, M. J. Peck, and E. D. Kalachek, Technology, Economic Growth, and Public Policy, The Brookings Institution, Washington, D.C., 1967.
   2. Roy Rothwell and Walter Zegveld, Reindustrialization and Technology, Longman Group, Ltd., Essex, U.K., 1985.
   3. New York Times, April 6, 1986.
   4. The Wall Street Journal, April 29, 1985.

2

National Policies
for High Technology Development
and Trade: An International
and Comparative Assessment

Henry Nau
George Washington University

Technology is the new "holy grail" of international economic competition. Countries of all economic sizes and political stripe are seeking to obtain, develop and exploit it. It is seen as the essential life blood of the modern state and world economic prowess.

What is the underlying policy rationale for this widespread interest in technology? Is this interest justi-fied? If so, what will be the consequences for inter-national economic relations? Is trade based on the new requirements of technological achievement, particularly in a few key sectors such as information and communication tech-nologies, a game of mutual benefits or a zero-sum game? Finally how does a nation succeed in this game? What are the different experiences and performances of individual countries, developed and developing, that have sought to harness technological change to national economic growth and competitiveness? What policy instruments have been most frequently used with what results?

This introductory paper and the case studies that follow address these questions of rationale, international consequences and national performance in the development and trade of high technology products, and focus specifically on information and communications technology. The introductory paper is deliberately critical of recent policies for tech-nology targeting and industrial policy in both developed and developing countries. This criticism does not overlook the enormous political appeal of these policies in a world eco-nomy beset by growing competition and government interven-tion. Nor does it overlook the evidence in the case studies that these policies have in some cases markedly influenced a country's ability to compete in world markets. Nevertheless, it seeks to set a high standard for these policies in

economic and practical terms, peeling away some of the
mythology that has been invested by national governments in
high technology development and trade. It raises a set of
broader considerations to evaluate and compare the very different experiences of Japan, France, Brazil, Taiwan, India,
South Korea and Mexico.

The information sector -- computers, semiconductors,
telecommunications and software -- is regarded by many analysts as the epitome of new high technology development.
This is true not only because developments in this sector
are on the edge of the technological frontier (lasers, new
materials, etc.) but also because communications and information services are essential to the modern economy and may
even exceed the importance of materials such as energy.
Every facet of a modern economy, not to mention essential
elements of political and social systems, depends on the
ability to communicate and to access, process and distill
the information in whatever form -- voice, data, video --
that is to be communicated. The information sector therefore may be a crucial test case of the role of high
technology in modern society and a nation's capacity to command that role.

Rationale for High Technology Development

The underlying economic rationale for high technology
development by the nation-state conceals two premises:
1) that high technology development produces economic advantages across a broad front going well beyond the specific
high technology sector in question; and 2) that these advantages can be captured by the nation-state, that is they are
divisible and appropriable in the language of collective
goods theory.[1]

The first premise enjoys increasingly solid support in
economic theory, even though the contribution of technology
to growth is still most often measured in terms of inputs or
residues, neither of which captures directly or precisely
the impact of technology. Traditional theories of comparative advantage have been modified to take into account
the increasing importance of technology. Ricardian and
Heckscher-Ohlin theories based comparative advantage on
slowly changing and relatively immobile (that is, among
nations) factor endowments such as land, labor and capital.
Technology, by contrast, was assumed to be unchanging and
perfectly mobile across national boundaries. All countries
had the same access to information and knowledge for

producing similar products. Nations achieved relative
advantage by concentrating production in those products that
employed the more abundant factors they possessed, while
importing products using scarce factors. Factor endowments
could change, for example, through conquest or population
growth, but government policies, other than warfare, were
not perceived as central to bringing about these changes.
Moreover, the relative immobility of factors such as land
and labor meant that trade might lead to a narrowing of product prices but not prices of factors, such as wage rates.
In some sense, comparative advantage was semi-permanent and
did not require constant national or governmental
attention.

The growing role of government in national economic
life changed all that. The late developers of the nineteenth century -- Germany, Italy, and Japan -- recognized
the important contribution national policies could make to
upgrade human (education) and physical (transportation,
communications, agriculture) capital endowments. Still
these governmental influences were long term, and the benefits were largely localized (and hence appropriable), as
growing nationalism at the turn of the century set new constraints on international labor and capital flows.

The critical role of technology in comparative advantage and of governments in promoting specific commercial
technologies was recognized only after World War II.
Leontieff's paradox revealed the importance of skill and not
simply the size of the labor force in comparative advantage.
The reconstruction of Europe and Japan, which could take for
granted the availability of human capital, paid more attention to technical assistance, enhancing productivity, and
quality control techniques. As a so-called start from
scratch, it also permitted more conscious national planning
and direction of industrial and technological development,
best reflected initially in France and subsequently in
Japan.

The liberalization of trade barriers further high-
lighted the important role of government domestic and especially technology policies in international trade competition. Today, these policies are viewed as critical not
only in their long term impact on human and physical
endowments but also in day-to-day choices concerning product
and industrial development. As Michael Borrus and John
Zysman argue in their study of Japan, "national comparative
advantage...can be created by national policy measures."[2]
Comparative advantage is, in short, available for the
asking. It is no longer the prisoner of relatively fixed
factor endowments.

Role of Government

It is little wonder then that nations worship the holy grail of technology. But is the new theology justified? Or is it misleading? The case studies of the information technology sector suggest a number of questions that might be raised about the wisdom or even possibility of governments selecting areas of comparative advantage arbitrarily apart from the context of more traditional factors affecting competition.

On what basis are these judgments made? The case studies reveal two somewhat different approaches. Brazil, India and at times France oriented their development efforts in informatics toward substitution for imports. Faced with increasing imports and strong foreign competitors in the domestic market, they established barriers to further imports and created national companies to design and produce wholly indigenous systems. The objective was to create a comparative advantage based on "national technology... defined in terms of the ability to produce independently of the technology acquired abroad." Development began with the design and assembly of whole systems; eventually, it sought to integrate backwards to more and more indigenously produced components and software. At the outset, considerable emphasis was given to local research and development (R&D) activities (as compared to imported technologies) and hardware production, relatively less to user requirements and software.[3] The approach emphasized sectoral policy factors and instruments, including specialized administrative mechanisms (such as SEI in Brazil), rather than broader cross-sectoral considerations, such as the competitiveness of user industries or the enhancement of overall market competition through regulation.

By contrast, Taiwan, South Korea and Japan pursued development strategies based more on existing indigenous production capabilities, especially in consumer electronics and semiconductors, and on domestic user requirements and export opportunities. Less emphasis was given to indigenous design and whole systems assembly. Taiwan, for example, produced and exported low cost components and computer peripherals such as monitors, building on its production capability in television sets. All three countries encouraged the import and adaptation of foreign technologies and tolerated a somewhat larger role for foreign multinationals than Brazil or India. As opposed to narrow sector policies, they stressed macroeconomic policies to restructure industries away from declining sectors such as light manufactures toward higher value added sectors such as informatics. Japan epitomized the use of market promotion policies to encourage yet control domestic competition and ensure early competitiveness in exports.

In both the import substitution and the domestic/export market approaches, the role of government is substantial. In that sense, the new theology correctly identifies government as a key actor. But the two approaches differ in the standards they apply to government choices. The import substitution approach assumes that governments face few restrictions in choosing the sectors in which they seek to compete. They can do so, for all practical purposes, independently of their existing or foreseeable factor advantages. Indeed they select sectors for technological development precisely because they possess few capabilities in that sector. They start with an import demand which, as Amar Gupta points out in his case study of India, may reflect foreign marketing strategies and techniques more so than indigenous user requirements, and seek to build backwards from this import demand to a comprehensive domestic production and technological capability. The link to traditional factors of comparative advantage, such as market size and local production and technological skills, comes only very late if at all.[4] As a consequence, in the case of Brazil and India, the limited economic size of the internal market and the licensing of numerous new companies to manufacture computers, rather than building on a smaller number of well-established producers, constitute major obstacles to efficient development in the informatics sector.

The domestic/export market approach follows much more closely the traditional logic of comparative advantage. Sectors, such as informatics, are selected for protection and accelerated development only after an indigenous competitive capability exists in relatively simple consumer electronic products and electronic componentry. The link to user needs, which reflect the country's broader comparative advantage, is more immediate. According to Simon and Schive, a principal motivation for the Taiwanese effort in informatics was to cut costs and increase productivity in manufacturing facilities and office management throughout existing industry in Taiwan. Similarly, awareness of market structure and assessment of both domestic and export market requirements were prominent features of Japan's informatics development. When the Japanese company NEC developed a digital switch primarily for export, it failed because this switch had not been designed, tested, and debugged in the more proximate domestic market.

Thus, high technology development does promise benefits across a broad front, and governments play an important role in this development. But it is not clear that governments are free of traditional factors of comparative advantage in making their choices. It is probably too strong to say that they can create comparative advantage. As Borrus and Zysman point out, they can "influence the accumulation of physical capital, the pace of research and development, and the development of labor skills and education, all of which underlie the factor 'endowments' and production technologies dear to classical theory" (emphasis added). And, over the long run, they "can steadily turn a competitive advantage in capital, education or research intensive industries into a national comparative advantage."[5] But the key words here are influence and long term and, one should probably add, some-times. Governments are still bound by the laws of scarce resources and relative factor endowments -- which is another way of saying they are bound by markets. The issue, however, is not government versus markets, as it is often posed, but governments, as well as private groups, operating on market versus open ended or arbitrary criteria for making technological and industrial decisions. Governments can influence but not deny market forces. In some cases, regardless of the effort they expend, they cannot convert any or every competitive (or absolute) advantage into a comparative one. That, after all, is what comparative advantage is all about; it holds even when one country has an absolute advantage in every factor.

National Control of High Technology Benefits

The proposition that nations can capture the benefits of high technology that they develop through government resources is much less well-founded in economic theory or data. This proposition depends heavily on the nature of international markets. Current international markets are becoming increasingly integrated, not only for products but also for capital, including investment capital. The multi-national company is now a permanent fixture of the inter-national economy. Indeed, growing competition among multinationals from all industrial countries and increasingly also from advanced developing countries may now be integrating international markets for technology as well as capital and products. If so, this development affects the ability of nations to capture the employment and earning benefits of specific technological advances.

The product life cycle theory offered an explanation of the flow and benefits of technology in international markets as the multinational company emerged in the 1950s and 1960s. According to this theory, technological change resulted in new products which were produced and sold initially in home markets where higher incomes oriented consumer tastes to more sophisticated products. As the price of these new products fell, foreign demand led to exports. During this early home production and export phase, the home country reaped the employment and earning benefits of the new technology. Eventually, however, as the technology matured and price competition intensified, companies shifted production overseas to take advantage of more traditional cost factors such as cheaper labor and transportation costs. In this way, the multinational carried technology around the world but only after a lag that enabled the home country to redeem its investment in the new technology.

Today, however, subsidiaries of multinationals exist in practically all major markets, and income differentials among the major industrial countries and even certain segments of advanced developing country markets have narrowed. A multinational company today may just as easily decide to introduce a new product abroad as in the home market where the product was developed. There is mounting evidence that the export phase, when a country could expect to capture the benefits of its investment in technology, is collapsing, perhaps even reversing -- that is, with the product initially imported into the home market (the latter defined by where the R&D were done).[6]

If the link between technology and production and jobs is being weakened, one of the major economic benefits from pursuing national technology development may be vanishing. As one analyst notes,

> these findings raise serious questions regarding the payoff from successful high-tech targeting strategies. The pay-off has often been alleged to take the form of the establishment of a high wage domestic export sector. The possibility also exists, however, that successful technologies, developed at public expense, will simply be exploited in other countries.[7]

The evidence suggests that successful countries have exploited the ease with which technology can be acquired on international markets. Japan, Taiwan and South Korea built their high technology development in large measure on imported technology, much of it from the United States.

16

Increasingly, Taiwan and Korea have sought Japanese technology. And the United States has now started to seek
Japanese technology as well as selected know-how from Taiwan
and South Korea -- for example, Chinese language software
capability from Taiwan. France, on the other hand, has been
more schizophrenic about importing foreign technology,
although as Brickman points out, even under the present
Socialist government opportunities are still available for
foreign imports. Brazil and India have relied much less on
foreign technology, and in informatics specifically are
seeking to master their own technology.

Given this experience, is the competition to develop
independent technologies accessible only to national firms
worth the cost? Borrus and Zysman suggest that national
pools of technology continue to exist, and that the Japanese
pattern of development in particular illustrates some of the
benefits of promoting internal development of technology
while closing off the domestic market to foreign participation and competition. Brazil and India have
consciously sought, with apparent success, to increase the
market share of nationally produced equipment and technology.

But, as the latter cases and also the French case
illustrate, these policies are increasingly costly, and in
capital and skill intensive sectors such as computer hardware and software, the employment gains are minimal.
Moreover, these gains presume a domestic market sufficiently
large and competitive to bring new technologies to market at
a competitive price and quality for both home and export
consumption. Brazil and India, and for that matter most
countries, have neither the vigorous internal market that
Japan has nor the likely future export opportunities that
Japan enjoyed at an earlier time. The Japanese model may
continue to succeed in controlling foreign participation in
the Japanese market, as Borrus and Zysman conclude in the
case of telecommunications, despite the privatization of
NTT. But the Japanese are unlikely to be able to export as
freely as in the past. Hence either Japan's internal market
must expand or the benefits of national development will
decline, even for Japan.

The limiting factor, in this case, is the saturation of
international markets at the high technology end of the product spectrum, as each country strives through domestic
market closure and internal technological development to
achieve international competitiveness in similar high technology goods. If most countries pursue this strategy,
international markets shrink and trade in high technology

products rapidly becomes a zero-sum game in which everyone seeks to export but no one is willing to import.

International Trade Consequences of High Technology Development

The push for national development of high technology and the conquest of international markets errs in two ways. It defines high technology development too much in terms of sophisticated goods and ignores the importance of high technology processes in manufacturing, management and marketing activities. And it overlooks the opportunities to develop national technologies more selectively and to bargain for other technologies through a reciprocal process of market liberalization.

Defined in terms of products, high technology markets are inevitably limited unless one can assume open borders and rising incomes around the world, which generate the demand for these products, and rapidly accelerating innovation to meet this demand. In fact, of course, high technology development affects productivity and output in all products, especially agriculture and including less sophisticated products such as textiles, steel and services. While final products in these industries may remain relatively traditional, manufacturing and marketing processes, as well as inputs, may become increasingly sophisticated. Textile products, for example, are not necessarily more sophisticated today than before, but inputs and automated production processes are. Or, steel and automobile manufacture can be significantly enhanced not only by automated processes but also by more sophisticated inventory and sales management and marketing techniques.

The case studies suggest that how a country defines high technology influences its strategy. India and Brazil and, to a lesser extent, France have tended to define high technology in terms of the technical mastery of sophisticated products. Taiwan, Korea and Japan, by contrast, have defined it more in terms of enhancing value added based on improved manufacturing, management and marketing techniques. The two strategies pursue the same goals -- for example, increased production and use of computers in industry -- but they do so from different angles. Taiwan, Korea and Japan put less emphasis on technical mastery of innovation and hence imported and adapted more foreign technologies. By thinking more in terms of broad competitiveness, they also paid more attention to end user requirements and hence marketing techniques. Brazil, on the other hand, sought technological self-sufficiency and thus far has cultivated customers almost exclusively in the banking sector, which also financially controls the largest computer firms. India and France likewise stressed technological independence; and, while India paid somewhat more attention to marketing through its regional user centers and maintenance services, both India and France have had inadequate commercialization strategies.[8]

The failure to view the development of informatics technology more broadly in terms of overall competitiveness and availability of markets is even more pronounced in export markets. India and Brazil, according to the case studies in this volume, have barely begun to think about export requirements. Amar Gupta notes, for example, that even in relatively simple electronic products such as calculators, India is far from being competitive in world markets. Ronald Brickman cites the disappointment in France because the European Community has failed to generate the international market dimension for French products. The desire to leapfrog to higher levels of technological development, without considering current competitive factors both in the home market and abroad, diminishes the home country's comparative advantage. For example, how much more competitive internationally might Indian and Brazilian manufacturers of consumer electronics be if they had access to higher quality and cheaper foreign computer products or information sources? But, what is more, this strategy, which reserves domestic markets for national firms, also reduces the comparative advantage of foreign competitors by forcing them relatively to maintain resources in more traditional product areas such as steel and textiles. Thus, one consequence of Brazil's exclusion of American computer firms from the Brazilian market is to limit Brazil's access to the American steel market. Or, put conversely, one consequence of America's protectionism in steel is to reduce Brazil's investment in this sector, where it probably has a comparative advantage over the United States, and to increase it in computers where it does not but where it now limits American access by policies of national market reserve. Through such policies, both countries push each other increasingly out of areas of relative strength, hurting themselves as well as overall world prosperity.

In many respects, this is the direction in which the trading system has been moving, in part driven by the fascination with high technology development. Protectionism has accelerated in the developed countries in product sectors

such as footwear, textiles, steel and automobiles, while
technological mercantilism in developing countries has led
to increasing output and exports in engineering and
electronic products.[9]
     Ironically, this growing government interference in
markets, which is usually justified in terms of market
imperfections, has taken place as international markets have
become more and more competitive -- and hence, relatively at
least, more and more perfect. Today developing countries,
in particular, face a buyer's market for technology, with
numerous potential multinational suppliers from industrial
as well as more advanced developing countries. The question
is whether this new market competition offers a better
opportunity for developing countries to acquire advanced
foreign computer and information technology than India and
Brazil experienced in the mid-1970s. At that time, IBM
withdrew from India rather than accept the terms India proposed. In Brazil and France, IBM remained (and actually
benefited from exclusion of other foreign firms) but faced
discriminatory treatment in favor of national firms and
technologies. By contrast, in the 1980s Taiwan negotiated
successfully with IBM to obtain design and development technology for its new firm, the New Development Corporation;
and Mexico concluded a new agreement with IBM to produce
microcomputers and establish a technology center in Mexico.
These examples suggest that it may be unnecessary to exclude
or isolate foreign firms in order to promote national competitors as was done in the past. An opportunity exists for
more active partnership -- joint ventures, licensing, etc.
-- between national and foreign firms. India seems to be
exploring this possibility in its new quest for advanced
technology, particularly from the United States.
     Developing countries, such as Brazil and India, not
only have more foreign suppliers from which to choose, they
also hold a trump card with which to bargain with these
suppliers, namely their highly protected domestic markets.
This may be the time to play that card to secure more
advanced foreign technology on better terms to stimulate
indigenous development. Interestingly, as Simon and Schive
point out, Taiwan in 1982 imported 97 percent of all its
hardware requirements in the informatics sector, while
exporting 94 percent of its hardware production. This trade
pattern reflected a strategy of national development and
bargaining with foreign firms that sought out market niches,
where Taiwan could develop a secure, comparative advantage.
While larger countries with bigger domestic markets, such as
Brazil and India, may not wish to go as far as Taiwan, the

Taiwanese strategy suggests an appropriate direction. In
return for access to their markets in certain sectors, India
and Brazil can obtain the most advanced technology for
indigenous development in other sectors. This selective
approach contrasts sharply with the comprehensive one which
led Brazil in 1978 to extend its market reserve policy
beyond minicomputers to medium-sized computers, or which led
France in the 1960s to attack IBM in its strongest products
rather than, as Brickman points out, "seeking out more
promising segments of the market."

There are the usual objections to this strategy of
bargaining for technology with domestic markets. Those
countries benefit most, it is said, that already possess the
necessary skills and resources. Or smaller countries benefit less because they have smaller markets with which to
bargain. These objections, however, are superficial. The
postwar trading record based on reciprocal bargaining for
markets speaks for itself. Trade and output grew faster
from 1950 to 1980 than in any comparable historical period.
What is more, growth was more evenly distributed than is
widely believed. The wartorn countries were rebuilt and
eventually caught up with U.S. standards. More significantly, some 60 middle income developing countries also grew
faster in this period than the industrial countries -- about
two times as fast in real terms. Others were left behind,
but, as seen in the last section of this paper, in part by
their own choice.

Moreover, even for smaller countries, it makes sense to
pursue technological strategies aimed to secure access to
foreign markets rather than to achieve technological self
reliance. Taiwan and South Korea represent two countries
that have successfully exploited this strategy. Philips of
the Netherlands represents a single company that has done
so. Philips does more than 50 percent of its R&D in Holland
but less than 30 percent of its production and six percent
of its sales. It exploits its technological edge in foreign
markets while offering an attractive market of its own for
sales and development of foreign technologies. Open markets
are not only more essential for smaller countries because
protectionism in small markets usually means monopoly, but
also permits small countries a free ride on the technological investments of larger countries.

Clearly, some indigenous technological capability is
required in bargaining for foreign technology. On a selective and temporary basis, infant industry protection remains
valid. But technological protection as practiced by many
countries is self-defeating and offers a bleak collective

future for the world's trading system. That these international consequences of national technology policies have
been relatively ignored is not surprising. As the next section of this paper suggests, many developing countries
pursued domestic and trade policies in the postwar period
that deliberately insulated them from international markets.
In certain key manufacturing sectors, such as telecommunications equipment, industrial countries did also. The
issue is whether these countries will learn from the unpre-
cedented success of postwar trade liberalization in most
sectors of manufactured goods and overturn the legacy of
protectionism in other manufacturing sectors, as well as in
agriculture and services.

National Policy Instruments for High Technology Development

National policy instruments for high technology
development can be grouped into four major categories:
1) domestic policies; 2) trade policies; 3) exchange rate
policies; and 4) capital market or financial policies.

Domestic policies include so-called macroeconomic or
aggregate policies -- fiscal, monetary and regulatory policies -- and microeconomic or sector and industry specific
policies -- policies for agriculture, the information sector
or individual state and private enterprises. The distinction between macro and micro policies is somewhat artificial
and hinges on how these policies are put together rather
than their generic differences. For example, tax and expenditure policy in the United States, while considered
macroeconomic fiscal policy in the aggregate, is really a
collage of individual tax and expenditure programs for specific interest groups, sectors, and even firms within the
U.S. economy. Conversely, policies for specific industries
or firms in many developing countries may follow largely
from broader sector or macroeconomic policies, such as telecommunications policy in Brazil or overall industrial policy
in Japan. The link between these two types of policies is
more important than the distinction.[10]

Trade policies include import and export policies,
exchange rate policies concern the particular regime for
currency transactions, and financial policies encompass the
incentives or restrictions on equity and portfolio investments, technology payments and international credit transactions by local banks, brokerage houses, pension funds,
insurance companies and the like.

Comparative policymaking is an important factor in comparative advantage. Countries differ in their capacity to formulate and implement coherent policies. In this respect, Japan appears to have a comparative advantage over, for example, France, where as Brickman notes, repeated policy shifts and reorganizations of industry have plagued high technology policy. This does not imply, as argued earlier, that any policy choice in a country such as Japan will yield a comparative advantage. Constraints always exist in the form of limited resources and international competition. And manipulation of these constraints becomes increasingly difficult as domestic politics become more and more pluralized and international markets more and more competitive.

Countries also exhibit different preferences for the use of various policy instruments.[11] Generally speaking, under the terms of the Bretton Woods system, industrial countries agreed to use primarily domestic and financial policies to influence comparative advantage. Governments gave up flexibility in the use of trade policy instruments by committing themselves to liberalizing and safeguard provisions under the GATT. They also accepted fixed exchange rate values under the IMF. On the other hand, they retained full use of domestic policy and financial market instruments, including controls on international capital flows. Financial policies appeared to play a large role in the postwar growth of France, Japan and West Germany.[12] The United States, on the other hand, liberalized its financial markets, allowing the dollar to become the world's principal reserve currency -- a development which increased the leverage of U.S. domestic, especially monetary, policy over that of other countries but also exposed U.S. financial markets to events abroad.

By contrast, Japan and the developing countries initially relied more heavily on trade policy instruments. Import substitution policies prevailed, while foreign capital, particularly direct investment, was also heavily regulated. Japan was the first country to initiate a strategy of export-led growth but without significant liberalization of import or financial markets. By the mid-1960s, the early NICs in the developing world -- Korea, Brazil, Singapore and Taiwan -- also began to promote exports while liberalizing some import markets, at least with respect to tariffs. In the case of Brazil and Singapore, foreign investment was also welcomed.

In the 1960s, the United States, having given up flexibility in the use of trade, exchange rate and financial policy instruments, found itself bearing the burden of

adjustment to new competitors in international markets.
Given its objectives in the late 1960s on both the domestic
(Great Society) and foreign policy (Vietman War) fronts, it
eventually refused to accept this burden any longer and
sought greater flexibility initially in the use of financial
market restrictions (the steps to stanch capital outflows in
the second half of the 1960s) and then in the use of
floating exchange rates and trade restrictions (such as the
Japanese textile agreement, MFA, etc.). Floating rates
eventually permitted the relaxation of capital market
restrictions in the United States and, to some extent, in
other major countries.

The oil crisis accelerated trends toward greater
government intervention in trade markets. Governments in
many industrial countries, including the United States,
postponed domestic policy adjustments to higher oil prices,
while developing countries exploited the freer flow of
international capital in the form of petro-dollars to
sustain growth despite huge oil-induced balance of payments
deficits. The NICs, including Brazil and Korea, tightened
import restrictions both directly and by maintaining over-
valued exchange rates. Japan liberalized tariffs but utilized numerous nontariff restrictions. Meanwhile, Japan,
the early NICs, and increasingly a second tier of NICs
accelerated manufactured exports, especially toward the high
technology or higher value-added end of the product
spectrum. With fewer countries willing to undertake adjustments through domestic policy changes, more countries turned
to trade, exchange rate and financial market policies to
compete for a larger share of less rapidly growing export
markets. By the end of the 1970s, the race was on for high
technology and other markets that were being increasingly
limited.

The overall record of growth performance during the
postwar period suggests that this shift toward increasing
use of trade, financial, and exchange rate policies has been
detrimental to world output. Growth slowed dramatically in
the 1970s for all countries and was sustained in the more
advanced developing countries only by virtue of the largest
transfer of financial resources -- petro-dollars -- in
modern times. Despite the overall slower growth of this
period, the protective and promotional policies of countries
such as Japan and the NICs came to be viewed as successful
models of development in a world in which free markets and
stable prices and exchange rates could no longer be taken
for granted. A closer look at the record of this period,
however, shows that those countries that based their

development strategies on domestic market factors, i.e.,
relative factor endowments, and government policies to
enhance those factors over the longer run did much better
than those that sought to substitute for international products and create the appropriate domestic factor endowments.
This record holds important lessons for current and future
development in the informatics sector.

Table 2.1 shows a calculation of revealed comparative
advantage in technology exports for five developing
countries.[13] Korea has by far the largest percentage share
of the total technology exports of these five countries.
Its revealed comparative advantage is most significant in
the export of construction services. This advantage,
according to World Bank investigations, lies primarily in
superior project management and organizational skills. These
skills have been developed less on the basis of local R&D or
technical knowledge, as in the case of India, or on the basis
of a domestic capital goods industry, as in the case of
Brazil, than on the basis of very high investments in technical human capital formation. The high educational level
of the Korean population in comparison to other countries
has enabled it to adapt (rather than substitute for) foreign
technologies and to move into more and more complex activities by participating in joint projects with foreign firms.

By contrast, India has the largest indigenous R&D
structure and the largest absolute stock of scientists and
engineers among the five countries. But India has also
fostered the most restrictive trade and financial environment for the application of Indian technology. According to
the World Bank,

> it has a highly regulated economy with many infra-
> structural constraints that stifle effective deployment
> of its high technical capabilities. For example, the
> growth of some of the most efficient firms is con-
> strained by controls on capacity expansion and maximum
> size. More generally, poor quality of local inputs,
> high local content requirements, difficulties in ob-
> taining imported inputs, unreliable local delivery
> schedules, power shortages, and transportation bottle-
> necks reduce its international competitiveness in
> product exports.[14]

As a result, India does relatively better than other
countries exporting technology--LCTS in Table 2.1--rather
than products. This is surprising when India's low wage and
abundant labor resources would suggest a comparative

TABLE 2.1

Analysis of Revealed Comparative Advantage of the
Five Countries' Technology Exports

	Argentina	Brazil	India	Korea	Mexico	Category subtotal
A. Percentage of grand total						
Construction	.76	5.29	7.44	54.28	1.22	68.99
Licensing, consulting & technical services (LCTS)	.07	.44	.62	.58	.06	1.78
DFI in manufacturing	.06	.02	.12	.08	.03	.31
Project exports	.23	2.04	2.29	3.17	.05	7.79
Capital goods	2.43	7.25	2.24	7.12	2.11	21.14
Country totals	3.55	15.03	12.71	65.24	3.47	100.00
B. Revealed Comparative Advantage*						
Construction	.31	.51	.85	1.21	.51	
Licensing, consulting & technical services (LCTS)	1.17	1.65	2.73	.50	1.02	
DFI in manufacturing	5.07	.53	2.99	.41	2.65	
Project exports	.83	1.75	2.32	.62	.19	
Capital goods	3.24	2.28	.83	.52	2.88	

* Revealed comparative advantage (RCA) is measured by the ratio $(X_{ij}/X_{wj}) / (X_{it}/X_{wt})$, where

i = country; j = type of technology export; w = exports of the relevant category for all five countries; and t = all technology exports. The greater the RCA ratio of country in a particular category, the greater its revealed comparative advantage in that category.

Source: Dahlman and Sercovich, Local Development and Exports of Technology. World Bank Staff Working Paper No. 667, 1984.

advantage in manufacturing rather than, for example, in
consulting.

Brazil has gone the farthest of the five countries in
developing its own technology-intensive capital goods sector, largely on the basis of import protection and direct
investment by foreign firms (unlike Korea, which imported
capital equipment). Its revealed comparative advantage is
strongest in this sector and in LCTS, mostly in the telecommunications sector. These advantages, however, reflect
foreign product and process knowledge as well as foreign
management. Brazil lacks a strong research base as in the
case of India or indigenous management class as in the case
of Korea.

Korea's superior performance appears to be grounded on
broadly-based human skills and early exposure to market competition, especially export markets.[15] Its performance
depended on access to foreign elements of technology, a
conscious effort to apply its own human skills to adapt that
technology, the opportunity to export its services and
actually gain new technology through joint ventures and projects with foreign firms, and the import of capital goods
that could be obtained at lower cost abroad.

The case studies of Japan and Taiwan in this volume
suggest similar conclusions. Although Borrus and Zysman
reject the thesis that Japan's high level of literacy is a
sufficient explanation for its postwar success, they note
that this rate is "quite remarkable" and that combined with
a high savings rate it means that Japanese exports might be
expected to concentrate in sectors in which capital
resources and an education work force count. Similarly,
Taiwan placed considerable emphasis on training and education and pursued the belief that general market policies
promoting technological advance were as important as the
technology policies themselves. Throughout the case studies, broader market instruments such as governmental education, procurement, and regulatory policies (e.g., the
controlled or structured competition practiced in Japan)
seemed to have been more effective than narrowly defined
sectoral R&D or industry-specific programs.

By contrast, the broader educational and economic
environment in Brazil and India, where literacy is confined
to a smaller elite and where protectionist policies have
been in vogue, was much less favorable to competitive
development. In such circumstances, the World Bank concluded,

much of the effort is deployed to overcome policy-
induced constraints and to substitute for imports....

For example, while some of the technological effort
that has been undertaken by firms in Latin America
is dictated by market needs and local input supply
conditions, much has been undertaken specifically
to overcome protectionist policies. These policies
have included local content requirements, promotion
of technological self-reliance, and restrictions on
imports of foreign technological elements. It appears
that some of the efforts induced by these policies
have been socially wasteful in the sense that they
would not have been warranted in a less restrictive
regime.[16]

Conclusion

Since the early 1980s, elements of two regimes have
been vying against one another to establish the dominant
policy directions for the world economy over the next
decade. The United States has made a determined effort to
lead the world back to pre-1970 regimes of domestic adjustment and freer trade and financial policies. It has failed
thus far to complete the course, particularly in terms of
its own fiscal policy adjustments, and currently threatens
the freer trade regime by tolerating a high and volatile
exchange rate for the dollar which is whipping up almost
certain Congressional protectionist retaliation. Meanwhile,
Europe has made less progress in terms of domestic adjustment, relying almost totally on exports to the United States
to achieve moderate growth in recent years, and remains
skeptical under current circumstances of high unemployment
and domestic structural rigidities about further trade and
financial liberalization. Japan moves rhetorically toward
more trade and financial liberalization but appears unable
to make the associated domestic policy adjustments.

How the industrial countries go will hold great consequence for developing countries. If the industrial
countries move toward more restrictive trade and financial
regimes, the developing countries, including the NICs, will
not find adequate future markets for their exports, high
technology or otherwise. As a result, they will face
serious debt servicing problems and wrenching domestic
policy adjustments that will make recent IMF programs, by
comparison, look attractive. These countries, therefore,
have a clear stake in encouraging further opening of international trade and financial markets. The NICs, in particular, cannot make their case any longer, as they did in

the 1970s, by arguing for a combination of discriminatory liberalization for their labor-intensive exports (GSP, etc.) and broad-scale protectionism for their high-technology imports (e.g., informatics sector in Brazil).[17] This kind of export skewed trade liberalization shrinks markets and hence growth.

Technological nationalism, while still a potent political potion, is economic poison for the world economy. Whether nations will learn this fact in time remains to be seen. How they proceed in the information sector will be critical. The case studies that follow shed some light on the choices they have already made and the crucial ones that loom ahead for them.

NOTES

1. See Richard R. Nelson, High Technology Policies: A Five Nation Comparison, American Enterprise Institute Studies in Economic Policy, Washington, D.C., 1984. The following discussion does not explore the national security rationale for high technology development. While military interests have been critical for the development of information technology in all the countries considered, the studies in this volume focus exclusively on the economic rationale for development.

2. See their contribution to this volume.

3. This generalization is less true for India than Brazil, but holds for both in comparison, for example, to Taiwan.

4. Brazil's policies to protect the domestic informatics industry from import competition apply for eight years (still a relatively long time) while other policies to provide various subsidies and incentives are open-ended.

5. See their contribution, p. 111.

6. See Edwin Mansfield et al., "R&D and Innovation: Some Empirical Findings," in Z. Guliches (ed.), R&D, Patents and Productivity. Chicago, IL: University of Chicago Press, 1984, pp. 127-48.

7. See D.G. McFetridge, "Recent Developments in International Technology Transfer: A Canadian Perspective," paper presented to the Workshop on International Technology Transfer: Promotion and Barriers, Six Countries Programme, Ottawa, Canada, May 6-7, 1985.

8. Recent policy decisions in India may be changing the balance more in favor of users. See Gupta's contribution to this volume.

9. See Donald B. Keesing, "World Trade and Output of Manufactures: Structural Trends and Developing Countries' Exports," World Bank Staff Working Paper No. 316, January 1979.

10. Borrus and Zysman distinguish a third set of policies -- market-promotion or organization policies. These policies, however, are not distinguishable from macro or micro policies except in terms of objectives. They represent macro and micro policies aimed at enhancement of the market.

11. For an elaboration of the terms and argument that follow, see the author's "Where Reaganomics Works, Foreign Policy (Winter 1984-85), pp. 14-38; and the longer version, "International Reaganomics: A Domestic Approach to World Economy," Significant Issues Series, Vol. VI, no. 18, Center for Strategic and International Studies, Georgetown University, December 1984.

12. See John Zysman, Governments, Markets and Growth. Ithaca, NY: Cornell University Press, 1983.

13. For the study from which this discussion follows, see Carl J. Dahlman and Francisco C. Sercovich, Local Development and Exports of Technology: The Comparative Advantage of Argentina, Brazil, India, the Republic of Korea, and Mexico, World Bank Staff Working Paper No. 667, 1984.

14. Ibid.

15. Richard Nelson finds the same results in his comparative analysis of five industrial countries. "The most important lesson here," he concludes, "is that nations aspiring to strength in high technology industries had better attend to their general strength in technical education and establish and maintain a set of policies and institutions supporting general economic growth." See High Technology Policies, p. 67.

16. World Bank, op. cit.

17. For an elaboration of NIC interests in a new trade round, see my article, "The NICs and a New Trade Round," in Ernest H. Preeg (ed.), Hard Bargaining Ahead: U.S. Trade Policy and Developing Countries. Transaction Books for the Overseas Development Council, 1985.

3

Brazil

Claudio Frischtak
The World Bank

INTRODUCTION

This paper presents a brief overview of the Brazilian
computer industry, as well as some of the policies and
institutions which have shaped its structure and influenced
its recent performance. The relevant literature, although
not extensive, presents substantial evidence that past policies have been instrumental in fostering the establishment
and growth of a sizeable number of national firms engaged in
the design and assembly of computer systems and
peripherals.[1] There is, however, insufficient discussion of
the implications of such policies for the competitive
status of the industry in the longer run. The relevant
question for sectoral strategy at this point seems to be:
once the industry surpasses its infancy stage, what set
of policies will be most conducive to simultaneously promote
growth, stimulate increased levels of efficiency, and limit
the technological gap to a relatively short time horizon?
The presumption is that the policies towards the
"informatics" sector, though sufficiently focused and
selective to attract resources and generate the development
of the computer industry in Brazil, have nonetheless been
unable to foster adequate overall levels of productive
efficiency, while national firms have not gone beyond
incremental innovations within well-known and relatively
open technologies. At present, the industry seems to be
uncompetitive in the international market in most
product-lines, if the assessment is made solely on price
comparisons of products with comparable levels of
performance, although prices have in fact come down
substantially for some of the more mature products (such as
8-bit home computers).[2] On the positive side, protection

from both imports and the entry of foreign firms, combined
with a fast growing market for data processing equipment
and services, has enabled national firms to increase in
number, size and market shares at very fast rates, acquire
some technological capability in the design and manufacture
of systems and peripheral equipment (particularly in the area
of micro and minicomputers), and led to the training of
substantial numbers of skilled personnel. Although these are
no small accomplishments for an industry de facto
established only in 1977/78, ultimately, as the
technological frontier moves and the use of computers
diffuses through the economy and becomes a necessary
condition for overall gains in productivity and efficiency,
the standards of price and technical performance of the
data-processing products available in Brazil will
necessarily be the main criterion for the survival of the
sector.

     In the next section, this paper focuses on the policies
and institutions which shaped the Brazilian computer
industry in the last decade, culminating in the "National
Informatics Policy" Law of October 1984. In this context,
we point to the multiple and at times conflicting objectives
of the Brazilian informatics policy, where economic efficiency, at least in the short- and medium-run, has been subordinated to the goal of stimulating national firms to
attain mastery in manufacturing and eventually in designing
data processing systems. In Section III, the structure,
levels of competition and performance of the sector are
discussed in relative detail. It is suggested that increased
levels of productive efficiency and continuous technological
updating are predicated on both static and dynamic forms of
economies of scale in production and R&D, and in the degree
of managerial or x-efficiency attained by individual firms.

     This paper concludes that a competitive environment and
large production volumes are both critical elements to
achieve international competitiveness. Given the economic
size of the Brazilian market and the minimum technological
and productive scales that firms have to achieve, it is
doubtful that the internal market will be sufficient to
accommodate large and technologically updated firms without
leading to monopolistic or non-contestable structures.
Under these circumstances, the proper set of incentives for
cost-constraining and quality-improving behavior will only
be found in the international market. This economic syllo-
gism points, therefore, to a strategy which increas-ingly
relies on the expansion of exports by individual firms as a
means of providing disciplines and stimulating productivity

gains and competitiveness in the industry. Protection, in
this context, should therefore not only be focused and time-
bound, but also predicated upon national firms being able to
penetrate the international market.[3] In addition, R&D
funding and resource needs will tend to increase substantially in the next few years. New generations of smaller
systems will be moving towards closed architectures, with
the utilization of custom-made chips and proprietary
operating systems, while larger systems will probably continue to be outside the reach of national industry unless
under some form of joint venture arrangement. In either
case, enlarged government support for R&D will be needed,
while resources may be better utilized within cooperative
forms of research organization.

POLICIES AND INSTITUTIONS FOR THE INFORMATICS SECTOR[4]

The radical transformation in electronics technology
has been marked by two major developments: the increasing
miniaturization of electronics components and the advent of
digital techniques. Together, they made possible enormous
price reductions and performance improvements in computers,
that is, in machines using electronic technology which
perform complex programmable operations on large volumes of
data in a time-efficient manner. Informatics, as used in
the Brazilian context, is the set of activities related to
data processing through machines: it encompasses,
therefore, a range of industrial and service activities,
including but not limited to the manufacture and use of
computers, their parts and components, peripheral equipment,
automated processes, software for both operating systems
and applications, etc. Here, we will be mostly limiting
ourselves to a discussion of the policy space which is
relevant to the manufacture of digital computers and
peripherals.

The establishment of a national computer industry in
Brazil can be traced to different, though eventually
converging, sets of forces. First, the consistent commitment
of policymakers dating back to 1968 to the promotion of
science and technology (S&T). To that end, an extensive
array of financial, industrial and academic agencies were
established or strengthened, resulting in an increased share
of the national budget earmarked for S&T development (rising
from .84 in 1970 to 3.64 in 1982), and an expansion of both
R&D expenditures as a proportion of GNP (.24 in 1971 to .65
in 1979) and in the number of scientists and engineers

engaged in R&D per million population (75 in 1974 to 208 in 1978). There are now an estimated twenty-five to thirty thousand scientific and industrial researchers and over one thousand graduate programs. The objective of national technological development was further pursued through the regulation of technology transfers, particularly through the 1971 Industrial Property Code and the Normative Act 15 of September 1976, which enabled the National Industrial Property Institute (INPI) to review and veto individual technology transfer contracts and insist on the unbundling of technology acquired abroad.[5]

The second major set of forces shaping a national computer industry can be traced to the interests of the Brazilian Navy in equipping its frigates with computers developed and manufactured in Brazil, which converged with the intentions of the National Economic Development Bank (now BNDES) of stimulating technological self-sufficiency in the Brazilian industry. The project of planning, developing and manufacturing a computer prototype to be later procured by the Navy went ahead with its political support and the financial backing of the BNDES; it was institutionalized and took the organizational form of a special working group created in February 1971. The importance of the event was twofold: it attracted the Brazilian military, which was then the politically most powerful institution in Brazil, to play a critical role in shaping a new industrial activity; and it led to the first Brazilian-designed and manufactured (mini) computer (the G-10), with hardware and software developed by two major Brazilian universities. This proto- type was later produced in industrial scale by Cobra, a pioneering enterprise created as a joint venture in 1974 (with state, national and foreign capital participation), which ten years later stood as the second largest manufacturer of systems in Brazil (after IBM, but ahead of Burroughs).

The third explanatory set of factors is linked to the rapid growth of the Brazilian informatics market and, in particular, the explosive demand of the public sector for computer hardware and services, which led to the creation of CAPRE in 1972, the predecessor of the Secretaria Especial de Informatica (SEI). Its initial objectives were both preventing unnecessary imports and increasing the efficiency in use of data processing equipment in the Brazilian government (which then accounted for over a half of total systems demand). In the period 1970/76, the number of imported computers increased at an annual average growth rate of 56.7 percent (see Table 1 in the next section); by

1974, this item was already the third largest manufactured import. This fact assumed special significance in the light of the first balance of payments crisis that Brazil faced in a decade. As a result, in December 1975, all imports of computers, parts, accessories and components required the prior authorization of CAPRE.[6] More important, in February of 1976, CAPRE was also charged with devising a strategy for the development of the local computer industry. Through Decision 01 of July of the same year, it created the basis for reserving the micro/mini computer market and related peripherals to national firms by recommending that the national informatics policy for the minicomputer and the microcomputer market, their peripherals, modern transcription and transmission equipment and terminals should be oriented in such a way as to allow the control of initiatives aiming at achieving conditions for the consolidation of an industrial park with total control of technology and decision within the country.
On the other hand, and still according to the same Act, the policy for "medium and large machines," would be based on "investment rationalization and optimization of installed resources," which basically meant relying on the productive capacity of multinational enterprises then located in Brazil. In addition, CAPRE, through Decision 02, was empowered to control the purchase of software and data-processing services by government agencies and enterprises.

At that point, therefore, CAPRE had three basic instruments to shape the production and sale of systems, peripherals and software: import controls, market reserve and government procurement. They allowed CAPRE (and later SEI) to attract domestic manufacturers into reserved market niches by slowing down the processing of import authorizations, which in combination with government procurement, created substantial pent-up demand to make domestic production by national firms a financially viable undertaking. Discretionary granting of import licenses was also an implicit threat and was effectively used against national firms attempting to exercise newly gained market power in order to extract monopoly profits within an environment of artificial scarcity. In the non-reserved areas of the market, granting and withholding import licenses, in particular, allowed CAPRE (and SEI) to establish operational goals for multinational firms, including obtaining a positive trade balance and relatively large ratios of exported over domestically sold systems.

By January 1978, CAPRE had chosen Cobra and four
private domestic firms to produce minicomputers: Cobra with
its own technology (an outgrowth of the G-10 project),[7] and
the others producing under license or through reverse
engineering (in one case). Technology was to be completely
transferred by 1982 (with royalty payments not exceeding 3
percent of net sales), and successive models were expected
to be locally developed. In addition, and as a way of
stimulating vertical disintegration and new entries in the
market, such firms were expected to manufacture only the
CPUs, but not peripherals, which were to be undertaken by
other national companies. A year later, in December 1978,
CAPRE issued new criteria for the manufacture of CPUs
beyond the minicomputer range, effectively prohibiting IBM
and Burroughs from producing medium-sized computers in
Brazil, thus expanding the scope of the market reserve
policy.

The recognition of the "strategic importance of
informatics to national development" and the increase in
CAPRE's responsibilities, led to the creation in October of
1979 of the Special Secretariat of Informatics (SEI) as
part of the National Security Council, an agency reporting
directly to the President and where the military have had a
preponderant voice. In addition to the tasks undertaken by
CAPRE, SEI was also to coordinate all activities in the
field of real-time control systems and microelectronics. A
series of Normative Acts followed the creation of SEI,
basically confirming and to a large extent strengthening
CAPRE's previous orientation. They allowed SEI to:

a. control the imports of finished products, parts
    and components as well as of capital equipment
    needed for the production of such goods through
    quota restrictions and tariff barriers, in order
    to stimulate local production and decrease the
    imports of hardware;

b. control the entry and expansion of firms into the
    various segments of the informatics market,
    promoting the establishment of national firms in
    those segments characterized by relatively less
    complex technology and high growth prospects,
    such as small, business, mini and desk-top
    computers as well as office word processors. For
    entry into a specific segment, a firm would need
    to prove that real decision-making power authority

over the strategies, operations and activities of
the company (including the control of its equity)
was permanently and exclusively held by
individuals living in Brazil, that the firm had a
capital endowment commensurate with the dimensions
of the project and used locally developed
technology (unless it was unavailable and the
product judged to be of special importance to the
national economy). For foreign firms, entry would
be allowed for the production of large systems and
of machines dedicated to scientific and engineering
applications, so long as they exported a
predetermined proportion of their domestic sales
and balanced their own trade account;

c.   control all government acquisitions of informatics
products and services, with preference given to
national suppliers. In addition, SEI was to
approve and supervise the annually updated three
year informatics plan that each federal agency is
obliged to develop;

d.   give preferential treatment for domestic suppliers
of numerical control equipment, programmable
controllers, systems of instrumentation, test
equipment, real-time control systems, especially
for automated production lines in industry and
supervisory control of service networks, and the
corresponding software;

e.   review and approve individual applications for
technology transfer contracts with foreign technology suppliers, therefore superseding INPI's
role; approve the import of parts, accessories and
components, other inputs and capital goods for R&D
projects, as well as the eligibility of the
project for financial incentives.

Most of those provisions and regulations framing CAPRE
and SEI's activities, and reflecting the concerns and intents
conveyed through these agencies, were incorporated in the
new Informatics Law of October 1984; it codified and gave
legitimacy to the existing regulatory structure, and
established the protective measures to be time-bound. The
Law is based on the following principles: that government
action is needed to guide, coordinate and encourage informatics activities; that State participation is warranted in

productive activities when national interests so determine
and where private Brazilian enterprises would not enter;
that State interference is justified to assure a balanced
protection to national production of certain goods and services, and to foster growing technological competence; that
monopolistic situations (either de jure or de facto) should
be forbidden, with free and unrestricted entry for national
firms using Brazilian technology; and that the national
government should provide incentives and protection of
Brazilian firms and encourage them to attain international
competitiveness.

In the Law, informatics activities are broadly defined
as connected to: research, development, production, import
and export of semiconductor electronic optoelectronic components, as well as their respective electronic inputs;
research, import, export, manufacture, marketing and operations of machines, equipment and devices based on a digital
technique whose technical function is the collection, processing, building up, storing, switching, recovery and pre-
sentation of information; import, export, production,
operation and marketing of software; building up and use of
data bases; rendering of informatics services.

Among the key features of the Law is the creation of a
National Informatics and Automation Council (CONIN), composed of representatives of government and non-government
entities, and headed by the President. CONIN will be
responsible for formulating and implementing the National
Informatics and Automation Plan, which will be submitted
every three years to the President to be approved, and will
be annually assessed by the Congress. Within the new
organizational structure, SEI is formally subordinated to
CONIN and will give administrative support and execute its
decisions.[8] It is to be noted that protection from import
competition is assured for a period of eight years, during
which SEI will have a prior say regarding imports of
informatics goods and services. However, the policy of
market reserve and prefer-ential procurement and incentives
for nationally controlled enterprises does not seem to be
time-bound, but to the contrary, open-ended. The Law has,
in addition, a precise and quite strict definition of a
national firm, which means corporations established in
Brazil, and which are under permanent, exclusive and
unconditional direct and indirect control of individuals
resident or domiciled in Brazil or of domestic public
entities. "Control" in the context of the Law has three
dimensions: managerial decision-making power; technological
development; and stock ownership.

CAPRE's and SEI's institutional trajectories and the policies emanated from those bodies should be referred to a basic set of beliefs, goals and objectives which have been formulated and gaining progressively greater cohesion over the last decade, and were finally given legitimacy and political support by the new Informatics Law.[9] The point of departure is that the possession and capacity to utilize information resources are increasingly becoming a form of national power, and require, therefore, the adoption of national policies that stimulate the emergence of national data industries and markets for hardware, software and services. In this context, two complementary aspects are worth stressing. First, the development of miniaturized, inexpensive, commercially available components has led to the emergence of completely new equipment markets; consequently, a policy of protecting the emergence of such markets in the interest of infant national producers would not harm established producers, which would tend to react with a longer time lag to new technologies and market opportunities. Second, the degree of technological complexity associated with the development of many parts and components suggest that the development of a national computer industry should proceed from the design and assembly of data processing system to, in a later stage, the design and manufacture of componentry.

As opposed to an approach of import substituting by backward integration, in the shortest possible time-frame, and irrespective of costs, SEI took a more cautious approach, separating final products from industrial inputs. In this perspective the agency states that

national technology is defined in terms of the ability to produce independently of the technology acquired abroad. The extensive use of imported components is not restricted, since this does not limit the corporation's autonomy and immediate capacity to manufacture for the market. At the same time, such imports allow corporations to maintain products near the international state of the art. In the longer run, however, a national component industry must be created through a parallel but separate policy to ensure the ultimate success of the equipment policy (see Note 9).

The industrial policy for informatics in Brazil may be thus summarized: among its general objectives are to maximize the amount of information resources located in

Brazil, no matter if produced in Brazil or imported; to
assure the national control over their production, implying
that the main decisions related to data industries are made
in Brazil and that their technologies are mastered by
national firms; to universalize access to information; and
to use information resources as a key instrument for the
enhancement of the cultural and political environment in
Brazil. To attain those general objectives, SEI followed a
strategy of creating the conditions under which an
informatics industry would be established and eventually
achieve industrial maturity. According to SEI, maturity is
perceived by the size of market shares that Brazilian
producers attain in national markets, and in the longer run,
by their ability to attain international competitiveness.
As the agency puts it:

> A well oriented industrial policy should, therefore,
> seek to attain a substantial share of the Brazilian
> informatics market for Brazilian companies, to
> consolidate that position and to ensure that national
> firms master technological developments in a manner
> that makes it possible for them to reach the ultimate
> goal of competitiveness in the international
> market...Before the threshhold of international
> competitiveness is reached, production is still at
> the stage of industrial learning. Consequently,
> product prices may be above, and corporate performance
> below international standards. Yet production is
> already based on Brazilian technology...The growth of
> this market segment depends upon support measures by
> the government, which gives domestic industry an
> opportunity to become competitive internationally
> (see Note 9).

Given the multiplicity and somewhat contradictory
nature of the objectives governing informatics policy, it is
unclear the extent to which CONIN and SEI will emphasize
economic efficiency and the needs of the users of goods and
services. The more immediate goal of CAPRE and SEI was to
establish and promote the growth of a national industry,
with respect to which they achieved a measured degree of
success. There is little question that in order to attain
this objective, users had to bear substantial costs;
yet, as the industry matures, and Congress takes a more
active participation in assessing the National Informatics
and Automation Plan, the tradeoffs between short-run
sectoral growth, and longer-run efficiency gains may be

evaluated in a somewhat distinct form. The Law already
reflects some of those concerns: it not only makes explicit
a time-bound commitment with respect to import competition,
but directs CONIN to aim not solely at "the growing
participation of private domestic companies," "the
substituting of imports and generating exports" and to the
"development of significant technology," but as well to
"properly meet the needs of users of goods and services of
the sector," "the development of applications that have the
best economic and social cost/benefit ratio," and the
"progressive reduction of the final price of goods and
services." In article 19 those objectives are evenly split
in number; it remains to be seen how the key Brazilian
informatics agencies will in the future strike a balance
between those two sets of potentially conflicting
objectives.[10]

MARKET SIZE, INDUSTRY STRUCTURE AND LEVELS OF
COMPETITION AND PERFORMANCE IN THE INFORMATICS
SECTOR

The Brazilian market for computers and peripherals is
of considerable size, with sales of about $1,700 million in
1984.[11]Shipments from the national segment of the industry
totalled $881 million in 1984, and included 1,082 mini-
computers; 61,680 home micros; 11,218 business micros;
25,857 serial printers; 1,114 parallel printers; 10,267
video terminals; 35,273 financial terminals; 1,824 cartridge
disk drives; 2,348 winchester disk drives; 20,965 floppy
disk units; 439 magnetic tape units; and 28,021 modems.[12]
Large systems, on the other hand, were mostly produced
and/or imported by multinational firms, with the exception of
Novadata (the sole and recent national entry in the market
for mainframes).

The rates of growth observed in the Brazilian market
have been quite high: during the 1970s, the market is
estimated to have grown 25-30 percent on a yearly basis.
Between 1981 and 1984, and in spite of the recession, total
sales increased at an average annual rate of 17.8 percent.
It has been suggested that for the rest of the decade, the
market for informatics products would expand at yearly
averages of 30 to 40 percent.[13] If the high growth
estimates (40 percent) were to be fulfilled, by 1990 total
sales would be in the order of $12.8 billion. This,
however, seems to be quite unlikely, in view of the fact
that since 1975, annual growth rates have been decreasing

and the industry is expected to become less insulated to the
environment of moderate economic growth predicted for the
rest of the decade. In those circumstances, a 10 to 20
percent range of average annual sales growth seems more
reasonable: in the "low-growth" scenario (10 percent),
industry sales would amount to $3 billion in 1990, whereas
in the "high-growth" case (20 percent), the figure would
come to $5 billion.

The Brazilian market for data processing equipment,
although substantial in size and offering reasonable
prospects of growth over the rest of the decade, is still
relatively limited by international standards. Although
Brazil is the largest market in Latin America (followed by
Mexico and Argentina), it represents no more than 20 percent
of the West German's, 10 percent of the Japanese and 3 percent of the U.S. markets. If commercially attractive and
financially rewarding for individual firms, its economic
size is such that most products are still manufactured by
batch processes and with low levels of automation. In fact,
indications arising from both the Brazilian and international experiences of the existence of substantial scale
economies in the production and R&D of data processing
equipment,[14] suggest that the internal market, although able
to support a number of product lines (such as financial terminals and some of the small systems), does not provide a
wide enough base and sufficient depth to sustain economically efficient and technically updated firms across a broad
range of products. This proposition, as will be discussed
below, has important implications for sectoral policy.

The physical dimension of the computer market and its
evolution in the last decade may be glimpsed from Table 3.1,
which points to the growth and transformation in the
installed computer capacity across different categories of
machines. Aside from the very high rates of growth in the
aggregate number of machines, and the notable increase in
the number of large and very large equipment at the
beginning of the decade (when class 5 and 6 machines grew at
annual average rates of 92.8 and 68.1 percent), the other
striking characteristic is the relative shift from the
larger and more expensive systems (classes 4-6) to smaller
and more flexible equipment. The number of minicomputers,
in particular, grew at an annual average rate of 50.8 percent between 1977 and 1981.

The changes in the configuration of the market brought
a corresponding change in the market shares of national vis-
a-vis multinational firms. In 1976, when the policy of

TABLE 3.1
Installed Computers in Brazil - 1970-81

Class[a]	1970	1973	1975	1977	1979	1981	Growth Rates		
							1970-75	1977-81	1973-81
1	-	586	2,143	3,846	4,791	8,576	-	20.1	33.5
2	-	19	173	356	1,015	2,719	-	50.8	62.1
3	378	639	1,057	1,296	1,494	1,858	25.7	9.0	15.9
4	122	250	327	353	377	408	24.7	3.6	12.1
5	2	45	82	122	226	374	92.8	28.0	52.3
6	4	33	61	87	97	134	68.1	10.8	35.1
Total	506	1,572	3,843	6,060	8,000	14,609	50.7	21.1	33.8

a The class sizes established by CAPRE/SEI are generally based on the size of the equipment, as well as upon prices and technical parameters (CPU speed, memory and input/output capacity). They have been generally identified, starting from Class 1, as micro, mini, small, medium, large and very large computers.

Source: SEI, Boletim Informativo, various numbers.

market reserve was established, virtually all equipment to
the Brazilian market was supplied by the subsidiaries of
multinational firms, in large degree through imports. In
that year, the only national firm supplying computers was
Cobra, which was then attempting to cater to the industrial
process control market offering systems using Ferranti
technology. At the end of 1978, after the establishment of
significant installed capacity in the two preceding years,
the national industry attained a 2 percent share (in value)
of computers installed in Brazil; by 1985, it had reached
one-fourth of the total computer base (or $1.1 billion). In
unit terms, the numbers are quite striking. SEI estimates
that at the end of 1985 there were 200,000 computers in
Brazil (whereas a year before there were 153,000, ranging
from home computers to mainframes), of which 96 percent were
manufactured locally. Table 3.2 presents the evolution of
gross yearly sales (net of exports) from 1979 to 1984 of
both national and multinational firms, establishing the
shrinking market shares of the latter; conversely, the
shares of national firms are shown to increase from nearly
zero in 1977 to an estimated 52 percent in 1984.

Entry and expansion of foreign producers have indeed
been significantly curtailed by the policy of market
reserve. Table 3.3 lists the name of the local subsidiaries
of multinational firms and the year in which they began
operations in Brazil. Significantly, except for Datapoint,
all foreign firms started operations in or before 1975. In
addition, production or expansion plans were blocked in at
least four instances: production of IBM systems 34, a
medium-sized computer, was stopped and moved to Japan;
application by Apple of production of Apple II was rejected,
and thus moved to Mexico; Hewlett-Packard plans for
production of its system 3000 was rejected and was similarly
displaced to Mexico; Texas Instruments' application for
expansion of facilities was denied and a plant was then
established in Argentina.

Although foreign firms have suffered a substantial
decline in market shares over the last five years, their
dominance in larger systems (classes 3 to 6 in SEI's
nomenclature) is still absolute. Table 3.4 shows the market
shares (measured by the value of the installed class 3-6
computers) in 1976 and 1982. Although IBM and Burroughs
suffered a slight decline in the period, market shares have
overall stayed virtually the same, except for the expansion
of Fujitsu and the entry of some Brazilian firms. As in
many other countries, sales are quite concentrated in the
two largest suppliers, with IBM in a clear position of

TABLE 3.2
Gross Sales of Computers and Peripherals, 1979-84
(in millions of current dollars)

Nationality	1979	(%)	1980	(%)	1981	(%)	1982	(%)	1983	(%)	1984	(%)
Brazilian	190	23	280	32	370	36	558	37	687	46	881	52
Foreign	640	77	580	72	670	64	950	63	800	54	841	48
Total	830	100	860	100	1,040	100	1,508	100	1,487	100	1,700	100

Note: 1984 figures are estimated

Sources: SEI, Panorama da Industria Nacional (1984), p. 8; ABICOMP, Brazilian
Informatics Industry Directory (1983), p. 5; and Ramamurti, op. cit.

TABLE 3.3
Subsidiaries of Multinational Firms
in Data-Processing in Brazil

First Year of Operation

Name of the Firm	Year
IBM	1924
Burroughs	1924
Sperry (Univac)	1950
Olivetti	1952
NCR	1957
Honeywell	1960
Hewlett-Packard	1967
Fujitsu	1972
Control Data	1974
Digital Equipment	1974
Data General	1975
Datapoint	1981

Source: Piragibe (1985), p. 111

TABLE 3.4
Market Shares for Mainframe Computers,
1976 and 1982

Name of the Firm	1976	1982
IBM	64.9	61.8
Burroughs	17.1	14.3
CII-Honeywell Bull	6.4	6.9
DEC	3.0	3.8
Univac	2.3	2.9
Hewlett-Packard	3.1	2.8
Fujitsu	0.8	2.6
Control Data, NCR Data General, DataPoint	1.6	2.4
ICL and Thompson	0.8	0.1
Cobra, Sisco, Labo, Medidata	-	2.3

Source: Piragibe (1985), p. 161.

leadership, followed by Burroughs.[15]

Market shares in segments dominated by multinational firms have shown considerable stability over time; however, the same cannot be said about mini- and microcomputers and some of the peripherals. If the policies instituted by CAPRE and SEI effectively blocked entry and expansion of foreign firms, thus reinforcing a market structure which as in other countries generally settles towards a form of concentrated oligopoly under single-firm price leadership, those policies, on the other hand, effectively stimulated entry by national firms. The number of national firms supplying data-processing equipment progressed from 13 in 1975 to over 100 at the end of 1984, denoting considerable sectoral dynamism. Among the national firms, the joint state/national private sector enterprise Cobra still retained, until 1983, overall sales leadership, as can be seen from Table 3.5.

Following Cobra, six of the ten largest national firms in terms of sales belonged to financially powerful economic groups, particularly of the banking sector, which have in the past been among the largest users in Brazil (together with the government) of data processing services.[16] Although the market is still quite concentrated, it has become less so in the national segment due to the number of new entries. Indeed, when we consider gross sales, the five and ten largest firms decrease their respective market share from 88.8 percent to 46.4 percent and from 98.0 percent to 65.8 percent in the four-year period 1979/83, while Cobra's leadership was being increasingly challenged by newly established firms. In addition, Table 3.5 presents evidence that over time, there was substantial vertical mobility among the ten largest national firms, being sufficient to compare their ranking in 1979 and in 1983.

If the degree of sales concentration of the five and ten largest firms in the sector appears to be decreasing and a significant level of vertical mobility exists across those groups, it is still not easy to evaluate how competitive are specific market segments. Taking the number of firms present in specific segments and changes in their respective market shares over time as evidence of competitive activity, we find that for a number of products it may be substantial. This is especially the case, as Table 3.6 puts in evidence, with minicomputers, microcomputers, modems and special terminals. In those segments, the degree of concentration at the beginning of the 1980s seems to have decreased with the entry of new firms and the expansion (or contraction) of existing ones, causing an instability in market shares which

TABLE 3.5
Gross Sales of the Largest National Firms
1979-83 (Ranking and Proportionate Shares)

Rank	Firm	1979	1980	1981	1982	1983
1	Cobra	58.8	30.4	27.7	22.3	16.6
2	Sid	16.1	13.3	6.3	7.3	12.1
3	Labo	3.8	10.8	8.3	8.4	6.8
4	Prologica	1.8	1.6	1.9	6.0	6.5
5	Digirede	-	-	1.5	4.3	4.4
6	Sisco	0.5	3.9	4.9	4.2	4.2
7	Itautec	-	-	1.2	0.4	4.1
8	Scopus	4.2	5.2	5.4	5.0	4.0
9	Elebra Informatica	0.4	3.0	5.8	7.1	3.9
10	Racimec	-	-	3.2	3.3	3.2

Source: SEI, Panorama da Industria Nacional (1984), p. 23.

TABLE 3.6

Market Shares for Main Product Segments, Selected Years[a]

Mini-Computers

	1979	1983
Cobra	47.1	33.3
Labo	11.2	27.7
Sid	24.5	19.7
Sisco	20.0	11.4
Edisa	13.2	3.4
Novadata	–	2.3
Medidata	2.0	2.2

Micro-Computers

	1981	1983
Microdigital	–	43.0
Prologica	15.8	37.0
Unitron	–	3.5
Polymax	25.7	3.2
Dismac	–	2.7
Digitus	–	2.2
Cobra	32.3	1.9
Scopus	6.1	1.4
Itautec	–	1.1
Sid	10.1	3.6
Edisa	9.3	0.3
Others	0.4	2.5

Disks

Magnetic

	1980	1983
Microlab	39	58
Elebra	13	42
Informatica		
Multidigit	48	–

Floppy

	1980	1983
Flexidisk	88	78
Elebra	12	14
Informatica	–	
Prologica	–	8

Printers

Serial

	1980	1983
Elebra	78.1	54.8
Informatica		
Elgin		–17.2
Globus	21.9	8.0
Others	–	20.0

Line

	1981	1983
Digilab	42	59
Globus	48	41

Special Terminals

	1982	1983
Sid	26.5	29.5
Itautec	22.2	27.3
Racimec	30.3	15.4
Digirede	17.7	17.6
Cobra	–	1.4
Digilab	3.6	5.1
Technodata	–	1.4
Edisa	–	2.1
Zanthus	–	0.2

Video Display

	1980	1983
Scopus	87.0	87.0
EBC	1.9	6.6
Cobra	10.8	3.6
CMA	–	2.8
Parks	0.3	–

Modems

	1980	1983
Elebra	48.8	54.4
Informatica		
Coencisa	48.7	40.6
Parks	1.7	3.6
Digitel	0.5	3.2
Moddata	–	2.0
CMA	–	0.2
Tropical	0.3	–

Source: SEI, Panorama, pp. 65–86.
[a] Except for the case of modems, the shares correspond to units shipped while the rank is established in value terms.

denotes both a significant degree of market contestability and of actual competition. Between 1983 and the beginning of 1986 additional entries occurred in a number of markets: for example, some 35 firms in the latter year were competing in the microcomputer segment, a net addition of approximately 20; the number of firms manufacturing floppy disk drives increased from 3 to 6, and of video displays from 4 to 12.

What implications can be drawn for the price-performance parameters of data processing equipment from the above discussion of market size, structure and contestability? We have suggested that the economic size and relative dynamism of the Brazilian market, although commercially attractive for an increasing number of firms, possibly does not provide the scales, if producers cater exclusively to domestic buyers, for manufacturing under efficient and contestable conditions a very wide range of technologically updated products. The presumption here is that price reductions and improvements in the performance characteristics of individual products are closely related to the extent of actual and potential competition in product markets and the possibilities of individual firms of exploiting both static and dynamic economies of scale in production and R&D.[17] However, if actual competition (denoted by new entries and corresponding shifts in market shares) is a stimulus for managerial or x-efficiency, it may also imply an undesirable degree of fragmentation of production units, due to a market of an insufficient size. In addition, a limited market is a constraint in the generation of funds and the internal accumulation of resources necessary for firms to finance and deploy R&D resources.

In the Brazilian case, unrestricted entry of national firms in a market of limited economic size may have been responsible for the large unit costs of data processing equipment. In view of the 1984 shipment figures and the production scales practiced internationally, we can adduce that the current production volumes in Brazil appear by and large insufficient for firms to fully reap potentially available scale economies (with the possible exception of special terminals for financial purposes). In fact, the manufacture of computers and peripherals is mostly characterized by its batch nature, which is incompatible with levels of productive efficiency necessary to make the industry internationally competitive.[18] Moreover, Brazilian firms do not command at present the resources necessary to bring them to new technological levels by way of discrete or significant innovations in systems design, components,

software or production processes; the available resources
are also rarely pooled by the lack of cooperative R&D
ventures among Brazilian firms.[19] As a result, and in spite
of the relatively low labor costs found in Brazil and the
substantial competition in some market segments, most data
processing equipment is price-uncompetitive for a given
performance specification. As an indication, exports from
national firms are still incipient, having reached 1.2
million dollars in 1983 and 1.5 million in 1984, or .17
percent of total sales in both years, and were mostly
composed of integrated circuits and special terminals.

These propositions need to be qualified. First,
concerning the relationship between market size,
contestability and scale economies in production: the
argument simply implies that observed yearly shipments of
individual products and the rate at which their production
volumes seem to be accumulating over time, combined with
fragmentation of production whenever institutional and
technological barriers to entry are absent, do not allow
national producers to fully exploit the economic benefits
arising from the existence of scale economies. It is not
implied, however, that productivity gains are absent and that
unit costs cannot fall over time. Indeed they do, as
documented for certain categories of equipment.

In the case of 8-bit microcomputers, Tigre and Perine
(1984) examined the evolution of prices paid by consumers
both in the U.S. and Brazil for Apple-IIs, HP-85 A and B,
and TRS-80 and their Brazilian-made clones, since the year
they were first offered in the Brazilian market. They
conclude that the Brazilian equipment is quite competitive
pricewise in the case of CPUs and somewhat less for the
whole system (CPUs, monitor and two drives). In May/June
1984, the Apple II CPU in Brazil was only 8.2 percent more
expensive in Brazil than in the U.S., whereas the whole
system was 36.6 percent; the TRS-80 CPU was 2 percent less
expensive in Brazil, but the price of the system in Brazil
was 18 percent higher; finally, the HP 85A and B were
respectively 37.5 and 48.8 percent more expensive in the
Brazilian market. It is noteworthy first, that the
Brazilian-made machines were initially 2-3 times more
expensive than their American equivalent, and suffered
substantial price reductions in a period of less than two
years. Second, the price differential was greatest in the
case of the HP systems. It is a subsidiary of Hewlett-
Packard itself which manufactures those systems, and, due to
technological barriers to entry imposed by closed
architectures in both microprocessors and operating systems,

it faces no internal competition.[20] In the case of the
TRS-80 and Apple-II clones, however, entry was facilitated
by open architectures. As a result, no less than six firms
were manufacturing the TRS-80 clone and 12 were involved in
the case of the Apple-II clone, indicating that the market
for home and small business computers was quite competitive.
By reaping the moderate scale economies available to them
(by increasing, in one case, from 10 to 400 units per
month), those firms were able to offer progressively lower
prices to the Brazilian consumers. Finally, the technological gap does not seem to be substantial, with innovations
introduced in the United States taking no more than a year
to be replicated in Brazil.

Is this experience generalizable to peripherals and
computers of a different technological "age"? Concerning
peripherals, Piragibe (1984) examined the case of serial
printers, for which the prices had a tendency to fall for
some types of equipment, but for others remained stationary
at levels substantially above prices in the American market.
The average price ratio between Brazilian-made products and
those offered in the American market varied, in June 1984,
from 2.073 (for 200 CPS printers) to 5.96 (in the case of
daisy-wheels), averaging 3.072. Thus, Brazilian-made
printers were, on average, three times more expensive than
those available in the American market. Those ratios,
according to Piragibe, may exaggerate the price differentials due to quality differences (the Brazilian printers
being more resistant) and the high incidence of taxes on
Brazilian products. In any case, the differentials appear
significant, and they seem to have stabilized at levels
considerably above what was the case with 8-bit systems.

Aside from problems related to the inadequacy of
production scales, the high price differentials in serial
printers seem to be associated with two related factors.
First, the scarcity of skills in the area of precision
mechanics, leading to considerably higher production costs
and import ratios for printers (as well as other
peripherals, such as magnetic tape units) than for CPUs.
Second, the serial printers' market apparently low levels of
competition, at least for some products such as
100cps/80cpl,340/400cps and daisy-wheels. The number of
producers catering to the non-captive market (that is, which
are not producing for their own consumption) were relatively
few, varying from 1, in the case of daisy-wheels, to 4, for
130/160 cps printers. The fact that producers of printers
faced relatively high technological barriers to entry,

reflected not only in their numbers and the prices of their products, but also in that some of the more recent product innovations (such as ink-jet, thermal and laser non-impact printers), are expected to be introduced in the Brazilian market with a 3-5 year lag.

A last case in point is of the 16-bit, IBM PC clones. The limited evidence that is available suggests that intense competition in the Brazilian market due to recent entries has driven down substantially their prices. In mid-1984, the basic configuration was selling for $10,500; by mid-1985, $6,650; and their price is expected to reach $5,600 by 1986. However, the price ratio between the American and the Brazilian market decreased from 4 to only 3 and is not expected to go much lower in the future. The reason, beyond the intense price competition in the American market, is that unit costs of the Brazilian PC clones are expected to settle around $3,000, which set a lower limit to the price the consumer would necessarily have to pay for the system.[21] The inability of producers to lower costs much further seems linked again to the limited economic size of the Brazilian market (15,000 units in all were sold in 1985), and therefore the very small scales of production of individual firms, the largest of which are in the 200 per month unit range.[22] The fact that the price differential between the Brazilian and American markets has yet (and is neither expected) to move much below a ratio of three, suggests that in comparison to the 8-bit machines, 16-bit systems may be subject to further economies of scale, not just in production, but also in R&D.

Thus, if for older generations of products characterized by open architectures, it may be in fact feasible to achieve international competitiveness (as in the case of 8-bit CPUs), it is less probable with newer machines due to changes in both the nature and rate of change of the technologies related to their design and production. In terms of design, there is a trend towards closed architectures in the newly enhanced 16-bit machines as well as in the ones employing 32-bit microchips. This means that smaller systems will tend towards an increasing use of customized microprocessors and proprietary operating systems, the most recent examples of which are Apple's Macintosh, Commodore's Amiga and Atari's ST.[23] Moreover, design changes are being accompanied by changes in production technology which are accommodating large production volumes by increasing automation and vertical disintegration. Finally, it is to be noted that changes in design and production processes occur in an environment of

relatively fast technical change, with product cycles of
shortened lengths.

As a result, research, development and engineering costs
tend to rise as producers move from 8 to 16 and then 32-bit
machines, and from the more open towards the more machine-
specific architectures. Efforts, therefore, to design,
manufacture as well as copy (through reverse engineering)
newer generations of machines, become increasingly expensive. Higher development and engineering thresholds for
national firms hold a number of implications. First, the
degree of competition in product markets would be negatively
affected by higher technological barriers to entry, as it is
already the case with some peripherals and newer machines.
Second, a larger entry "fee", in the form of higher minimum
R&D expenditures, tend to bring larger price differentials
between the Brazilian and the markets of the more advanced
countries, in direct proportion to the fixed costs firms
would have to amortize. Third, the compression of the
product-cycle length implies a shorter time period for the
national industry to catch up, making it considerably more
difficult to manage the technological lag.

In this new, and technologically more hostile environment, the links between market size, competition, and scale
economies in R&D and other technological activities are the
second critical dimension determining the price-performance
characteristics of data processing equipment (the first
being the extent to which scale economies in production are
effectively exploited). The Brazilian market does not seem
to be sufficiently large to support firms which, in isola-
tion, would have the financial means to conduct R&D in the
scale and depth necessary to introduce major innovations;
neither would most firms be able to undertake the efforts to
go inside the "black box" and unlock the proprietary technologies characteristic of newer systems. In fact, technological activity and expenditures need to be substantially
increased if the technological lag is to be maintained in
the 2-4 year range.[24]

This proposition relating the possibilities and need of
exploiting scale economies in R&D in a fragmented market
of limited economic size also needs to be qualified. Most
national firms have in fact introduced a substantial number
of incremental innovations, most often after an initial
effort at reverse engineering enabled them to copy products
displaying open architectures, or once they obtained a
license, transferred and effectively absorbed a new technology. Some of this adaptive R&D involves modifying foreign
designs and specifications to local conditions, which

generates high social pay-offs. Those efforts, moreover,
consume significant human and financial resources. As in
most countries, the data processing industry is quite
skill intensive: in 1983, 24.7 percent of the employees had
a university degree, and the largest proportion of them
(30.3 percent) were deployed in R&D activities. Although
multinational firms operating in Brazil had an equally large
proportion of graduates among their employees (28.1
percent), it is noteworthy that only a small proportion of
them were engaged in development activities (4.3 percent).
Most of them were deployed in marketing (42.8 percent), a
category which absorbed only 12.8 percent of professionals
in Brazilian firms. Seen from a different perspective,
national producers engaged in 1983, 171 employees in R&D per
100 million dollars of sales, whereas the corresponding
ratio for multinational producers was 15.

The importance of R&D activities for national firms is
also captured from their R&D expenditures which, in 1983
corresponded to 9.8 percent of total sales, and have
averaged 11 percent between 1979 and 1982.[25] Further, their
R&D expenditures per employee have increased an average of
78.3 percent per annum between 1979 and 1982 in real terms.
By contrast, the manufacturing sector in Brazil spent just
over .6 percent of its sales in R&D. The proportion of R&D
expenditures over sales varied somewhat according to the
market segment: 9.8 percent for minicomputers, 12.2 percent
for micros, 5.6 percent for peripherals, 8.1 percent for
modems and 15.2 percent for other equipment.[26] These high
R&D intensities should not be surprising as producers have
faced strong incentives to develop on their own, or at least
continuously upgrade their products. This has led to a
variety of technological strategies involving both imported
and local designs generally requiring relatively large R&D
expenditures.

In the case of minicomputers, the five national
producers opted in 1977/78 for three different strategies:
Sisco decided to emulate through reverse engineering DEC's
PDP-8 and Data General's Nova-3; Edisa, Labo and SID were
licensed respectively by Fujitsu, Nixdorf and Logabax; and
Cobra went for its own development on the basis of the G-10
design, originally developed at the university. Cobra's
ability to successfully launch in 1980 the C-520/30/40 minis
(of which by the end of 1983 Cobra had sold 537 units) was
however not independent of the experience it had obtained
in producing two other series of minicomputers under license:
the C-700, introduced in 1974 for industrial process control
and utilities using Ferranti technology; and the C-400

series, a mini suited for data entry and general business
applications, built with Sycor technology. Sycor was a
relatively unknown American firm which had supplied
technology to Olivetti, which prior to the 1975 import
controls was a major supplier of equipment to Brazilian
banks; the C-400 series had, as a result, wide acceptance
among financial institutions (over 1300 sold between 1978,
when first introduced, and 1983). Although all producers of
minicomputers had therefore primary or secondary reliance on
foreign technologies, still they followed CAPRE's original
directives of relying on their own capabilities for
up-gradation and further development. Edisa, for example,
up-graded its ED300 through reverse engineering and the use
of more powerful devices such as Motorola's 32-bit 68000
micro-processors. Generally, local firms have been able to
keep up with incremental innovations abroad by migrating to
more powerful microprocessors and memories available off-
the-shelf and by an expansion of R&D activities.

If national firms have been able to successfully bring
significant improvements within a given generation of products, as with minicomputers in the period 1981-84, a recent
example points to the technological difficulties of introducing new generations of data processing equipment. In
1984, all five producers of minicomputers competed with independent projects for the production of superminis: Cobra,
SID and Labo with their own technology, and Sisco and Edisa
under license of IPL Systems and Fujitsu respectively. In
addition, three other national firms had requested SEI's
approval for their projects, which were also based on
foreign technologies: Elebra, Itautec and ABC Sistemas,
with licenses from DEC, Formation and Honeywell Bull. At
first, SEI approved the production of superminis only by the
three firms with production based on local technologies; in
the end, a more pragmatic and result-oriented view prevailed
and all eight projects were approved. That led SID, Labo
and Cobra to drop their plans and the latter two to sign
collaboration agreements with Nixdorf and Data General,
respectively. The fundamental reason was economic. To
compete with the most reputable technology for superminis,
which is DEC's (Elebra will be initially producing the Vax
11/750), Cobra and others realized they would require timely
access to technology beyond their present R&D capabilities.
Licensing then became the most feasible alternative to enter
a market estimated to be worth $1.4 billion in the period
1985-90.[27]

The licensing strategy which predominated in the case
of minis and superminicomputers, was also the means of

obtaining technology for magnetic disk drives, tape drives
and high speed modems. Other sources of technology,
including local design and reverse engineering, were
utilized for equipment of lower levels of complexity, such
as microcomputers, electronic accounting machines, data
entry terminals, keyboards, low speed modems, word
processors, and bank terminals. On balance, it appears that
a diminishing proportion of total data processing equipment
sales is from goods produced under license (this proportion
fell from 69 percent in 1979 to 41 percent in 1982).[27]
Nonetheless, among the eighteen largest national producers,
11 still had licensing agreements which, in 1981, were either
classified as "important: or "very important" and no radical
shifts in sourcing technology have been received since
then.[28] Most of the licensees in that year were firms
linked to financial and other large economic groups with
little or no previous experience in informatics. Although
benefiting from their financial backing, those producers
have lacked the technological capabilities to develop their
own designs independent of foreign technology suppliers. In
addition, licensing agreements were seen as a way to meet
competition by compressing the time that would normally be
required for product development, avoiding large R&D costs
while attaining an acceptable standard of quality. In sum,
despite the technological efforts undertaken by national
producers, which are substantial by the standards of
Brazilian industry, they still seem unable to move beyond
adaptive R&D efforts and improvements in the engineering of
systems and peripherals manufacturing. A larger and more
focused deployment of R&D resources will probably be needed
in the future to significantly reduce price differentials
between the national and international markets and avoid a
widening of the technological gap.

What we are therefore suggesting in this section is
that in order for the national industry to produce equipment
of competitive price-performance characteristics, firms need
to feel compelled to exploit economies of scale of both
static and dynamic sorts in production and R&D, while facing
the constraint and the discipline imposed by a competitive
environment. In this perspective, and in view of the
limited economic size of the domestic market, the sector
should first, be encouraged to expand its exports as a way
to overcome the domestic scale limitations and move towards
more contestable market structures. As part of such export
development strategy, a higher degree of vertical
disintegration and horizontal specialization in production
and R&D may be called for, as firms shift their attention to

specific market niches.[29] Second, given the financial,
informational and human resource constraint which national
firms individually face in conducting research, development
and engineering activities, cooperative arrangements should
be stimulated, and closer links and more efficient
interfaces need to be established between industry and
universities or other research centers. Third, the
insufficient flow of highly qualified scientific and
technical personnel into the industry to face its enlarged
R&D needs require measures oriented to strengthen the
training and education components of the informatics
policy.[30] Fourth, licensing arrangements should not be per
se discouraged, but used as a strategic instrument to
complement local technological activities. The presumption
is that for more complex or idiosyncratic technologies,
licensing is a means to effectively provide for their
transfer, being economically superior to costly attempts at
reverse engineering and similar modes of technological
acquisition.[31] Finally, protection from entry of foreign
producers and equipment should not only be focused and
time-bound, but its implementation should be gauged against
policy-defined targets, particularly the price-performance
differentials between products offered in the Brazilian and
the international market.[32]

CONCLUSIONS

     The growth prospects for the Brazilian computer
industry are, in the next 5-8 years, quite bright. SEI's
policies are not expected to shift significantly during the
period, now that the Brazilian Congress has given them the
political seal of approval by passing the Informatics Law.
There is little question that CAPRE's and SEI's policies
were instrumental in bringing about the establishment and
growth of the national informatics industry with the entry
of over 100 firms in the last 8 years. Those policies have
also led to the progressive compression of both direct and
indirect imports; in fact, the import content of total sales
by national producers decreased from 28 percent in 1979 to
7.5 percent in 1982.[33] Simultaneously, foreign investment
in the sector has been curtailed by the market reserve
policies; the exact decrease in capital flows are, of
course, hard to estimate, as they depend on corporate data
unavailable to the public.
     In the near future, the two most pressing issues will
be the extent to which the national industry will be able to

increase its level of productive efficiency and how effectively will the technological gap be managed, so that a
growing price-performance lag does not develop. As we noted
in this paper, batch production processes, a still narrow
R&D base, and an insufficiently competitive environment in
some product markets are probably a major cause of
inefficiency, high unit costs and the inability to move
beyond established technologies. Large production and R&D
scales and long runs are not however compatible with
the present size distribution of firms for most market
segments and, even more important, with the inward orientation of the industry. In order to achieve international
scales in R&D, output volumes and length of production runs,
a change in the policy framework and the way industry is
organized are needed.

The central question for policy regards the nature of
incentives and constraints which may lead to cost efficient
and technologically progressive behavior. The external
market is generally regarded as an arena where firms face
the discipline of the market to a much larger extent than in
the (generally protected) domestic market. However, to
penetrate those markets, producers have to surpass a minimum
threshold of technical competence and price competitiveness.
For that, the firm must not only mobilize large volumes of
resources to be invested in product development, but need to
reap significant economies of scale before it reaches competitive price-performance levels. Although cooperative R&D
ventures among firms and in close collaboration with government would help to overcome the R&D budget constraint, a
similar concept is less applicable to production activities, which would still be submitted to a minimum scale
constraint. New mechanisms will probably have to be devised
to push firms into export markets; unrestricted entry of
national producers and internal competition per se, although
desirable from the point of view of stimulating x-efficiency,
are not sufficient for firms to approach international
levels of production efficiency and technological performance. The economic size of the external market combined
with an expanded R&D effort hold the key to competitiveness
for the Brazilian informatics industry.

NOTES

*The World Bank does not accept responsibility for the views
expressed herein which are those of the author and should
not be attributed to the World Bank or to its affiliated

organizations. The findings, interpretations, and conclusions do not necessarily represent official policy of the Bank.

1. The most comprehensive description of the policy space within which the Brazilian computer industry operates is found in Transborder Data Flows and Brazil: Brazilian Case Study (1983). A detailed investigation of the industry, with a particular focus on problems related to technology transfer and development, was undertaken by P. Tigre in Technology and Competition in the Brazilian Computer Industry (1983).

2. Note that performance is a non-trivial quantum to define, as it is the combination of many operating and other characteristics of data processing machines, including speed of input/output operations, internal memory capacity, reliability, flexibility, etc. In addition, there is the question of product appropriateness to local environment, which should be factored in when comparing performance levels of "equivalent" products.

3. That export activity can hasten the process of maturation of infant industries is a proposition found, for example, in Westphal (1982), who notes that "it is very likely that infant-industry exports will yield sizeable net benefits because export activity appears to accelerate the acquisition of technological mastery and hence to hasten productivity improvement and efficiency gains" (p. 271).

4. For illuminating accounts of the origins and evolution of the policies towards the computer industry see C. Piragibe, Industria da Informática: Desenvolvimento Brasileiro e Mundial (1985), Chs. 5 and 6; R. Ramarmuti, State-Owned Enterprises in High Technology Industries: Studies in India and Brazil (forthcoming), Ch. 6; E. Adler, The Quest for Technological Autonomy: Computer and Nuclear Policies in Argentina and Brazil (forthcoming); S. Helena, A Industria de Computadores: Evolucão das Decisões Governmentais, Revista de Administracão Publica (1980).

5. Normative Act 15 classified contracts into five categories: for license of patents; for license of trademark use; for the supply of industrial technology (consumer goods and raw materials); for technical and industrial cooperation (technical assistance for capital goods production); and for technical services (up to the limit of 20 thousand dollars). A separate contract is needed for each category. In addition, payments for use of patents, trademarks and for technical assistance should not exceed 5 percent of gross sales, with maximum term for

contracts being 15 years for invention patents, 10 years for model patents and 5 years for technical assistance (renewable for capital goods production). For a detailed description, see C. Ganz (1983).

6. In allocating import licenses, CAPRE gave highest priority to spares for existing equipment, then to parts and assemblies for local manufacturers, equipment required to expand existing systems, and lastly to new systems.

7. Cobra was created in 1974 as a joint venture with equity equally owned by government, through Digibras; by Ferranti, a U.K. supplier of computers to the British Navy; and by EE Equipamentos Eletronicos, a local firm. In 1976 its ownership and control structure changed dramatically in order to restructure its finances and face internal competition in the production of minicomputers. Cobra's share capital was increased in that year from $4.4 million to $30.8 million, with the additional capital coming from three state-owned banks as well as from the largest government computer services bureau (Serpro) and a consortium of 14 private banks. The private banks, which were going to become Cobra's largest customers, owned 39 percent of the stock but had a voting majority on the board.

8. Actually, to the extent that CONIN's majority is made up of representatives of various ministries, probably lacking the technical expertise and institutional backing to effectively challenge SEI's plans and programs, it is doubtful that CONIN will in fact shape the future course of informatics policy.

9. What follows is based on SEI's Transborder Data Flows, op. cit., p. 13 and seq.; and pp. 67-68.

10. In this connection, Schwartzman in his paper "High Technology vs. Self-Reliance: Brazil Enters the Computer Age" (1985) notes that "...the field of computer production and operation is being organized in Brazil according to the views and interests of its promoters, producers and professionals. [H]ow long this tendency will hold depends on their capacity to confront three challenges: the changes in the political system, which threatens bureaucratic insulation; the pressure of a growing user's market, which requires quality, services and low prices; and the pressure of international competition, which looms behind the market pressure in its demand for universalism. Success will depend, in part, on political variables; but it will also depend on the computer industry's capacity to step up its research effort and respond effectively to the internal demands and foreign competition." (p. 14)

11. For a detailed discussion of this theme see Tigre, op. cit., Chs. 6-9 and Piragibe, op. cit., Chs. 7 and 8.

12. Informe ABICOMP, March 1985, and Ramamurti, (1985).

13. According to its vice-president, these are the rates of growth with which Prologica, a leading computer manufacturer, plans its operations. See Senhor, March 27, 1985, p. 46.

14. In discussing the economics of computer production, O'Connor (1985) suggests that as the industry moves towards standardization and automation, the "economies of large-scale production appear to be assuming increasing importance in many types of hardware..." (p. 314), particularly peripheral equipment, in spite of the act that "rapid technological change and short product life cycles ...(serve) as a disincentive in the short run to investment in highly automated equipment for equipment production/assembly." (p. 316)

15. With the exception of Japan, England and the USSR, IBM has commanded absolute market dominance in the category of large systems in virtually all industrial and semi-industrial countries. In Brazil, its traditional dominance in that segment of the market may have been in fact reinforced by the institutional barriers to entry regarding other foreign producers, as well as trade restriciton concerning imports of large systems.

16. Sid, Labo, Digirede, Sisco, Itautec, Elebra Informatica.

17. Static economies of scale, as projected in the shape of the long-run envelope cost curve, reflect the impact of different rates of output per unit of time on average cost curves; dynamic economies of scale are related fundamentally to the length of the production run as it affects the acquisition of skills, the possibilites of mechanization and automation, and the spread of R&D, engineering and set-up costs.

18. Note, in addition, that the levels of labor productivity, as denoted by the value of output per employee, do not seem to be rising over the period 1979-83. In current dollars, they were respectively: 47076, 38456, 44689, 44342, 43663, and 38291.

19. The human resource base as well as public infrastructure and funding for R&D are also limited. Schwartzman, op. cit., drawing from a recently proposed three-year national research plan in computer sciences, notes that "...There are five institutions providing doctoral degrees for 10 persons a year. The total number of researchers with doctoral degrees is 108. There are also 15

64

institutions providing master's degrees...On average, 15 new
doctors enter the field each year. The total number of
researchers is estimated as 750, 500 of which are working on
software. The research plan projects a total increase in
the number of doctors to 500 by the end of 1987, as against
300, if the current growth rate is kept. The total cost for
research projects, infrastructure, ...is estimated to be
around 40 million dollars in three years. The amount
required by the plan is quite small by international
standards. However, Brazil would not have the capacity to
absorb a much larger sum, given the current small basis of
computer research." (p. 21) For a detailed account of R&D
programming objectives, see Seplan/CNPq, Acao Programada em
Ciencia e Tecnologia 17, 1984).
    20. Hewlett-Packard is the only foreign firm authorized
to manufacture microcomputers in Brazil, catering to the
engineering and scientific market.
    21. Informatica Hoje, June 18, 1985.
    22. In comparison, Compaq in 1984 shipped 139,000 units
of its portable and desktop models; Apple shipped 250-300,000
units of its Macintosh, although the highly automated
Freemont plant is capable of producing 1,000,000 units per
year; and IBM produced approximately 2,000,000 PCs. It is
worth noting that Commodore, at the beginning of 1985, estimated that it would take sales of 300-350,000 units to break
into the market with a sufficiently inexpensive machine and
make its production a profitable operation. Even allowing
for factor price differentials between the USA and Brazil as
they affect the choice of production technology, optimal
scales for production of micros would certainly be beyond
the present 1-3,000 units per year which most Brazilian
firms practice, probably in the order of 50-100,000. This
in fact is the type of range found, for instance, among the
S. Korean producers of word processors and microcomputers.
    23. Although all three have in common a 68000 CPU
operating with a 32-bit internal architecture and 512K of
memory, each uses a number of advanced custom chips and
offers features (including high clock speed and imaging
possibilities) which characterizes their technology as part
of a new generation of personal computers.
    24. In 1982, national firms spent approximately $69
million in R&D; by contrast, Data General and Apple
individually spent respectively $84 and $38 million,
(although they only cater to the small systems market
segment), whereas IBM total R&D expenditures were over $2
billion. Even allowing for the large wage differentials of
R&D personnel in Brazil and the United States, those figures

denote the nontrivial problem of containing the
technological gap in informatics, let alone closing it.

25. The 1983 figure refers to the 48 largest producers,
which were included in SEI's Panorama (1984). For other
years see Piragibe (1985), p. 197.

26. Panorama, p. 53.

27. Table 3.7 summarizes the characteristics of the
superminis which were being introduced in the Brazilian
market at the end of 1985.

Note that none of the technologies are state-of-the-art
but 3-4 years old. Data General has launched more powerful
models since (the MV 10000 and 10000SX) and so has DEC (the
11/780, 11/785, the 8600) and others, within a general
strategy of outcompeting in price and performance mainframe
equipment (such as the IBM 4381 series). In any case, the
capability of national producers to effectively absorb the
2-5 year old technology they have licensed and migrate in a
relatively short period to more advanced models will depend
very much on the extent of assimilative and other types of
R&D they undertake. Minor efforts, in this case (and as
opposed to 8-bit home computers, for instance) would not be
sufficient to acquire technological proficiency in the
production and servicing of minicomputers.

28. ABICOMP, Directory (1984), p. 6.

29. SEI, Transborder (1983), pp. 211-213. See also the
discussion on licensing in Tigre, op.cit., pp, 105-114.

30. Among the possible options to expand exports,
serious consideration should be given for original equipment
manufacture (OEM), joint venture and co-production
arrangements. East Asian Economies are now major suppliers
of OEM equipment for American producers. Japan's Kyosera,
for example, exports portable computers to Tandy which sells
it under the Radio Shack brand; similar arrangements can be
found for larger machines and peripheral equipment. In
Japan, OEM contracts have become so common that a 1983
government survey of 300 major corporations in precision
instruments, electric machinery and transport equipment,
found that virtually all had entered into OEM contracts.
Even Fujitsu, the sixth largest producer of data processing
equipment in the world in 1984 (with revenues of $3.5
billion), continued a path of 'oeming' to partners with
stronger sales and services networks in the Asian regional
market. See Fukushima (1985), p. 25. It is telling that
out of the IBM PC manufacturing cost of $860, nearly 50
percent ($395) worth of equipment are supplied under OEM,
which rises to over 80 percent ($625) when including system
components made by U.S.-owned plants. Japan supplies the

66

TABLE 3.7
Characteristics of New Computers Introduced in 1985

Firm	Technology	Equipment	Basic Architecture	Year of Introduction	Performance (MIPS)
ABC-Bull	Honeywell	DPS6/95	32 bits	1980	0.62
Cobra	Data General	MV-4000	32 bits	1982	0.60
		MV-8000II	32 bits	1983	1.26
Edisa	Hewlett-Packard	HP-3000/48	16 bits	1983	0.56
		HP-3000/68	16 bits	1983	1.10
Elebra	DEC	VAX 11/750	32 bits	1980	0.72
Itautec	Formation	F-4000/200	32 bits	1980	0.72
Labo	Nixdorf	8890/72	32 bits	1981	0.70
Sisco	IPL	4460	32 bits	1982	1.30

Sources: Revista Isto E, Nov. 27, 1985; ComputerWorld and Auerbach.

MIPS - Millions of Instructions per Second

graphics printer, semiconductors, power supply and the
keyboard; the monitor is South Korean, and the floppy disk
drives from Singapore (Business Week, March 11, 1985, p.
48). In fact, IBM export-oriented OEM purchases from
Brazilian manufacturers have increased fairly rapidly from
$5 million in 1984 to $15 million in 1985, and are expected
to reach $30 million in 1986. They are, however, still
small relative to IBM's captive market, having therefore
very high growth potential. It has also become increasingly
common for joint venture agreements to involve cross-OEM
contracts, as between ATT and Olivetti, with one supplying
computers and the other printers to each other's markets,
taking advantage of a larger measure of horizontal
specialization and expanded volumes.

    31. Those last two points have in fact been addressed
by the first National Informatics Plan approved September
30, 1985 by the Council on Informatics and Automation (to
which SEI is now formally subordinated). The Plan calls for
a strategic focus on the training of human resources and the
strengthening of R&D activities through integrated R&D
programs involving research centers, universities and firms.
These activities will be supported by the concession of
fiscal incentives conditioned on a formal commitment of the
beneficiary to invest a certain percent of its sales in R&D.
In particular, the Plan allows for a deduction from income
taxes of up to twice the proven expenditures in R&D
projects; and for accelerated depreciation of fixed assets
used in either R&D or production, together with their
exemption from sales, financial operations and import taxes
(whenever those assets are imported and there are no
national 'similars'). In addition, foreign firms will be
required to invest 5 percent of their annual sales in R&D
priority areas determined by the Council. For training of
staff, firms are allowed a deduction of income taxes of
twice the proven expenses. The fiscal incentives to be
granted during the three year life of the Plan are estimated
to total 125 million dollars per year, two thirds of which
will be in R&D projects.

    32. More generally, the experience of many newly
industrializing countries suggest that local efforts in
technological development and transfers of foreign
technology more often than not stand in complementary
relationship to one another. There would, in other words,
be a combination of imported and internally generated
know-how that would bring countries to the desired goals of
technological and industrial maturity. See, for instance,
the essays on the experience of Korea, Japan and India in

N. Rosenberg and C. Frischtak (eds.), <u>International</u>
<u>Technology Transfer: Concepts, Measures and Comparisons</u>
(1985).

33. This concept could also be incorporated in
negotiations with multinational producers, which tend to
charge in the Brazilian market, prices markedly superior to
those charged for equivalent equipment in their home market.
A case in point is the IBM 4341 system, which with a typical
configuration, was in mid-1984, between 2.4 (according to
IBM) and 3.02 (according to the association of national
producers - ABICOMP) times more expensive in Brazil.
Further, its prices were raised in real terms by 38 percent
between August 1981 and February 1983. See ABICOMP, <u>A</u>
<u>Politica de Informatica, A Industria Nacional e o</u>
<u>Desenvolvimento Tecnologico</u>, (1984). In order to bring down
similar price differentials, the Foreign Investment
Commission of Mexico recently worked an arrangement with IBM
along the following lines: in order for this corporation to
manufacture its "System 51" microcomputers, the Commission
requires that the prices of IBM micros be no more than 15
percent higher than prices in other countries for the same
products. In addition, the agreement calls for IBM to
introduce its most advanced products in Mexico within 6
months of their commercial introduction in the U.S. See <u>The</u>
<u>Washington Post</u>, July 24, 1985, p. D3.
    34. ABICOMP (1984), p. 6.

BIBLIOGRAPHY

ABICOMP, <u>Brazilian Informatics Industry Directory</u>, 4th
    (1983) and 5th (1984/1985) Editions, Rio de Janeiro
    (1984, 1985).
ABICOMP, <u>A Politica Nacional de Informatica, a Industria</u>
    <u>Nacional e o Desenvolvimento Tecnologico</u>, May 1984.
Adler, E. <u>The Quest for Technological Autonomy: Computer</u>
    <u>and Nuclear Energy Policies in Argentina and Brazil</u>,
    University of California Press, Berkeley, (forthcoming).
Fukushima, K. "Japan's Real Trade Policy," <u>Foreign Policy</u>,
    p. 59, Summer 1985.
Ganz, C. "Regulation of Technology Imports: An Alternative
    to Market Reserve Policy," <u>mimeo</u> (1983).
Government of Brazil, <u>Diario Oficial da Uniao</u>, October 30,
    1984.
Government of Brazil, Secretaria Especial de Informatica,
    <u>Boletim Informativo</u>, various numbers.

Government of Brazil, Secretaria Especial de Informatica, Panorama da Industria Nacional - Computadores e Perifericos, Brasilia (1984).

Government of Brazil, Secretaria de Planejamento/CNPq, Acão Programada em Ciencia e Tecnologia 17 - Comunicacões, Eletronica e Informatica, Brasilia (1984).

Helena, S. "A Industria de Computadores: Evolucão das Decisões Governamentais," in Revista de Administracão Publica, Oct/Dec 1980.

O'Connor, D. "The Computer Industry in the Third World: Policy Options and Constraints," World Development, vol. 13, p. 3. March 1985.

Piragibe, C. "Competitividade dos Equipamentos Perifericos Fabricados no Brasil - Impressoras," Instituto de Economia Industrial/UFRJ, Texto de Discussao n. 61, December, 1984.

Piragibe, C. Industria da Informatica - Desenvolvimento Brasileiro e Mundial, Editora Campus, Rio de Janeiro (1985).

Ramamurti, R. State Owned Enterprises in High Technology Industries: Studies in India and Brazil, Praeger, New York (1985).

Rosenberg, N. and C. Frischtak, eds. International Technology Transfer: Concepts, Measures and Comparisons, Praeger, New York (1985).

Schwartzman, S. "High Technology vs. Self-Reliance: Brazil Enters the Computer Age," IUPERJ, Serie Estudos, n. 36, Rio de Janeiro, May 1985.

Tigre, P. Technology and Competition in the Brazilian Computer Industry, St. Martin's Press, New York (1983).

Tigre, P. and L. Perine, "Competitividade dos Microcomputadores Nacionais," Instituto de Economia Industrial/UFRJ, Texto de Discussao n. 60, November 1984.

United Nations, Transborder Data Flows and Brazil - Brazil Case Study, prepared by the Special Secretariat of Informatics, Government of Brazil, New York, 1983.

Westphal, L. "Fostering Technological Mastery by Means of Selective Infant Industry Protection," in M. Syrquin and S. Teitel, eds., Trade, Stability, Technology and Equity in Latin America, Academic Press, New York (1982).

4

France

Ronald Brickman
Vanderbilt University

On February 3, 1985, Newsday revealed a secret
agreement between the American and French governments providing for the sale of U.S. supercomputers to aid French
deployment of MIRV missiles. According to the Long Island
newspaper, the 1982 deal was arranged in exchange for
France's commitment to increase its participation in the
Western military alliance.

The Newsday item provides an ironically fitting
postscript to the French government's twenty-year effort to
develop a viable domestic industry in computers and related
high technologies. Most students of this fascinating
history of political determination and economic frustration
concur that the starting point was the refusal of the
American government in the mid-1960s to authorize the export
to France of two giant U.S.-built computers, for fear that
their use would be diverted to nuclear arms development.
The episode, coming on the heels of General Electric's
takeover of the leading national computer firm, Machines
Bull, demonstrated France's weaknesses in information technology and revealed the strategic importance of an independent national capability. Thus was born the Plan Calcul, a
massive program of state-funded and directed aid to favored
national firms that continues in different forms to this
day.

After twenty years, the essential features and results
of the program can be summarized as follows:

a) The French state, notwithstanding several changes in
government and dominant political ideology, has not wavered
in its commitment to bring French high technology industries
into the ranks of leading world competitors;

b) Its preferred policy instruments to achieve this

goal have been, with similar constancy, substantial government investment, especially in capital contributions and R&D
aid, industry rationalization and reorganization, and preferential public procurement;

c) Government policy over this period has shifted most
noticeably in the degree of cooperation sought with more
technologically advanced foreign firms; in turn, the government has for the most part condoned the establishment and
expansion of foreign subsidiaries in France;

d) Despite sustained public commitment and assistance,
French firms in many areas of information technology have
yet to win a substantial share of the world or even the
domestic market; the most heavily subsidized companies show
almost chronic losses. Yet the prolonged effort has served
to keep French industry in the international running;
current areas of strength, abetted by favorable trends in
international markets and in the underlying technology, may
even give certain segments of the industry a long-awaited
edge.

The history of French policy toward the computer and
allied industries falls conveniently into three stages: the
Gaullist period from the launching of the Plan Calcul to its
demise in the mid-1970s, the 1975-1981 period under the
government of Giscard d'Estaing, and current policy under
the Socialists.

THE PLAN CALCUL

Like much of French industry, the electronics sector in
the 1950s and early 1960s was composed of small, specialized
companies geared to serving the domestic market. Some
foreign-controlled firms, including IBM, ITT and later Texas
Instruments, had already found French soil an attractive
staging ground to conquer the European market. The
establishment of the European Community encouraged both a
policy of mergers among French firms and further penetration
of American firms to avoid EC tariffs. Yet the financial
and technical difficulties of Machines Bull that led to the
GE takeover in 1964 illustrated the continued weaknesses of
the French electronics industry in a rapidly changing technological and commercial environment.[1]

The central objective of the Plan Calcul was to promote
selected "national champions" that could meet these international challenges. A new company, Compagnie
Internationale de I'Informatique (CII), was formed through
the merger of two small French firms and designated the pri-

vileged beneficiary of government aid. The strategy was to
take on IBM where the American firm was strongest and the
French industry weakest, in the medium- to large-sized computer market. In 1967, a five-year agreement between the
government and the company was signed that promised some $80
million in state aid for R&D and another $8 million in other
assistance.[2]

The following year, the government launched a similar
effort to stimulate the fledgling semiconductor industry.
General Electric was pressured to give up its 49% equity
share in SESCO, which then merged with COSEM. The resulting
independent firm, SESCOSEM, was promised some $18 million
over the next five years for developing integrated circuits
for computer applications.[3]

While the policy of national champions was a direct
corollary of the Gaullist government's independent line on
foreign and military policy, it did not foreclose a more
indulgent attitude toward foreign subsidiaries in France.
IBM-France, which in 1967 already employed over 12,000, was
a major exporter, maintained an important research center
and trained several thousand Frenchmen a year in computer
design and applications.

By the mid-1970s, the government had invested some $350
million in the two programs but the results were disap-
pointing. CII, suffering annual losses, still ran far
behind IBM even in the domestic market; its principal
clients were government agencies or government-influenced
businesses and services. American firms and Philips dominated the market in semiconductors with SESCOSEM, now
absorbed into the Thomson group, ranking only fifteenth in
world production. Analysts cite several reasons for the
lagging performance: a misconceived strategy for CII that
attempted to challenge IBM in its strongest product lines
rather than seeking out more promising market niches; insufficient investment in view of the ambitious goals;
weaknesses in product development and commercialization, and
the reluctance of domestic end-users to buy domestic components over foreign products.[4]

THE GISCARD ERA

Recognizing the failure of the Plan Calcul and its counterpart effort in components, the government of Giscard
d'Estaing embarked upon a new course whose distinguishing
feature was a greater reliance on foreign technology. In
computer manufacturing, an earlier attempt to find a

European solution in the form of a consortium associating CII, Philips and Siemens was aborted in favor of an alliance of CII with Honeywell's French subsidiary, Honeywell-Bull (the descendent of the GE takeover). The new company, CII-HB, was 47% owned by Honeywell, which retained significant voting power over major decisions. Over the 1976-1980 period, the government poured some $440 million into the venture, with Honeywell's investment amounting to $44 million. Government funding covered the cost of buying Honeywell's shares, absorbing the merged company's losses, and financing research. In addition, the government promised the firm that it would pay 55% of the difference if government purchasing orders fell below $1 billion in the 1976-80 period.[5]

CII-HB's product strategy continued CII's line and, with government encouragement, also expanded into minicomputers and office automation. In partnership with Thomson and Télémécanique, CII formed SEMS, a venture in minicomputer manufacturing that, with the help of $11 million a year in state aid, captured 40% of the domestic market in 1979.

The government's new policy for components, revealed in 1977, demonstrated a similar eagerness to forge international alliances. American firms were enticed with easier access to French markets in exchange for technological know-how. The major poles of cooperation were three joint ventures, with the French holding a majority interest in each, aimed at the development and production of MOS integrated circuits: Thomson and Motorola, the French aerospace firm Matra with Harris (later joined by Intel), and Eurotechnique associating the glass and chemicals giant Saint Gobain with National Semiconductor.[6] Unlike the government's continued championing of a single firm in computer manufacturing, the new policy for components reflected a greater faith in market competitiveness by supporting a more diversified and less centrally controlled array of companies.

The government's renewed interest in market forces did not extend, however, to a curtailment of public financial assistance. Over $150 million was allocated to the three ventures and to two other initiatives: a subsidiary of Philips, and EFCIS, a former unit of the French atomic energy authority that became part of the Thomson group. Additional state aid went to several peripherals firms, most of which were affiliated with either Thomson or the electrical equipment firm CGE.[7] The government also endeavored to protect its domestic efforts by selectively discouraging independent foreign investments. An application by Digital Equipment to build a computer manufacturing plant at Annecy

was refused on the grounds that CII-HB was not up to the
competition.

Giscard's version of <u>la politique informatique</u> produced
somewhat mixed results. Analysts agree that the part-
nerships with American firms paid important technological
dividends. Eurotechnique produced its first integrated circuits in 1980, helping to reduce the country's chronic
weaknesses in the sector.[8] By 1978, CII-HB, with a turnover of $900 million, had captured about a quarter of the
French market in mainframes; cumulatively, CII-HB and its
parent companies accounted for 29% of the installed base in
small, medium and large computers by number and 13% by
value.[9] The French performance was most impressive in software and computer services; with over 400 active firms and
$450 million in 1978 sales, the industry had become Europe's
largest.[10]

These advances notwithstanding, market share continued
to be a problem for most segments of French information
technology. IBM still held on to 55% of the $5.2 billion
domestic market in computers, with Burroughs, CDC, Univac
and NCR also taking significant shares. In minicomputers,
the three largest French firms (SEMS, CII-HB, and
Intertechnique) were unable to overtake the 45% market share
of the four leading American imports. In semiconductors,
the largest French producer, Thomson, ranked far behind
Philips and Siemens among European producers, with 1980
sales of $190 million. Although exports of computers and
peripheral equipment rose 110% in the 1976-79 period,
imports rose 80% and still accounted for nearly half of the
domestic market (see Table 4.1).

HIGH TECHNOLOGY POLICY UNDER THE SOCIALISTS

The arrival in power of Francois Mitterand and the
Socialist party in 1981 signaled less a radical departure
from previous policy than yet another fiddling with the
controls of the state's industrial policy machinery in the
information sector. The nationalization of the major
electronics firms provided drama but did little to alter the
underlying relationships of dependency and direction to
which the principal recipients of state largesse had long
grown accustomed. The key players in the government's grand
designs over the past fifteen years, Thomson, CGE, and Saint
Gobain, fell under state ownership. In addition, the
government took a controlling interest in Matra and in
CII-HB, reducing Honeywell's holding in the latter company

TABLE 4.1
Trade Flows for Computers and Peripheral Equipment, 1976-79
(in millions of U.S. dollars)

	1976	1977	1978	1979
Minicomputers				
Production	164	150	237	350
Imports	62	80	90	130
Exports	60	61	77	85
Market Size	166	169	250	395
Small, medium and large computer systems				
Production	510	550	620	675
Imports	276	308	400	500
Exports	219	244	320	400
Market Size	567	614	700	775
Peripherals and data communications equipment (sold separately)*				
Production	348	356	500	580
Imports	180	250	290	300
Exports	110	243	300	330
Market size	418	363	490	550
Totals				
Production	1,022	1,056	1,357	1,605
Imports	518	638	780	930
Exports	389	548	697	815
Market size	1,151	1,146	1,440	1,720

Source: U.S. Department of Commerce, International Trade
Administration, "Computers and Peripheral Equipment," p. 4.

Size of market equals production (ex factory value), plus
imports (c.i.f.), minus exports (f.o.b.). Figures include
leased equipment counted at its market value as if sold
outright in the initial year of lease. Parts are not
included.

*Excluding equipment sold as components of integrated com-
puter systems.

from 47% to 20% at a cost of $147 million. With these acquisitions and other holdings, the French state came to control some 70% of the national capability in electronics.[11]

With nationalization came further restructuring. CII-HB was split into four specialized subsidiaries: a revamped CII concentrating on large and medium mainframes; a peripherals subsidiary, strengthened by the transfer of the data processing peripherals concern Transac from CGE; mini-computers, merging Thomson's SEMS into the CII-HB effort; and an office automation subsidiary incorporating elements of CGE's CIT-Alcatel. Saint Gobain's involvement in electronics was eliminated altogether and its venture with National Semiconductor, Eurotechnique, sold to Thomson. Thomson and Matra were retained as leaders in components.[12]

The nationalized industries, conceived as direct instruments of the state's economic policy, were expected to align their activities with the state's objectives in investment, technological development, employment and foreign trade. Each industry signed "planning contracts" with the state in which strategic options, employment projections and financing requirements were set forth. The contract of the renamed CII-HB, Machines Bull, for example, established the goal of doubling its turnover and becoming by 1986 the largest European producer in office automation, minicomputers and peripherals. Priority was placed on quality improvements and a policy of "systematic openness to the outside." In turn, the state committed itself to a $110 million subordinated loan and a $221 million capital contribution. Over the same 1983-86 period, the government promised an additional $750 million in assistance to integrated circuit technology.

State efforts to promote both computer manufacturing and components are part of the comprehensive Government Program for the Development of Electronics (Filière Electronique), the culmination of an interministerial study whose high-level official endorsement elevated electronics technology to the status of a prime national mission. Projects receiving special emphasis in this ambitious effort include consumer electronics, the design and fabrication of large-scale integrated circuits, and the development of consumer systems related to user needs in education, engineering and translation. Overall, the plan projects an investment of $20 billion over five years from both private and public sources, with the state share representing some 40%.[13] Of that amount, about 10% was slated to go to computer

technology, 7% to components, and 3% to software. About
half of the plan is to be carried out by the nationalized
groups, Thomson, CGE, Matra and Machines Bull (23).

The Socialists' policy toward foreign cooperation has
been to nurture such relations when they are perceived to be
in the best interests of the domestic effort. The government bought out a major share of Honeywell's interest in
CII-HB (this interest fell further to 8% in 1984 when the
American firm failed to meet the $47 million capital infu-
sion required to retain its 20% share) and acquired ITT's
telecommunications subsidiary CGCT as a means to strengthen
Thomson's effort in telephone exchanges. But other decisions reflect a desire to arrange technological agreements
and encourage foreign investment. Hewlett-Packard, Digital,
Mitel, and Sony were allowed to build or expand plants in
France during the 1981-85 period.[15] Technological
agreements include Matra with Tandy, Tymshare and GCE and a
Machines Bull licensing agreement with Vertex Peripherals.[16]
But the government also reportedly blocked a bid by SEMS to
produce mini- and microcomputers with the American groups
Fortune and SEL in order to promote closer cooperation bet-
ween SEMS and Machines Bull.

The performance of the principal high-technology firms
in the first years of the Socialist government was hardly
promising. Most of the nationalized companies, including
Thomson and Bull, suffered heavy losses. The balance of
payments deficit in components reached 2 billion francs in
1982, with Thomson, the leading French producer, dropping to
twenty-fifth in world ranking. Exports of electronics and
computer products fell the same year to 74% of imports, compared to 88% in 1981 and 102% in 1980.[17] In 1983, however,
there were signs that the situation was beginning to turn
around. Under aggressive new management, Thomson's semiconductor division raised its world ranking to twenty-first.
Bull cut its losses in half in 1983 over 1982; the trade
deficit in electronics was reduced from $1600 million in
1982 to $800 million in 1983. The following year, semicon-
ductor sales rose 35% to $620 million, capturing 15% of
the European market.

THE EUROPEAN CONNECTION

One of the major disappointments of the European
Community is its failure to stimulate the development of
strong intra-European industries in key technological sectors. In electronics, the largest European firms, like the

French, have looked more to American firms than to each
other to pool resources and exchange technological know-how.
National rivalries and restrictive practices, especially
protectionist procurement, have impeded collaboration and
fragmented the European market.

While the Brussels institutions considered for years
initiatives that would improve the situation, nothing much
happened until the announcement of the ESPRIT program in
1982. ESPRIT attempts to coordinate industrial R&D efforts
by selectively cofunding projects with two or more firms
from different member countries. After a one-year pilot
program, the Community budgeted $1.5 billion over five years
in the areas of advanced microelectronics, information processing, software technology, office information and
computer-integrated manufacturing. In early 1985, funding
contracts were announced with some 270 companies participating in 104 projects; American firms based in Europe
were allowed a small participation. Another, more complex
program labelled RACE has been launched to stimulate coordination and integration of telecommunications markets.

Whether these programs will produce tangible results is
a matter of some debate. Many European industrialists
remain skeptical of technology-promotion efforts in the
absence of any overarching EC policy of industrial development or guaranteed markets for the resulting products. Some
prefer EC assistance in forging intra-European joint ventures rather than R&D subsidies. Some member governments,
including the French, are accordingly pressuring the EC to
raise tariffs, which now range from 9% on computers to 17%
on semiconductors. Others point out that even a 17% duty on
components has not allowed European firms to attain self-
sufficiency and world leadership.

Wearing another hat, the EC Commission has taken an
often critical view of the French government's tendencies to
favor national firms. In 1984, the Brussels authorities
commenced legal proceedings against France under Article 30
of the Treaty of Rome which prohibits, at least implicitly,
"buy national" policies of member governments. Also, under
Article 93, the EC has condemned the French policy of
granting investment subsidies to encourage the application
of microelectronics in manufacturing; the EC alleges that
the funding gives French firms an unfair competitive advantage.

Standardization is another EC activity having important
long-range implications for French information technology.
Only 30% of the technical specifications of phone systems,
for example, are common to all EC countries. The diversity

is undoubtedly due in part to the efforts of member governments to set standards that favor domestic firms; EC-wide
standardization would encourage competition and economies of
scale that would help European producers challenge the
larger American and Japanese competitors. Standardization
could also be used as a novel means of Community-sanctioned
protection: the largest European manufacturers of data communications equipment are seeking a common language that
would displace the dominant IBM system.

CONCLUSION

    A great deal of French political and economic history
over the past twenty years can be read into the nation's
policy toward information technology. With remarkable
constancy, changing governments have reaffirmed a high
national priority to the sector and have convincingly indicated their willingness to deploy the full powers of the
state to achieve an independent and competitive industry.
The objectives have scarcely changed: the development of a
French presence in all major segments of the market, technological self-sufficiency, independence from foreign
control for reasons of national security and prestige, and a
determination to guide French society into the electronic
age. Neither has the overall strategy: successive governments have deployed the same familiar tools of massive R&D
assistance, strong-arm restructuring, capital infusions
wherever necessary, substantial involvement in management
decisions even when firms are nominally under private
control, and high levels of public or government-induced
purchasing.
    Yet the evidence strongly indicates that unwavering
governmental commitment, direction and financial support are
insufficient to secure a self-sustaining presence in this
rapidly changing, intensely competitive industry. By the
mid-1980s, French industry in the information sector is at
best a second-string player in the international
marketplace. The country ranks a distant fifth in world
electronics production, accounting for just 5% of global
production. While 72% of domestic production is now in
French hands (with American-owned subsidiaries producing
19%), the domestic market is highly penetrated: imports and
products of foreign subsidiaries account for 52% of sales.[18]
In only telecommunication equipment and computer services
do French firms capture more than 50% of the local
market. Moreover, French firms remain highly dependent

on foreign technology. Foreign patents represent some
three-quarters of all patents registered in France. In
information technology, the United States receives 97% of
all royalty payments.[19] (See Table 4.2.)

Aggregate market-share statistics do a better job of
describing the problem than explaining it. Given the continuity in objectives and strategy, it is not surprising
that the underlying reasons for the poor performance have
changed little since the demise of the Plan Calcul: overam-
bitious goals, the cross-signals coming from market
pressures and political objectives, ill-conceived product
lines, a continual "catch-up" mentality in technology, inadequate commercialization, and the limited--despite
substantial state aid--availability of capital. The French
government has placed extraordinary emphasis on R&D
assistance, yet the research funds available to French
industry still lag behind the most powerful international
competitors. According to one study, the French electronics
industry spent 12.5 billion francs on R&D in 1982, 60% of
which came from the government. But American industry the
same year spent over 130 billion francs ($18.5 billion), 44%
of which was provided by the government. Even within
Europe, French public assistance for R&D is less than that
provided by the West German government and about equals that
of the UK.[20]

Another, more characteristically French problem is the
almost constant restructuring of the industry. Although
there has been more continuity in product development and
market strategies than the frequent reorganizations would
suggest, the repeated reshufflings of affiliates, equity
shares, and personnel have undoubtedly taken their toll on
morale and long-term planning. At present, French managers
must contemplate the likely policy consequences of another
change in government.

French high-technology firms have encountered a number
of less visible but still significant obstacles to growth.
These include:

a) lack of venture capital. Aside from those
firms benefiting from the public treasury, French firms
have had difficulty finding the necessary venture capital from the nation's traditionally risk-averse financial
institutions. It is undoubtedly no coincidence that the
most dynamic and successful segments of the information-
based industries in France are in software and services
where capital needs are less critical. Further nationalization of the banking sector in 1982--resulting in a situation
where three-quarters of all deposits pass through state-

82

TABLE 4.2
French Production and Market Shares, Selected Electronics
Industries, 1982

	French Production ($ million)	French Market ($ million)	World Production ($ million)
Data Processing[1]	3600	4400	64000
Automation Equipment[2]	1000	1300	22800
Office Automation[3]	100	700	17000
Computer Services[4]	1600	1500	28000
Total	6300	7900	131800
Total, electronics sector)	(15500)	(17700)	(327000)

Source: French Telecommunications and Electronics Council,
"The Electronics Industry, USA/France 1982," April 1983.

Market share of country X = France production sold in France by
X controlled subsidiaries + imports from X.

[1]Includes mainframe, small, mini- and micro-computers with
peripherals.
[2]Includes process control equipment, numerical control systems,
robots, industrial computers and CAD/CAM.
[3]Includes electronic typewriters, word processors, micrographics,
calculators, etc.
[4]Includes data processing consulting companies, computer services
apart from manufacturers.
[5]Includes 5% of foreign origin.

Market Share in France (%)							
French	Foreign	USA	Japan	West Germany	Nether-lands	UK	Italy
25–30[5]	70–75	58	1	5	2	4	4–5
60	40	12	5	10–15			
4	96	15	25	14	12	16	4
90	10	4				3	
(47–48)	(52–53)	(22)	(7)	(7)			

owned banks[21]--raised fears that investment opportunities
would be restricted to state-favored firms. Recognizing the
dearth of incentives for entrepreneurship, Prime Minister
Fabius created a special credit fund providing tax-free
interest on deposits that is intended to grant below-
market-rate loans to high-technology and energy-saving ventures. The government has also imposed a three-year tax
moratorium on new companies.

      b) shortage of skilled manpower. Despite long-
standing government support for training and research, the
country's supply of skilled manpower is insufficient to meet
the government's ambitious goals. The electronics plan projects the creation of 80,000 jobs by 1990, but already in
1985 there was an estimated shortfall of 5,000 computer
engineers.

      c) government coordination. Government machinery
for overseeing the electronics industry has undergone as
many reorganizations as the industry itself.
Interministerial coordination is a chronic problem, with the
key players--the ministries of industry and defense and the
PTT--often pursuing independent lines. The governmental
effort is further dispersed among an array of second-level
institutions, including INRIA (a public research center on
computer applications), CNET (the PTT's research arm in
telecommunications), CNRS (the national science council),
LITI (the atomic energy authority's components laboratory),
and ADI (a special institute associating users with the
Ministry of Industry's R&D program). The Socialist government has attempted to centralize many of these efforts in
its filière électronique. It also created a "world center
for microcomputers and human resources" charged with
carrying the benefits of information technology to the Third
World.

In view of the government's persistent efforts to nurture domestic firms to the ranks of world competitors, it is
noteworthy that foreign companies have not fared badly on
French soil, and now account for 28% of domestic production.
IBM-France is the nation's nineteenth largest firm and the
eighth largest exporter.[22] But it is undeniable that
the government has favored its own firms through such
restrictive practices as public procurement and targeted
assistance. The recent refusal of the government to buy
250,000 Apple personal computers in favor of the domestic
product to supply the public education system is simply the
latest in a long string of examples of governmental favori-
tism.

The decidedly mixed results of the government's twenty-
year program to make France a world power in high technology

suggest that a continued policy of "more of the same" will
scarcely fare better in the future. It would be premature,
however, to count the French out completely. The industry
stands poised to profit from some undeniable strengths,
including a highly skilled workforce, a flourishing
computer-services sector, pockets of managerial brilliance,
and a relatively undeveloped but rapidly expanding market at
home and in selected regions abroad. Moreover, certain
underlying trends in high technology, particularly the
fusion of data processing with telecommunications, are
potentially quite favorable to a national industry whose
government knows how to use its full powers to marshall
supplier and customer in the service of collectively defined
objectives.

NOTES

    1. John E. Tilton, International Diffusion of
Technology: The Case of Semiconductors (Washington, D.C.:
Brookings, 1971) and John Zysman, Political Strategies for
Industrial Order (Berkeley: University of California Press,
1977).
    2. John Walsh, "France: First the Bomb, Then the 'Plan
Calcul'," Science, Vol. 156, May 12, 1967, 767-770.
    3. Tilton, op. cit.
    4. J. K. Paul, ed., High Technology International Trade
and Competition (Park Ridge, N.J.: Noyes, 1984); OECD, The
Semiconductor Industry: Trade Related Issues (Paris: OECD,
1985); Tilton, op. cit; Zysman, op. cit.
    5. International Management, May 1983.
    6. Paul, op. cit. and OECD, op. cit.
    7. Business Week, March 21, 1977; Paul, op. cit.
    8. Paul, op. cit.
    9. U.S. Department of Commerce, International Trade
Administration, "Computers and Peripheral Equipment:
France," Country Market Survey, International Marketing
Information Series CMS, 81-313, July 1981.
    10. Ibid.
    11. Gareth Locksley, "Europe and the Electronics
Industry: Conflicting Strategies in Positive
Restructuring," West European Politics, Vol. 6, April 1983,
128-138.
    12. Jacques Blanc and Chantal Brule, Les nationalisa-
tions françaises en 1982, Notes documentaires nos. 4721-4722
(Paris: La Documentation Française, 1983); OECD, op. cit.;

86

Julien Savary, French Multinationals (New York:
St. Martin's Press, 1984).
  13. Locksley, op. cit. and Savary, op. cit.
  14. H. J. van Houten, ed., The Competitive Strength of
the Information and Communication Industry in Europe (The
Hague: Martinus Nijhoff, 1983).
  15. OECD, op. cit. and Savary, op. cit.
  16. French Telecommunications and Electronics Council,
"The Electronics Industry, USA/France 1982," New York, April
1983 and OECD, op. cit.
  17. Locksley, op. cit.
  18. French Telecommunications and Electronics Council,
"La recherche et le développement en électronique,
Etat-Unis/France, 1982/1983," New York, March 1984.
  19. René-Francois Bizec, "La technologie francaise est-
elle compétitive?" La Recherche, No. 114, September 1980
and Locksley, op. cit.
  20. Tilton, op. cit.
  21. Paul, op. cit.
  22. Savary, op. cit.

BIBLIOGRAPHY

Bizec, René-François,"La technologie française est-elle
    compétitive?" La Recherche, No. 114, September 1980.
Blanc, Jacques and Chantal Brule, Les nationalisations
    françaises en 1982, Notes documentaires nos. 4721-4722
    (Paris: La Documentation Française, 1983).
Business Week, March 21, 1977.
Clairvois, Marc, "Le Who's Who de I'Informatique en France,"
    L'Expansion, September 18-October 1, 1981.
Les Echos, November 9, 1984.
Ernst, Dieter, The Global Race in Microelectronics
    (Frankfurt: Campus Verlag, 1983).
Frank, Lawrence G. and Jack N. Berhman, "Industrial Policy
    in France," in Robert E. Driscoll and Jack N. Behrman,
    eds., National Industrial Policies (Cambridge, Mass.:
    Oelgeschlager, Gunn & Hahn, 1984), 57-71.
"France's Social Agenda for the Computer," Computer-world,
    Vol. 17, No. 19, May 9, 1983.
French Telecommunications and Electronics Council, "The
    Electronics Industry, USA/France 1982," New York, April
    1983.
_____, "La recherche et le développement en
    electronique, Etats-Unis/France, 1982/1983," New York,
    March 1984.

Hazewindus, Nico, The U.S. Microelectronics Industry
     (New York: Pergamon, 1982).
International Management, May 1983.
Locksley, Gareth, "Europe and the Electronics Industry:
     Conflicting Strategies in Positive Restructuring,"
     West European Politics, Vol. 6, April 1983, 128-138.
Le Monde, April 19, 1977.
National Academy of Sciences, National Research Council,
     The Competitive Status of the U.S. Electronics
     Industry (Washington, D.C.: National Academy Press,
     1984).
Nelson, Richard R., High-Technology Policies: A
     Five-Nation Comparison (Washington, D.C.: American
     Enterprise Institute, 1984).
Paul, J. K., ed., High Technology International Trade
     and Competition (Park Ridge, NJ: Noyes, 1984).
OECD, The Semiconductor Industry: Trade Related Issues
     (Paris: OECD, 1985).
Savary, Julien, French Multinationals (New York: St.
     Martin's Press, 1984).
Tilton, John E., International Diffusion of Technology:
     The Case of Semiconductors (Washington, D.C.:
     Brookings, 1971).
U.S. Department of Commerce, International Trade
     Administration, "Computers and Peripheral Equipment:
     France," Country Market Survey, International
     Marketing Information Series CMS 81-313, July 1981.
     _____, "High Technology Industries: Profiles and
     Outlooks--The Computer Industry," April 1983.
van Houten, H. J., ed., The Competitive Strength of the
     Information and Communication Industry in Europe
     (The Hague: Martinus Nijhoff, 1983).
Walsh, John, "France: First the Bomb, Then the 'Plan
     Calcul'," Science, Vol. 156, May 12, 1967, 767-770.
Wright, Vincent, "Socialism and the Interdependent Economy:
     Industrial Policy-making under the Mitterand
     Presidency," Government and Opposition, Vol. 19,
     Summer 1984, 287-303.
Zysman, John, Political Strategies for Industrial Order
     (Berkeley: University of California Press, 1977).

5

India

Amar Gupta
Massachusetts Institute of Technology

INTRODUCTION

Since their advent in the late forties, electronic computers have had a revolutionary impact on almost all sectors of human endeavor. Initially used primarily for defense applications, the fifties witnessed growing usage of computers in commercial enterprises for payroll and accounting applications, activities that had so far been done using human resources.

Computers in India are a relatively recent phenomenon. The first digital computer was installed in 1956 at the Indian Statistical Institute, Calcutta, and the first commercial computer was installed at Esso Standard Eastern Inc., Bombay in 1961. During the next three years, 14 computers were installed, of which 12 were in research and development organizations. The subsequent years saw an annual doubling of total number of computer installations, and the newer ones were predominantly in commercial enterprises. On the developmental side, the first indigenous computer, ISIJU, was fabricated jointly by the Indian Statistical Institute and the Jadavpur University in July 1964. India is among the first ten countries to develop computers indigenously.

The initial thrust into the computer era was provided by foreign computer vendors. Their marketing strategy was based on their experiences in the West, and the focus was on selling software packages for payroll, accounting and inventory control. User technical expertise was minimal, and "computers were introduced in many cases as mere status symbols and to keep up with the 'Joneses' and not with any clear-cut and calculated assessment of their benefits as an

effective management tool."[1] Similar experiences have
been reported from other developing countries.[2]

 With 40 million unemployed persons, the labor sector
was naturally upset at this new threat. The Committee on
Automation[3] described the two views:

> For some it is a harbinger of an age of plenty and
> progress—a development which opens up new vistas
> of greater productivity and higher standards of
> living. Some others have viewed it as an unmitigated
> curse which would deprive man of his employment and
> functions and ultimately dehumanise him, making
> him a slave of these machines.

There were numerous agitations against computerization, and
several organizations postponed the installation of computer
systems.

 Another significant development was the total polariza-
tion of the market between two companies, IBM of the USA and
ICL of the UK with a market share of 65% and 25%, respectively. In particular, the number of IBM 1401 computer
systems was larger than all the other models of all manufacturers put together. These IBM 1401 computer systems were
all second-hand systems rented out by IBM at $4,000-$5,000 a
month. Incidentally, this rate continued until 1978 even
though the international sale price of such systems had
dropped to as low as $10,000.

 There are a number of reasons for the success of IBM
and ICL. Market survival is critically dependent on effective computer maintenance. India is located far from the
computer manufacturing plants, and permanent location of
engineers to support one or two installations becomes a
costly proposition. At that time, only one institution
(Tata Institute of Fundamental Research) was prepared to do
in-house maintenance and they bought a CDC-3600 directly
from USA. IBM and ICL got a headstart, and set up strong
local organizations—IBM India as a branch office of IBM
World Trade and ICL (India) Ltd. as an Indian company
fully owned by ICL, UK. Other firms found it impossible to
penetrate this market. And since the computers were transferred at almost zero book value, IBM and ICL circumvented
the government ban on release of foreign exchange for computer imports. As India has never restricted repatriation
of profits, the local offices were able to pass much of
their rental income to their respective parent companies,[4]
and the total annual repatriation (and "head office
expenses") far exceeded the aggregate fair market value of

the obsolete computers.

POLICY OF SELF RELIANCE

In 1970 the government set up the Electronics
Commission to undertake the following major tasks:
   a) to lay down policy guidelines for the entire field
      of electronics;
   b) to plan a positive and balanced growth of the
      electronics industry; and
   c) to promote self-reliance.
Electronic systems consist of several subsystems and
assemblies which in turn are made up of components; these
components (resistors, transistors and integrated circuits)
are made from a diverse range of materials (like silicon and
germanium). A totally indigenous electronics industry could
mean production of all sub-assemblies, all components and
all materials in the country. Apart from involving collosal
investments, such a strategy could be uneconomic as it
involves production of items at the low levels needed for
internal use. The emphasis was therefore placed on self-
reliance, that is, to build up complete systems using the
best ingredients available in international markets at prices most favorable to the country. The intent was that as
the market demand picked up a backward integration strategy
would enable increased levels of indigenisation.[5]

Calculator Industry

An excellent example of the self-reliant strategy is
provided by the calculator industry. This industry was non-
existent in India in 1971. By 1975 India was manufacturing
calculators of all sizes, shapes and capabilities, comparable to the best in the world. The industry developed
using internal resources alone, right from the stages of
research and development to final testing and marketing.
Contemporariness continues to be maintained by using the
latest chips on the international market. In 1985 the
public sector Semiconductor Complex started providing chips.
Although indigenous expertise has built up, the limited
market potential is a severe constraint in cost effective
production. In the U.S., capital intensive industries
require large amounts of electronic inputs. In India,
industries are labor intensive, and as such market demands
have been inherently low. Unlike Japan, which has increased

volumes by catering to world markets, India has had very
limited success in increasing production volumes. Thus,
calculators in India sell at a higher price than in many
other countries.

Computer Industry

In the field of computers, the Electronics Commission
decided in the early seventies that:
   a) the import of second-hand obsolete equipment by
      multinationals would be discontinued;
   b) computational requirements would be met through
      outright purchase of computers on the basis of
      global tenders;
   c) key sectors of computer industry would be freed
      from monopolistic influences;
   d) a viable program of production of computer hardware
      and software would be built up to meet domestic
      requirements and also to generate surpluses for
      export.
As a consequence of this policy, indigenous computer manufacturing activities grew substantially during the seventies. The public sector Electronics Corporation of India
Ltd., ECIL, started manufacturing the first TDC 12 (second
generation computer with a 12-bit word size), and then the
TDC 316 (third generation computer with a 16-bit word size).
Subsequently, the 32-bit TDC 332, with overall system performance comparable to an IBM 370/145, was introduced at the
high end and the microprocessor based MICRO-78 system at the
low end. Today ECIL computers form one-fifth of the
country's total computer population.
At the end of 1983, forty-two companies were manufacturing computer systems including microprocessor based
systems. In most cases, the development has been nucleated
by Indian citizens employed in research activities in developed countries. These entrepreneurs act as technology
transfer agents, and the government assists in their return
to India by permitting liberal import of capital equipment,
and preferential investments by governmental funding agencies like IDBI, IFCI, ICICI, and others. However, the
largest private sector enterprise, ICIM, is a subsidiary of
ICL, UK. ICIM manufactures the ICL 2904 computer, a 24-bit
system primarily geared towards business applications.
Between 1973 and 1983 the annual production of computers and allied equipment increased from Rs 220 million to
Rs 3290 million. The latter figure is still higher if one

includes the output of units in the export zones. (See
Table 5.1.) As seen from Table 5.2, the computer industry
has grown at an annual compound rate exceeding 30%,
significantly higher than other segments of the electronics
industry.

Large Computers

Large computational facilities are needed for supporting many applications. For example, in flutter analysis
of aircrafts, the size of matrices and equations is so large
that it is physically possible to solve the problem only on
a large computer system. The mathematical techniques for
splitting up the problem into several smaller size problems
results in an intolerable loss of accuracy. In many instances significant computing power is required, not on a continuous basis, but from time to time in the design and
optimization stages.

Early in the seventies, a conscious decision was taken
not to produce such computers indigenously because of the
low volumes involved. Large systems were, and continue to
be, imported mainly from the U.S. (Burroughs, DEC, Univac,
CDC) on the basis of the best price-performance ratio. In
order to permit the maximum multiplier effect, several of
these large systems have been set up as common user facilities for catering to a wide spectrum of users, and also to
tackle problems of national and regional importance. The
primary activities of these centers are described below:

i) National Centre for Software Development and
Computing Techniques, Bombay: Generally abbreviated as
NCSDCT, this center was established in 1975 with UNDP
assistance for catalyzing development of sophisticated software. In the Close Coupled Network project, NCSDCT
integrated several indigenously produced TDC systems to permit execution of large programs. Also, an interface unit
was developed that allows the indigenous TDC system to
serve as an RJE (Remote Job Entry) station for the larger
host computer system. The original experimental link used
the telephone line between NCSDT and VJTI, an educational
institute located 16 miles away. NCSDT has also undertaken
several activities in computer education, training, promotion of application, and technology development in the area
of computer aided design and computer graphics.

ii) National Informatics Centre, Delhi: Established
with UNDP assistance, the main CDC Cyber-171 computer system
was installed in 1979. Until the establishment of NIC, data
of various governmental agencies were handled in an ad hoc

94

TABLE 5.1

Production of Electronic Goods In India
(in millions of rupees)

	Sector	1973	1978	1983
1.	Consumer Electronics	640	1,585	3,300
2.	Communication and Broadcasting Equipment	580	1,265	2,700
3.	Aerospace and Defense Equipment	330	620	1,260
4.	Computer, Control, and Instrumentation	220	1,190	3,290
5.	Electronic Components	510	1,170	2,300
	SUB-TOTAL (DTA)	2,280	5,830	12,850
6.	Export Zones	0	75	750
	TOTAL	2,280	5,905	13,600

Source: Annual Reports, Department of Electronics, 1970-71 to 1983-84.

TABLE 5.2

Growth Rates for Electronics Industry in India

	Sector	Annual Compound Growth Rate (%)		
		1 Year 1982–83	5 Years 1978–83	10 Years 1973–83
1.	Consumer Electronics	−2.9	+15.8	+17.8
2.	Communication and Broadcasting Equipment	+5.8	+16.4	+16.6
3.	Aerospace and Defense Equipment	+16.1	+15.2	+14.3
4.	Computer, Control, and Instrumentation	+62.5(a) +29.4(b)	+22.6	+31.1
5.	Electronic Components	+7.5	+14.5	+16.2
6.	Export Zones	+54.6	+58.5	Indeterminate
	OVERALL	+12.9	+18.2	+19.6

Source: Annual Reports, Department of Electronics, 1970–71 to 1983–84.

(a) Computers
(b) Control & Instrumentation

manner, and the varying standards and systems severely
constrained inter-agency use of data files. This center
serves as a centralized facility for such use. It has developed methodologies for designing and implementing national
information systems in government and associated agencies,
and has installed terminals in different ministries for
inputting data and retrieving information.

iii) Regional Computer Centres: RCCs cater to the computational requirements of the respective regions. In these
centers, users have access to contemporary facilities at
guaranteed rates. To permit professional management of
these facilities, these centers have been established as
fully autonomous units jointly sponsored by the central
government, the respective state governments, and the
premier educational institute in the region. As the needs
of individual users increase, such users are encouraged to
purchase their own in-house facilities.

The regional centers have been helpful in nucleating
the growth of computer awareness, and now each state has
access to such facilities. Incidentally, the concept of
such centers has been used in developed countries, too, for
example, the chain of National Computer Centres (NCC) in the
U.K.

Incentives for Development

Soon after its own inception, the Electronics
Commission set up a Technology Development Council (TDC) to
undertake the following activities:
   a) identify areas where technological gaps exist
      within the framework of the country's requirements;
   b) assess capacities of organizations engaged in R&D
      in electronics; and
   c) finance projects at appropriate institutions with
      proper monitoring and evaluation.
Being the primary channel for encouraging development of new
electronic concepts and products, the TDC has provided
grants to national laboratories, public sector companies,
joint ventures, private sector organizations and educational
institutions. Of all the activities supported, more than
one-fifth relate to computers (more than Rs 60 million).

A cross section of TDC supported projects is shown
below:

Project	Institution	Sector
a) Development of hybrid computer	ECIL, Hyderabad	central government
b) Development of 18 column printer	KSEDC, Trivandrum	state government
c) Computerized information system for steel distribution	SRI, Pune	private
d) Cassette CRT printer terminal	IIT, Kharagpur	educational

The TDC funds support research and development up to the
stage of prototype fabrication and testing. The mechanism
for the transfer of this technology to the industrial sector
is rather weak. Public sector enterprises, like ECIL and
BEL, are at an advantage in terms of turning their research
work into production capabilities. In the case of computers, most TDC funds have gone to public sector organizations.

Software

   Most vendors sell computer systems in India on a
"bundled" basis, that is, the software costs are already
included as part of the deal. In a few cases it has been
necessary to import specialized software, e.g., for seismic
exploration. Most software is now developed indigenously,
and a substantial amount is exported, too-- worth Rs. 170
million during 1983 from Domestic Tariff Areas (DTA) alone.
   Software development is a labor intensive industry, and
since manpower costs in India are significantly less than
those in Europe and the U.S. (see Table 5.3), export
potential is excellent. As compared to other countries in
the region, India alone has an abundant availability of
highly trained technical manpower, and the government
permits liberal imports of contemporary computer systems for
software export activities. This has also encouraged
Indians abroad to return and set up viable industrial units.
   Human effort can be transformed into an exportable commodity at varying levels of sophistication. There are three
major classes:

TABLE 5.3
Cost Structure of a Programmer/Analyst in India
(in U.S. dollars)

	Costs	A*	B**	
1.	Salary	$ 3,600	$ 2,400	
2.	Statutory Benefits (85%)	3,060	2,040	
3.	Overhead	4,890	4,440	
4.	SUBTOTAL	$11,550	$ 8,880	
5.	Utilization (4) x 1.33	15,360	11,810	
6.	Profit @ 30% (5) x 1.3	19,970	15,350	
7.	Communication and Travel	2,750	2,750	work done in India
8.	TOTAL	$22,720	$18,100	work done in India
9.	Communication and Travel	$ 2,000	$ 2,000	work done outside India
10.	Living Expenses @ 1,500/mo.	18,000	18,000	work done outside India
11.	TOTAL (6+9+10)	$39,970	$35,350	work done outside India

Source: Report of EEPC Computer Software Delegation to USA,
Engineering Export Promotion Council, New Delhi, December
1982, p. 74.

  *Level A: M.S. (Computer Science), 3 years experience
 **Level B: B.S. (Engineering), 2 years experience

a) Routine programming and data entry. This provides vast employment potential to persons with minimal computer background. There are over a hundred companies, all in the private sector, which are involved in this class of activity.

b) Application software ranging from elementary applications to sophisticated data base management systems. This requires more specialized effort, and the work is concentrated in 20 organizations; the predominant ones are TCS, EIL, Computronics and ASCI.

c) Systems software, e.g., operating systems. This activity is rarely done for export purposes. NCSDCT, computer hardware manufacturers and a few software houses are involved in this effort.

Software is exported to the U.S., the U.S.S.R., the E.E.C., Middle East Arab countries, Australia, New Zealand, and Singapore. The advent of satellite communications is opening up new avenues of exporting software without the overhead of transportation costs and delays. India today generates about 0.1% of the total world software and this percentage is expected to increase.

Maintenance

It was realized in 1973 that in order to develop an indigenous industry, it was necessary to promote independent maintenance activities to enable users to buy computers of other makes. With this in view, the Computer Maintenance Corporation (CMC) was established in 1976 as a public sector unit to undertake maintenance of all imported computer systems in the country.

Today CMC maintains almost 400 computer systems consisting of 100 models and 20 makes. Such a diverse maintenance base is probably without parallel in the whole world. In spite of this heavy job, the average computer uptime exceeds 96%. Indigenization of maintenance activity has enabled users to purchase add-on units on an OEM (Original Equipment Manufacturer) basis at 10%-25% of the prices charged by the multinationals for the same equipment. Also, CMC was able to smoothly manage the transition when IBM quit India in 1978. Recently CMC took up the INDONET project involving implementation of a national computer network and the INTERACT project involving training and mutual assistance to computer professionals from other developing countries.

Education

In the sixties there were very few institutions providing training in the computer field. Today, about 40 universities and institutions have undergraduate and graduate
programs in computer sciences, and they train about 4,000
persons every year. In addition, lower level training is
provided by various Industrial Training Institutes, private
sector and public sector organizations to about 10,000 persons every year. Several developing countries in Africa and
the Middle East use Indian experts to train their own
people. The educational aspects are thus completely indige-
nized.

Labor Angle

In Section I, the labor aspect was mentioned. Until
1984 the government permitted commercial enterprises to
import computers only if the labor union concurred with the
computerization. As expected, this concurrence occurred in
cases where the interests of both management and labor were
clubbed together, for example, in software export, weather
prediction (cannot be done by hand), space research, educational applications, etc.

In many important sectors such as banking and
insurance, the interests conflicted. In such cases the role
of computers was limited to new applications. For example,
the railways used computers for wagon allocation and traffic
studies but not for ticketing and reservations.

In June 1984 the government scrapped the time-consuming
procedure for grant of no-obligation certificates from the
labor angle. At the time of acquisition of computer
systems, the management of the company is now required to
certify that:

a) there would be no retrenchment as a result of
   computerization and any worker rendered surplus
   would be absorbed;
b) there would be no loss of earnings or wages of
   the existing workers;
c) there would be no adverse effect on the conditions
   of work, promotion prospects, etc. of the workers;
d) there would be adequate safeguards to protect the
   workers' interests, including sharing of possible
   benefits; and

e) the proposal to import computer equipment has been
explained to the workforce of the establishment
where it is to be installed.
This new policy is encouraging computerization in areas such
as railway reservations, maintenance of banking and
insurance accounts, and inventory control.

ANALYSIS AND DISCUSSION

Before analyzing specific government policies and their
long-term ramifications, it is pertinent to outline broad
statistical data relating to the information industry.

Statistical Details
----

a) Value of Output: The production figures for computer hardware and software have already been summarized in
Table 5.1. Since these figures do not include the value of
other products generated using computer systems, one must
exercise caution in using these figures as a basis for comparison with other countries.
b) Employment: The number of persons employed directly
in computer related activities (such as system analysis,
programming, operations, data preparation, etc.) has
increased from 5,000 in 1973 to 125,000 in 1983 (25-fold).
c) R&D Expenditures: Apart from TDC grants, educational institutions and public and private sector organizations have utilized other resources to fund R&D activities.
The total expenditures are estimated at Rs. 1 million in
1973 and Rs. 25 million in 1983.
d) Profits: Most public sector units operate close to
a break-even point. CMC had a pre-tax profit of Rs. 12.1
million on a turnover of Rs. 101.9 million during the year
1982-83. As regards operations of private companies, the
example in Table 5.4 shows the figures in 1973. Currently,
most companies manufacturing computers usually have other
activities as well. This makes it difficult to estimate
profits of computer operations alone.
e) Market Share: In 1973 IBM and ICL accounted for 90%
of the market, and the public sector accounted for under 5%.
In 1983 the public sector accounted for two-thirds of the
market and the private sector for about one-third. Foreign
representation was to the extent of the supply of a few
imported computers.
f) Trade Flows: In 1973 India exported virtually no
computer software. IBM exported key punches and verifiers

102

TABLE 5.4

Revenue and Profit Statement for Operations
of IBM in India During 1973
(all figures in millions of rupees)

	Revenues
Machine Rentals	119.884
Export Sales	33.394
Sales – Cards	16.243
Data Processing Charges	18.332
Sales – Imported Items	22.736
Sales – Indigenous Equipment	3.303
Ribbons, Control Panels, etc.	2.268
Miscellaneous	5.293
	221.453
PROFITS (before taxes)	96.0
PROFITS (after taxes)	20.5

Source: Computerisation in Government Departments, 221st
Report of Public Accounts Committee, LOK Sabha Secretariat,
New Delhi.

and these figures are summarized in Table 5.5. In 1983 the export figures were Rs. 24 million for computers and allied equipment and Rs. 170 million for software. SEEPZ alone exported goods worth Rs. 750 million, more than half of which were computer-related (see Table 5.6). The import bill for mainframe computers and parts was around Rs. 90 million.

Legislation Affecting Informatics

The Industries (Development & Regulation) Act of 1956 lays down the basic framework governing industrial policy. Some areas have been reserved for the public sector and some others for the small-scale sector. Licenses are needed before major manufacturing plants can be set up. Very large units are subject to the provisions of the Monopolies and Restrictive Trade Practices Act of 1969.

Heavy repatriation of profits by cosmetics, beverages and other non-essential industries led to the Foreign Exchange Regulation Act (FERA) of 1973. All companies, except those producing for export only or involved in high technology (e.g., drugs), were required to increase Indian equity shareholding to at least 26% (for manufacturing units) and 60% for non-manufacturing units. The step was not an indirect nationalization, nor an attempt to control the executive boards. It was designed to limit economic exploitation through windfall repatriation.

Many segments of the informatics industry have been exempted from the provisions of the MRTP Act. However, except for Tatas who formed a joint venture with Burroughs (Tata-Burroughs), other leading industrial houses have not invested in the computer industry. Apart from the provisions of the FERA Act, the government has never restricted remittance of profits. However, remittance of recurring service fees is discouraged.

Non-resident individuals and non-resident companies (companies incorporated outside India) are taxed at a higher rate as compared to resident individuals and companies. Non-residents prefer the export zones where the earnings of their companies enjoy a tax holiday.

Until recently the government disallowed the use of foreign brand names for goods produced and sold in India. However, such names could be used for goods exported abroad. Wide dissemination of new technology is encouraged. For example, less customs duty is levied on software imported in source form based on the premise that it is more likely to be distributed within the country.

104

TABLE 5.5

Impact on Foreign Exchange Due to Operations
of IBM in India During 1973
(all figures in millions of rupees)

(a)	CIF Cost of Imports	
	"AS IS" Machines	1.557
	Total Imports Sold "AS IS Machines," Other Imports, Maintenance Parts and Literature	34.096
(b)	Remittances	
	Administrative Charges	11.115
	Profits (after taxes)	20.471
	TOTAL OUTFLOW	65.682
	Exports	38.083
	NET OUTFLOW	27.599

Source: Computerisation in Government Departments, 221st
Report of Public Accounts Committee, LOK Sabha Secretariat,
New Delhi.

TABLE 5.6

Exports from India During 1981-83
(in millions of rupees)

	Sector	1981	1982	1983
1.	Consumer Electronics	40.0	41.0	30.0
2.	Computers, Control, and Instrumentation	30.0	16.0	24.0
3.	Aerospace and Defense	95.5	132.0	65.0
4.	Communications	19.5	17.0	20.0
5.	Components	80.0	96.0	86.0
6.	Computer Software	44.0	103.0	170.0
	SUB-TOTAL (DTA)	309.0	405.0	395.0
7.	Export Zones	255.0	485.0	750.0
	TOTAL	564.0	890.0	1145.0

Source: Annual Reports, Department of Electronics, 1970-71 to 1983-84.

In India indirect taxation is the primary source of
revenue for the government. Custom duties have ranged between 40% and 200% on computers during the ten-year period
under review (1973-83). Indigenously produced systems have
been subject to an excise duty of 15%. No duties are levied
on goods produced for export, or on equipment imported to
generate items exclusively for export. Companies can pay
duties at time of production and subsequently claim duty
drawback for the subset of the products exported.
Alternatively, they can produce goods under bond and no
duties are paid.

The Industrial Development Bank of India (IDBI), the
Industrial Finance Corporation of India (IFCI), and the
Industrial Credit and Investment Corporation of India
(ICICI) are three major governmental agencies responsible
for providing financial assistance to set up new industrial
projects as well as to expand, diversify, renovate, or
modernize existing ones. A recent study[6] shows that 25%
of the shares of leading industrial enterprises is held by
these investment agencies. Almost all of the informatics
concerns in the private sector have availed themselves of
financial and/or technical assistance from federal or state
agencies.

Administrative Restraints

In September 1970 the government announced that it will
allow computers to be imported to develop software. The
only requirement was that during the first five years of
operations the software exports must be to the tune of 200%
of the c.i.f. value of the imported equipment. Subsequently,
in July 1976 persons importing systems using their own
foreign exchange were obliged to commit to exporting software only to the tune of 100% of the c.i.f. value. More
than 200 computers have so far been imported into India for
purposes of developing software for export.

The government announced the minicomputer policy in
1979. Almost 150 companies were permitted to manufacture
computers, each at the rate of a few hundred units a year.
The general industrial policy permits automatic capacity
enhancements at the rate of 5% per year. Recognizing that
there is no way in which companies can produce at such low
volumes and still compete in the international market, the
government announced major policy changes on November 19,
1984 to "enable manufacture in the country of computers
based on the latest technology, at prices comparable with

international levels and progressively increase indigenisation consistent with economic viability."[7] In terms of the
new policy:

a) any Indian company will be permitted to
   manufacture micro/mini computers;
b) CPU of mainframes and super minicomputers
   will be reserved for manufacture by the public
   sector for a period of two years;
c) all existing capacity restrictions on the
   organized sector will be lifted;
d) liberal import of knowhow will be permitted to
   companies supplying CPUs and peripherals on
   original-equipment-manufacture (OEM) basis;
e) tarrif structures will be modified to enable
   components to be available at near-international
   prices. Specifically, components not
   manufactured in India will be permitted to
   be imported at very low levels of import duty.
   For other components which are manufactured in
   the country or can be manufactured within a
   short period, liberal manufacturing facilities
   will be allowed to be set up to take advantage
   of economies of scale;
f) actual users will be permitted to import
   standardized EDP systems as complete systems
   costing less than Rs. 0.1 million c.i.f.
   on the basis of liberal procedures;
g) import of higher-capacity systems will continue
   to be controlled by the government; and
h) a Software Development Promotion Agency will
   be set up.[8]

The government has targetted for an overall growth of the
electronics industry at an annual compound rate of 35% for
the next five years, with the private sector contributing up
to 70% of the growth in the case of computers.
     According to a press report,[9] the new policy has
made users happy since computers are now available at much
lower prices. The traders are also happy at the increased
volume of sales. However, the manufacturers of indigenous
systems are unhappy since their systems can no longer be
marketed in the face of the flood of imported systems. In
the short run, a liberal import policy is disheartening to
individuals and companies who have worked hard to implement
systems with maximum indigenous content.
     The liberal policy of the government can have several

108

different long-term ramifications. Ideally, a number of
companies will develop hardware and software for internal
use as well as for export. At the other extreme, the possibility exists that the liberal import policy will cause a
severe imbalance in the trade position and the government
will be compelled to revert back to the old conservative
policies. Incidentally, the present government has made far
reaching changes in sectors other than computers. A number
of leading multinational companies, including
Hewlett-Packard, Texas Instruments, Data General Corporation
and Digital Equipment Corporation, are currently embarking
on establishing substantial computer-related manufacturing
and service activities in India.

Overall Impact

     The policies followed by the government have been
largely successful in meeting the original set of objectives. The Indian computer industry is no longer dominated
by a few monopolies, indigenous manufacturing facilities
have come up, computers are now acquired on the basis of
outright purchase, and contemporary computational facilities
now exist in a number of locations. Whereas in 1970 prices
for imported computers were higher than in other countries,
many recent deals have been made at below U.S. list prices,
partly because of the lower marketing and manpower costs in
India.
     Because of low production volumes, prices of indige-
nously manufactured computers have been high. Relatively
little has been invested in research and development. The
industry has been dominated by public limited companies
whose overall return on capital invested has been very low.
Despite the advantage of large numbers of trained persons
and low wage rates, exports of computer-based services are
still in terms of millions (see Table 5.6), not in billions.
     In his three volume study entitled Asian Drama,[10]
Gunnar Myrdal concludes that nations are poor because they
are poor. He argues that in India and other neighboring
countries, the low capital intensity of the primitive
methods of production results in low productivity. This in
turn results in very low savings, and hence hardly any capital for investment purposes. Democratic election processes
usually result in power being shared by people from rural
backgrounds. Thus political stability inherently implies
stagnation, making the vicious cycle difficult to break.
     The fate of the computer industry is an illustration.

Computer development has an immense potential for creating
new job opportunities. But the mass of unemployed people
hindered extensive computerization. Thus, offices and
industries continued to operate using antiquated methods
with low overall productivity and implicit time delays.
Successive governments had been unwilling to touch this
thorny issue, until the policy statement on the labor angle
in June 1984.

The situation has been compounded by the peculiarities
of the computer industry. In a world of inflation it is
astonishing that the cost of computation continues to
decline by about 20% per year. In India the government as
well as the private sector have been reluctant to import
foreign manufacturing technology; rather they would prefer
to re-invent the wheel. The production activities of ECIL
and other enterprises have been driven entirely by indigenously developed products; the final products reflect a time
lag of almost 5 to 10 years since the time of introduction
of similar systems in the U.S. Even if these systems were
mass produced, they will be 2 to 4 times as costly as the
comparative U.S. products because of the "negative" inflation rate for the computer industry.

Most major electronic companies, e.g., DEC, National and
Intel, have preferred the pro-American political and
industrial climate of Taiwan, South Korea and Hong Kong.
However, labor costs in these places have escalated enor-
mously, and there is great potential for encouraging these
companies to manufacture in India. India possesses the best
manpower and is politically the most stable country in the
entire region. The multinationals would assist infusion of
contemporary technological skills, and their own benefit
would be primarily in terms of low labor costs.

In March 1980 BusinessWeek presented a comprehensive
article on the industrial climate in various Southeast Asian
countries. This article had commented that India alone
possessed enormous trained manpower for jobs at all levels.
On the negative side it had pointed out that government
decisions took time. In a fast moving industry like
electronics, such delays motivated international companies
to locate elsewhere in the region. The liberal policies
announced in 1984 and the high labor costs in Japan, Korea,
Taiwan and Singapore, are encouraging these companies and
many others to seriously consider relocating manufacturing
facilities in India.

CONCLUSION

Over the past fifteen years, the emphasis has been on
an increasing level of indigenization. This policy of self
reliance has made India capable of both manufacturing and
maintaining computers. The country has attained limited
success in the production of advanced semiconductor chips.

In spite of having large numbers of educated persons
and a growing infrastructure, India has been able to capture
only a small part of the world computer market. The government hopes that the recent changes will encourage growth at
a rapid pace. There exists a vast potential for joint ventures involving India and countries like Japan, Taiwan,
Korea and Singapore. The latter countries possess contemporary manufacturing capabilities. India can provide
excellent expertise for software, training and translation activities. This cooperative approach is likely to
bring in quicker benefits for all concerned parties.

NOTES

* I thank A. V. Raj for his valuable comments on an
initial version of this paper.
1. Report of the Committee on Automation, Ministry of
Labor and Rehabilitation, New Delhi, 1972.
2. R. C. Barquin, "The Transfer of Computer Technology:
A Framework for Policy In Latin American Nations," Ph.D.
Thesis, MIT, 1974, and The Computer and Africa, Praeger
Publications: New York, 1977, pp. 27-28.
3. Report of the Committee on Automation, op. cit.
4. Computerisation in Government Departments, 221st
Report of Public Accounts Committee, LOK Sabha Secretariat,
New Delhi.
5. M. G. K. Menon, Inaugural Address, CSI Annual
Convention, 1976; A. Gupta, Computers in India - State of
the Art, Proc. of CSI Annual Convention, 1979; and Annual
Reports, Department of Electronics, 1970-71 to 1983-84.
6. Economic Times, Bombay, April 13, 1985, p. 1.
7. Press Note on the New Computer Policy, Department of
Electronics, Government of India, November 19, 1984.
8. Ibid.
9. "Computer makers fear closure; users happy,"
Economic Times, Bombay, April 16, 1985, p. 1.
10. G. Myrdal, Asian Drama, Penguin Press: London, 1956.

6

Japan

Michael Borrus and John Zysman
University of California at Berkeley

Japan has pursued a conscious strategy of industrial
development that has influenced its pattern of domestic
growth and international trade, and its internationally
competitive position in informatics. We elaborate here the
mechanisms by which government shaped the dynamics of a
highly competitive market system. We see it not as miracu-
lous, not as a product of distinctive Japanese cultural
characteristics, and only partly as the result of distinctive political institutions. Our position differs sharply
from many of the standard interpretations of the so-called
Japanese miracle. Government and market cannot be disen-
tangled in the story. We argue that the Japanese government
has played and continues to play an important role in
creating advantage for Japanese firms in world markets. Our
intent is to explain how the process works, using informatics as our primary example.

This discussion proceeds in four steps. First, we present an interpretation of the interplay between government
and market during the high growth developmental years.
Second, we consider the institutional base on which this
approach to policy rests. Third, we consider whether the
strategies and arrangements of the developmental years have
been altered. Finally, we examine the present pattern of
Japanese trade and consider whether it is simply a product
of market forces or is shaped by policy.

THE DEVELOPMENTAL YEARS: AN INTERPRETIVE SKETCH
OF THE INTERPLAY OF GOVERNMENT AND MARKET

Explanations of all sorts have been found to account for
Japanese success.[1] They fall loosely in categories: the
cultural arguments that run from the features of Japanese

management style to the attitudes of Japanese workers; the
institutional arguments that point variously to the production cartels, to the lax or relaxed rules for antitrust and
to the Ministry of International Trade and Industry (MITI);
the economic arguments that consider such things as high
savings rates and the convoluted workings of the distribution system; and the political arguments that point to the
concerted political will required to mobilize the state
policy that supported and promoted growth. None of these
individual elements in and of themselves were critical to
the success of Japanese policy. It is the web of policies
and purposes to which the elements are put that we must
understand.

Government and Market

During the period of orchestrated development from the
mid-1950s to the late 1960s, the Japanese government's primary commitment was to economic growth and the transformation of the economic base from agriculture to light
industry and then to heavy industry. To do this, in our
view, the government sought to establish the infrastructure
necessary for private firms to expand, develop, and compete.
Infrastructure was very broadly defined. It included
sectors, such as steel and shipping during the 1950s-60s,
and microelectronics and computers later, that reduced the
cost of imported materials, could generate foreign exchange
through export, and were critical to the entire economy's
development. The government assured critical sectors the
financial resources they needed to expand competitively,
both by providing budgeted funds and by manipulating the
financial system to do this. Similarly, it encouraged the
importing and domestic development of basic technologies.
In this sense, in the parlance of the trade debate, Japan
targeted certain industries. But that metaphor is
misleading, and it understates the complex web of arrangements that underlay the competitive drive for success within
Japan.

The Japanese government exerted influence on the
industrial economy during the boom years in two principal
ways. First, it was a gatekeeper, controlling external
access to the domestic economy; perhaps more accurately, it
patrolled the channels that tied the national to the international market.[2] The discretion to decide what to let into
Japan permitted the government to break up the packages of
technology, capital, and control represented by foreign

multinational corporations. MITI was the primary func-
tionary in these gatekeeper activities. As Chalmers Johnson
explains:

> Before the capital liberalization of the late 1960s and
> 1970s, no technology entered the country without MITI's
> approval; no joint venture was ever agreed to without
> MITI's scrutiny and frequent alteration of terms; no
> patent rights were ever bought without MITI's pressuring
> the seller to lower the royalties or to make other
> changes advantageous to Japanese industry as a whole;
> and no program for the importation of foreign technology
> was ever approved until MITI and its various advisory
> committees had agreed that the time was right and that
> the industry involved was scheduled for 'nurturing'.[3]

A crucial proposition in the debate is that the closed
market gave Japanese firms a protected base of demand that
facilitated the rapid expansion of production and innovation
in manufacturing; this served to negate the product or production advantages foreign firms would have used to enter
the Japanese market in a range of products including automobiles. The Japanese automobile market was quite closed to
foreign firms. Indeed a reciprocal agreement limited Fiat,
a firm quite capable of producing small cars that were in
demand in Japan to selling 3,000 cars a year. Later such
restrictions did not matter, but as we shall see they played
a role in creating advantage. The controversy over the consequences of market closure continues. To many observers
Japanese policies and practices restricting access still
negate the advantages in research and innovation on which
many foreign firms in many sectors depend. This is particularly true of informatics, where anecdotal evidence
abounds.[4] Cray Computer would note that only two supercomputers were sold in Japan during the 1970s and 1980s.
However, in the year that Hitachi announced its rival to the
Cray, it sold at least 5-10 supercomputers. Corning Glass
would note that it has been unable to receive patent protection on optical fibre lightguide in Japan for 12 years. It
now faces a Sumitomo product developed in conjunction with
NTT in the American market. Similarly, U. S. semiconductor
firms argue that their Japanese market share has remained at
just over 10% for over a decade, despite a flood of innovative new product developments during that time.

Second, agencies of the Japanese government--notably
MITI, and later NTT in informatics--sought to influence the
development of the domestic economy. Seen from the

perspective of the firm, government policy helped provide
cash for investment, tax breaks to sustain liquidity,
research and development support, and aid to promote
exports. We shall examine these policies in a number of
informatics cases as we proceed. These public policies--the
web of policies rather than any individual elements in it--
changed the options of companies. Without external debt
finance, the funds to expand production rapidly would not
have been available to firms. Importantly, with a protected
market the easy availability of capital and imported technology was bound to attract entrants to favored sectors.
Protection and promotion in Japan served to produce real
domestic competition.

MITI was not so much a director as a marketplace player,
with its own purposes and its own means of intervening in
the market to achieve them. Most important, the Japanese
government's industrial strategy assumed that the market
pressures of competition would serve as an instrument of
policy. It is not simply that the government made use of
competitive forces, but rather that it often induced the
very competition it sought to direct. There was (in the
phrase used by Professor Murakami of Tokyo University)
intense but controlled competition. The promotional policy
attracted market entrants, and the stampede for entry and
the resulting battle for market share were then termed by
MITI as excessive competition which had to be controlled.
The intensive domestic competition was controlled by a
variety of mechanisms that included expansion plans agreed
to jointly by government and industry, debt financing of
rapid expansion that made the bankruptcy of major firms a
threat to the entire economy and hence unthinkable, and the
oft cited recession cartels. Equally important, joint
research and development programs for the development of
generic technologies assured wider diffusion of a technology
base than might have occurred from purely private programs,
whether government subsidized or not. Similarly technical
standard-setting served to channel competition into applications and manufacturing.

This intense but controlled domestic competition substituted for the pressures of the international market to force
development. The competition is real, but the government
and private sector worked together to avoid "disruptive" or
"excessive" competition. It is important to note that the
complex of policies that encouraged rapid entry and a
scramble for market share rather than short-term profits,
also encouraged surges of exports. These surges, in fact,
began to lead to criticisms of Japanese economic policy.

We do not need to select between cartoon images of Japan, Inc. or of a land of unfettered competition. It is the particular interaction of state and market in Japan that is interesting.

The interaction of market and state in Japan rests on a very particular set of institutional arrangements in politics and business. We must summarize them briefly both to understand the dynamics of the Japanese economy and to clarify why the particulars of the Japanese strategy cannot easily be copied in other countries.

The Institutional Base of Japanese Policy for Industry and Trade

Japanese policy for industry and trade and the strategy of controlled competition for development rest on a very particular institutional and political base. That base has three components: First, the administrative apparatus is structured in a fashion that permits a group of elite bureaucrats at MITI and Finance to formulate a strategy. The administration is centralized, which eliminates conflicts between, for example, state and national officials. The executive branch dominates the legislative, so that there is little detailed scrutiny of administrative decisions. The administration has extensive discretion in determining and applying rules, which gives it extensive power in bargaining with the private sector. The elite bureaucrats themselves form something best called a caste, recruited from the same schools and rising within the system together. In the informatics area, the key bureaucratic players include MITI, the Ministry of Posts and Telecommunications (MPT), MITI's Information Technology Promotion Agency (IPA), the Science and Technology Agency, and, prior to its privitization, Nippon Telegraph and Telephone (NTT).

Second, the structure of the financial system gives the bureaucracy the ability to intervene selectively as a player in the industrial economy. As Ueno has argued the financial system might be the crucial instrument in the government's repertoire of domestic policies. It permitted the government to direct not just budget funds but the flow of savings and investment in the economy.[5] As Ueno summarized the situation:

> Broadly speaking, the total supply of funds in Japan was controlled by the Bank of Japan, the level and

structure of interest rates were artificially regulated
by the Ministry of Finance, and <u>private funds were allocated, under the guidance of public financial institutions, by city banks which competed for market shares.</u>
In this process, the Bank of Japan followed the
guidelines of the Economic Planning Agency and the MITI
and determined the total amount of funds so as to
satisfy the demands to growth industries. At the same
time, the Ministry of Finance maintained the low
interest policy inasmuch as the policy did not lead to
large deficits in the balance of payments or to sharp
price rises.[6]

Zysman has summarized the importance of the financial
instrument:

The credit-based financial system served the government
as a powerful instrument of policy. The political and
policy strategies of the Japanese government would have
been difficult to accomplish within the constraints of a
capital market-based financial system with freely moving
prices and an elaborate securities market. The
financial instrument in Japan served several purposes.
Most generally, it helped force the household sector to
bear the costs of expansion in the form of artifically
low interest rates. At the same time, the system
socialized those costs by diffusing or absorbing the
risks of investment and corporate failure. It also
reduced the price of expanding and stockpiling goods in
anticipation of market development, which has been a
constant Japanese market tactic. Access to credit was
selectively manipulated to provide preference to favored
sectors and to push the economy slowly toward
capital-intensive and knowledge-intensive production.
In all sectors there has been a constant effort to push
and tempt firms onto what the government sees as the
paths of competitive righteousness. The degree to which
government's view prevails within particular sectors
depends on the international competitive strength and
financial position of their major companies. The
government's view prevailed when companies needed
capital, imported technology, and sought assistance in
market development. In sum, the economy is not
administered but the government seeks to act to affect
the terms of competition in order to create outcomes it
favors. In essence, the state is another powerful
economic player shaping market development in pursuit of

competitiveness but not of profits. Finance is a vital
instrument--in Ueno's view the crucial instrument--in
the government's repertoire of domestic policies. The
Japanese case closely parallels the French in which a
credit-based, price-administered financial system is at
the core of a state-led industrial strategy.[7]

Thus, from the time that the information industry was
designated as strategic in a 1957 law (to be discussed
below), the credit-based financial system was manipulated to
extend credit to Japan's major informatics firms (including
NEC, Fujitsu, Hitachi, Toshiba, Mitsubishi and others).
Although direct government assistance to informatics in the
form of loans and subsidies was relatively small--see
Table 6.1--the major firms nevertheless had easy access to
capital at preferencial rates through the banking system.

TABLE 6.1
Direct Government Assistance to Informatics
(billion yen)

Period	Loan Amount	Loan/Total Investment
1961-65	7.5	2.5%
1966-70	8.4	1.4%
1971-75	8.9	1.0%
1976-79	9.2	0.8%

Source: MITI and Japan Development Bank, "Plant and
Equipment Investment Plans of Key Industries".

Third, a conservative coalition of organized agriculture
and business insulated the bureaucracy from radical
political shifts. The Liberal Democratic Party, the
instrument of that coalition, was based on rural and small
town votes and big business finance. It has been in power
continuously since its creation early in the post-war
period. Power shifts have occurred between factions within
the party, but the party itself has been the government. As
Chalmers Johnson has remarked, "The politicians reigned, but
the bureaucrats ruled."[8] This was certainly true in the
center of government priorities, industrial development.

Controlled Competition Muscle and Flexibility

The structure of business, as well as the system of
state administration and policy, supports an arrangement of
controlled competition. The notion of controlled competition was one we adopted to account for the interplay of
market and politics we observed in many sectors in Japan.
Having begun to use it we found that Professor Murakami of
Tokyo University had chosen that term to describe the
central characteristics of the Japanese economy. The
dynamics and mechanisms of controlled competition are crucial to understanding the role of government in the pattern
of rapid growth and emerging international competitiveness.

Much has been made of MITI's structure councils where
private business, government officials, academics, and even
press leaders meet to formulate policy directions. That
pattern of interaction rests on the structure of government
on the one hand and of business on the other. As we
discussed above, at the core of the state system in Japan is
a highly centralized bureaucracy staffed by elite civil servants. These career servants of the state were recruited
from the top graduates of the most prestigious national universities. Their positions gave them social status as well
as administrative power. Responsibility for promotional
policies was inevitably spread across several ministries,
but at the core of the system, informatics no less than
elsewhere, was the Ministry of International Trade and
Industry. Chalmers Johnson's excellent book traces the evolution of MITI's role from adjunct to an agriculture
ministry, to keeper of the cartels, through administrative
control during the war and into the system of administrative
guidance we have been describing.[9] This bureaucratic system
was relatively insulated from detailed political control by
the domination of the Liberal Democratic Party and was armed
with instruments of selected economic intervention through
the financial system that were entirely outside of legislative control.

Japanese state developmental policy rested, as well, on
a business community that, before the war, developed giant
hierarchical firms, inter-company group linkages, and some
international orientation.[10] The business community was not
only the vehicle but the political support for the efforts
of postwar development.

Equally important, the structure of business provided
the basis of collaboration between firms. This was not so
much because Japan is an economy of giant firms, although

levels of concentration in the economy as a whole and of
sellers in specific markets are as high as in the United
States. Rather, a number of mechanisms drew the large firms
together in common institutions.[11] The trading companies,
an early link between the insulated domestic economy and its
external sources of supply, represent one such mechanism. A
second mechanism, the Zaibatsu groupings of companies, was
dissolved in the American occupation. However groupings
around large banks (keiretsu) based on earlier zaibatsu ties
have been established that now tie firms together. There
are several forms of keiretsu, ranging from groups with
close inter-company ties to loose, basically financial
arrangements. While there is a debate on the precise form
or degree of operating cohesion in these groups, the fact is
that a majority of company stock in Japan is held by other
companies or banks. This provides still another set of
inter-firm links. The world of small firms is not anarchic
either, because many of the small firms are linked as
suppliers to larger companies. Small firms are not inevitably relegated to subordinate supplier status; some independent small firms have grown to compete directly with the
giants. But the well known and much publicized examples,
Sony and Honda, are rather exceptional. Lastly, while cartels are nominally illegal, an enormous number are in fact
exempt from the general prohibition. These several forms
of inter-company links provide the organizational
infrastructure for controlled competition.

Japanese industry combines, in an innovative manner,
strengths of both the muscular large firms able to mobilize
substantial resources in pursuit of long term objectives and
the flexibility and mobility of small firms. Much has been
made of the ability of large Japanese firms to raise low
cost capital and to often lever a strong position in one
market into entry into another. Indeed, the advantages of
interfirm cooperation in research and development have led
some American observers to argue for a relaxation of
antitrust laws in order to permit coordination among
American firms.[12] Less has been said about the flexibility
that has made the Japanese an agile, not a lumbering, giant.
The agility comes in two forms. First, small firms that are
suppliers and contractors to larger firms play a vital role.
In the American system many of the tasks these small firms
play would be integrated into the parent company.
Subcontracting ties component suppliers to the parent
assembler by market ties rather than hierarchy inside a
firm. The small firm must scramble to adjust to changes in
the market demands of the large parent firm.

Second, many Japanese companies begin as spinoffs from larger firms[13]. Elsewhere they might be structured as divisions or tightly controlled subsidiaries. In Japan, firms like Fujitsu Fanuc are organized as quite independent operations. Marketplace ties rather than purely administrative relations are at work again. Yet we must not be lost in the Anglo-American dichotomy between market and administration. The Japanese system combines both along lines different from those with which the West is familiar.

The system of controlled competition permitted the government to pursue a strategy of creating enduring advantage in the international market. Production technologies and factor availabilities, unlike mountains, are not immutable features of a nation's economic topography. There are only a few industrial sectors such as coal or oil in which comparative advantage is given in the form of fixed natural resource availability, and even there production and transportation facilities may alter a seemingly self-evident calculus. Japanese transportation policy gave its basic industries a cost advantage by importing raw materials. In most sectors--particularly the manufacturing sectors which dominate the production and trade of advanced industrial countries--comparative advantage is partly the product of national economic policies. For example, such policies in Japan influence the accumulation of physical capital, the pace of research and development, and the development of labor skills and education, all of which underlie the factor "endowments" and production technologies dear to classical theory. A concerted long range policy can steadily turn a competitive disadvantage in capital, education, or research intensive industries into a national comparative advantage. In short, national comparative advantage, the sectors at which relative to other domestic uses of resources a country gains the most in international trade, can be created by national policy measures. From this perspective, a nation that subsidizes its exports may transfer wealth to other countries in the short term but it may build its own wealth in the long term if it promotes an enduring comparative advantage for domestic firms in the sectors with high value added that are growing the most rapidly.

Although government policies were critical, the direct engine behind growth was domestic competition in a rapidly expanding market[14]. Structured competition in a rapidly growing domestic market, closed to outsiders, generated the product and production strengths that the Japanese have taken into world markets. Elements of Japanese culture, and more importantly of the business structure, may have

facilitated these market innovations, but the driving force
was marketplace incentives. Many supposedly "Japanese"
elements--including the pursuit of market share and the tactics of internal organization--follow logically from the
nature of the market situation, even though they have roots
in policy. The achievements of Japanese companies are real;
they are not mysterious. Those strengths are now entrenched
in corporate strategies for the market and the tactics of
production organization in the factory.

Consider how structured competition in a rapidly growing
market will generate the product and production advantages
the Japanese have taken into world markets. Those strengths
are rooted in corporate strategies for the market and the
tactics of production organization in the factory. Given
the same market conditions, producers of many nations would
likely have responded in similar ways.

During the 1970s, through a series of government
orchestrated cooperative research and development projects,
Japan's major electronics firms developed state of the art
semiconductor memory capabilities.[15] The cooperative R&D
helped to focus the firms, and ensured diffusion of a common
level of technical expertise. Preferential loans and
targetted tax incentives for production (more on this topic
later) encouraged the rapid addition of manufacturing capacity. With all of the major firms at a common technical
level, the race for market advantage focused on refinement
of the manufacturing process to increase yields and quality,
and decrease costs. Each additional increment of factory
capacity installed was interactively built on the manufacturing advances that preceeded it. With foreign competition
in the domestic Japanese market limited both by policy and
by the structure of the market (Japan's largest producers
also account for about 60% of domestic Japanese semiconductor consumption), the domestic market provided an insulated
base in which to reach scale economies, refine manufacturing, bring costs below world market levels, and then
export. The result, by the early 1980s, was that five major
Japanese producers were able simultaneously to move to
volume production of certain kinds of semiconductor memory
devices that boasted higher quality and lower costs than
their international competitors. Japanese firms rapidly
became, by the mid-1980s, the world's leading memory
producers.

A simlar story is evident in automobiles. From 1960
automobile production jumped from 160,000 cars to some
10,000,000 by the end of the 1970s. Each new assembly line
was an experiment station for production, and the Japanese

companies could innovate and come down that infamous production learning curve. In essence, the Japanese imported the best available production technology and then improved on it. The marginal improvements accumulated into a fundamental manufacturing innovation. Rapidly expanding markets meant that they then had occasion to learn how to improve on the imported practices.

Nowhere are the attributes and occasional risks of Japan's orchestrated development better illustrated than in the telecommunications segment of the informatics industry.[16] Until April 1985, Nippon Telegraph and Telephone (NTT) was Japan's domestic, public, common carrier communications monopoly under the adminstrative control of the Ministry of Posts and Telecommunications (MPT). In addition to its just-ended monopoly over common carrier communications, including data transmission, NTT offers data-processing time-sharing services, licenses all communciations and runs five very advanced electronics R&D and systems engineering laboratories (which are currently being reorganized into nine labs). Since its formation in 1952, NTT--under MPT's direction--has engaged in joint R&D and systems engineering to develop microelectronics, computers and software, optoelectronics, and network equipment for Japan's public-switched communications infrastructure with a favored 'family' of major Japanese electronics companies (normally, NEC, Fujitsu, Hitachi and Oki, but others like Sumitomo Electric depending on the particular product). NTT has helped to develop and finance pilot and mass production systems for manufacture of the products jointly researched and developed. Crucially, NTT has procured high volumes of equipment and systems at premium prices from its family companies--which serves both to make demand highly predictable and stable, and to subsidize price competition for those Japanese firms in export markets. It has even engaged in direct export-finance. Of course, all of these developmental activities have been closed to foreign firms. Indeed, until the 1980 U.S.-Japan Agreement on NTT Procurement, the Japanese market was formally closed to foreign producers. In telecommunications, as in steel, autos and consumer electronics, Japanese success on world markets has rested on the ability of Japanese producers to move rapidly to volume production with limited risk in a domestic market insulated from foreign competition.

NTT's industrial policy role enabled favored Japanese telecommunications companies to develop and commercialize new technologies in a protected and subsidized, risk-minimalized way. With NTT coordinating common standards development and allocating markets among its favored family, Japanese producers developed a small number of related product families that share common components and automated production facilities, and hence, lower overall costs. When combined with procurement from NTT in high volumes at premium prices, the costs of the resulting equipment have been driven to or below world levels, enabling rapid competitive penetration of world markets by major Japanese firms. As data processing and telecommunications have converged, NTT has emerged as an important element in electronics development.

There are numerous examples of the impact of NTT's developmental role in helping to establish Japan's telecommunications equipment producers as world class competitors. The example of fiber-optic light-guide is illustrative.[17] In the early 1970s, Corning Glass held generic patents on the production of light-guide and attempted to register its patents in Japan prior to moving into Japan through licensing or export (as it did in Europe). The patent applications were administratively stalled in Japan for ten years. During that time, NTT entered into a crash development program with its family of favored cable producers, Sumitomo, Furakawa and Fujikura, to develop a different mass production method for light-guide, the vapor-phase axial deposition (VAD) method. NTT then entered into high-volume, premium-price procurement at levels far above its own immediate needs. This forced Japan's cable producers to reach a scale of production that brought their costs below world market levels, created excess capacity destined for export, and provided the profits to subsidize price competition on world markets. Indeed, in 1983, Japan's total fiber market was estimated at about 60,000 fiber kilometers while Japanese producers had an estimated production capacity of 575,000 fiber-km; and NTT was paying Japanese producers a price some 3-4 times higher than they were selling at in the United States. Today, the Japanese industry is a highly competitive world class producer of light-guide.

Quite similar stories with similar competitive outcomes are true of Japan's push to become a leading producer of optoelectronic components for fiber-optic transmission, where NEC and Fujitsu were chosen as the favored suppliers, and of microwave transmission equipment, where NEC was chosen as the leader. The same story is true of fast facsmilies, where NTT pioneered developments in data compression, solid-state array scanning, and printing techniques, and then transferred the technology to Japanese producers.[18] In each case, the Japanese producers are

currently among the world's leading suppliers. Procurement
of high volumes at premium prices, and component/sub-system
production shared across product families, permitted
Japanese firms to recoup high R&D costs early in the product
cycle in their closed home market. By the time they hit
world markets, Japanese costs were substantially below the
prevailing levels of their competitors, who needed to price
to recoup development costs.

The contrasting example of Japan's relative failure in
digital switching equipment markets also illustrates how
critical the NTT developmental system has been for Japanese
firms. NEC entered the U.S. digital central office switch
market relatively early in 1979 with its NEAX 61. After a
quick start in sales to smaller independent and rural telcos
primarily as a result of its habitual lowest-bid pricing
strategy, NEC ran into trouble largely because of software
problems with the switch. It was in fact forced to rip-out
the switches it had installed for Rochester Telephone, a
larger independent. NEC ran into problems primarily because
it had not had a chance to install and de-bug digital
central office switches in Japan. This, in turn, was the
result of NTT's late move to digital switching for Japan's
public network--it began commercial installation and testing
of the D70 digital central office switches in Japan only in
1984. Indeed, the NEAX 61 was an export-only switch, the
result of early prototype development by NEC with NTT for
export markets, and was never destined for use in Japan. In
short, without the benefit of procurement and use in a
closed domestic market, NEC was at a decided disadvantage in
competition on world markets.

While there are downside risks like the creation of too
great a dependency on such a highly organized developmental
system, Japan's past orchestrated development policies have
on the whole helped to create a highly competitive and world
class informatics industry. This can be seen by examining
domestic Japanese markets for microelectronics, computers,
telecommunications and optoelectronics, and by highlighting
the international competitive position of Japanese producers
in these areas.

Japan's domestic market for semiconductors reached about
$10 billion in 1985, and ranked second in size only to the
U. S. market.[19] With the appreciation of the yen against
the dollar, it is likely to surpass the U. S. market in size
by early 1987. The primary reason for this is Japan's
extremely high per capita consumption of microelectronics
(see Table 6.2). Though imperfect, Table 6.2 gives some
indication of the degree to which informatics related

technology has penetrated Japanese society compared to other major industrialized countries.

TABLE 6.2
Semiconductor Consumption Per Capita
(dollars)

Country	1978	1984
Europe Total	7	14
France		(15)
Germany		(22)
U.K.		(20)
Italy		(8)
U.S.	16	52
Japan	22	61

Source: Dataquest.

Because Japanese producers capture roughly 90% of the demand for semiconductors in their own market, Japan's major semiconductor firms have been the primary beneficiaries of the explosive growth in usage of microelectronics in Japan. As a result of the experience and economies gained serving their own market, Japanese firms led by NEC, Hitachi, Fujitsu, Toshiba, Matsushita, and Mitsubishi, have made rapid competitive inroads on world markets. Indeed, Japan's semiconductor industry has risen from relative obscurity at the start of the 1970s to become the second largest industry in the world, and the only one that has been gaining market share rapidly at the expense of U.S. producers. Over the past ten years, Japan's share of world semiconductor markets has doubled to just over 40% in 1985, while the U. S. share has fallen from over 60% to under 50%. At current investment and growth rates, the Japanese industry will overtake the U. S. by the late 1980s.

Although Japan's computer industry has not fared quite as well on international markets, its growth has nevertheless been impressive, and its firms offer the only serious competitive challenge to U. S. computer makers.[20] Indeed, many of the second tier U. S. producers, like Burroughs, Honeywell and Sperry, now rely partly or entirely on Japanese producers to supply them on an OEM basis with computer hardware ranging from peripherals to PCs to entire

mainframes. Table 6.3 indicates the domestic Japanese
market for computers in 1984, broken out by supplier firms
and by production for domestic consumption and export. In
addition to the companies listed below, Matsushita,
Seiko-Epsom, Sharp, Sony and Sanyo are major producers of
personal computers and computer peripheral equipment.
Overall, Japan's domestic computer market is the world's
second largest national market. Japanese firms, largely on
the basis of OEM deals with U. S. and European producers,
are the only national industry offering competitive hardware
supply to IBM, DEC and the few other leading U. S. producers.

TABLE 6.3
Japanese Computer Sales - 1984
(yen = billions)

Supplier	Total	Domestic	Export
Fujitsu	857	687	170
IBM Japan	768	545	223
NEC	662	569	93
Hitachi	532	428	104
Toshiba	231	192	39
Oki	185	128	57
Mitsubishi	165	132	33
Japan NCR	66	66	--
Others	204		
Total	3670		

Source: Japan Economic Journal and Japanese Industry Sources.

On the telecommunications side, Japan's industry is also
a world class supplier, particularly of microwave
transmission, fiber-optics, and customer premises
equipment.[20] In 1984 the domestic Japanese telecom equipment industry shipments reached about $6.5 billion.
Table 6.4 breaks out these shipments by equipment type.
Of these shipments, Japan exported about $2.3 billion of
equipment, making the Japanese telecom equipment industry a
rival to the U. S. industry as one of the world's largest
national exporters of telecom equipment. As suggested
above, Japanese export competitiveness resides largely in
transmission and customer premises equipment. By contrast,

Japanese producers do less well in the export of switching equipment to world markets outside of Asia, largely as a result of the digital switching story described before. This may change, however, as Japan moves to digitize its public switched telephone network during the remainder of the century.

TABLE 6.4
Domestic Japanese Telecom Equipment Demand
(1984 - billions of yen)

Equipment Type	Value
All Equipment	1615.1
Wire Total	1261.7
Telephone Sets	76.9
Telephone Systems	296.6
--Key	(229.7)
Telegraph and Graphic	278.3
--Telegraph	(8.5)
--Facsimile	(263.7)
Switching	283.0
--Electronic CO	(141.2)
--Electronic PBX	(89.1)
Carrier Transmission	263.6
--Digital Transmission	(118.8)
--Wide-band Terminal	(48.2)
Parts	63.3
Radio Communications Total	353.4
Fixed Radio Stations	179.7
Mobile Radio Stations	148.9
Personal Radio Equipment	24.9

Source: Communications Industry Association of Japan

Japan's optoelectronics industry is another bright spot in the country's informatics' firmament. With production of approximately $4 billion in 1985 (over 864 billion yen), we believe that Japan's industry has surpassed the United States to become the world's largest producer of optoelectronics (total production of components, equipment and systems) for commercial market applications. Table 6.5 breaks out the 1985 industry production by market sub-
In short, Japan's orchestrated developmental strategy and system have helped to produce a highly internationally

128

TABLE 6.5
Japan Optoelectronics Industry Production
(1985 - billions of yen)

Type	Value
Optical Components Total	278.7
Light emitting elements	(121.8)
Light receiving elements	(21.9)
Complex light devices	(39.2)
Solar batteries	(9.1)
Optical Fibers	(50.5)
Other	(36.0)
Optical Devices and Equipment Total	283.3
Optical transmission	(31.8)
Optical measuring	(16.7)
Installation equipment	(4.6)
Optical fiber sensors	(1.3)
Laser-based sensors	(6.9)
Optical disk memories	(47.4)
Optical digital audio disks	(66.9)
Optical input-output	(53.8)
Medical laser	(4.3)
Laser processing and other	(49.1)
Optical Application Systems Total	80.1
Optical communications systems	(73.2)
Other	(6.9)
TOTAL	864.4

Note: Figures are estimated. Numbers may not add due to rounding.

Source: 1985 Production Survey of Optical Components, Devices and Equipment, and Systems, Japan Optoelectronics Industry and Technology Development Association.

competitive informatics industry. 'Controlled competition' in the market among major Japanese firms, aimed at achieving costs that are competitive around the world, has carried forward Japan's informatics development, even as the developmental system has changed. We turn now to examine the significance of those changes.

IS THERE NOW AN INDUSTRIAL POLICY IN JAPAN?

As the Japanese economy has evolved, its developmental system has loosened. Government-led policy no longer seems to try to control the evolution of the whole economy; instead, its interventions are intended to ease the transition of declining sectors and to promote the expansion of new industries. In other words, there are sectors in which Japan has lost advantage or would like to create it.

There have been genuine efforts at removing formal tariff barriers and other forms of direct discrimination against foreign imports. However, some of the arrangements that have given structural advantages to the Japanese in their home markets, and often in international markets, have endured.[22] The capacity to resist foreign competitors in crucial sectors remains, even though there is a marked reduction in the government's ability to control the domestic economy. The high-technology informatics sectors are not, in our view and that of many others, open to full foreign competition. To judge the extent of liberalization we consider the sets of policies intended to promote "sunrise" industries.

Policies for "Sunrise" Industries

Japanese policy is committed to developing the industries of the future, the sunrise industries. It has, roughly since the first oil shock of 1973, avowed a determination to shift the country's industrial structure away from the base of heavy and chemical industries upon which it is currently grounded and to move toward knowledge-intensive industries.[23] Here we look horizontally at the range of policies used to promote informatics industries. These include formal government legislation and pronouncements, measures to capitalize on certain features of the domestic market structure for competitive gain, collaborative research and development (R&D) measures, subsidies and tax incentives, and finally, measures to foster industry rationalization and the creation of cartels in designated sectors.

From the perspective of world trade, and of the potential adoption of these tactics by developing countries, the important issue is whether the Japanese efforts to hurry toward the industrial future unfairly affect the development of the same industries in other countries. The question, of course, is what is "unfair." The fact of promotion is not in itself improper or illegal. Indeed, the definition of proper and improper promotion policy is unclear under the international trade rules. Discrimination against foreign firms, however, is in most cases improper. Such discrimination invokes the image of the developmental years, and this suggests to some that the domestic market is still being used as a protected preserve for government-promoted expansion. MITI's proposed software protection law (which would have forced foreign producers to unbundle their software), the intensive software, computer, component and optoelectronics coordinated research and development projects, policies for satellite development, and NTT deregulation, all raise concerns that Japan intends to use government policy to create advantage in world markets. In other words, the fear is that the objectives and policies of the developmental period persist, and that only the choice of sectors to promote has changed.

Policy development often begins with a "vision" usually formulated by MITI. MITI's visions (bijon) are merely government-sponsored studies that present a coherent but purposely sketchy outline of likely future trends. These have served not only as public relations ventures--intended to draw attention to concerns the government deems significant--but also as tools for building a genuine consensus of expectations among these groups most directly concerned with the problem at hand.[24] Once a political consensus has been reached the formal legislation enacted to "give teeth" to those visions and policy statements follows. The case of Japan's computer and other information industries shows these visions do not remain mere pronouncements once a broad consensus has been reached. In a series of three laws--the Law on Extraordinary Measures for the Promotion of Electronics and the Machinery Industry (April 1971), and the Law on Extraordinary Measures for the Promotion of Specific Machinery and Information Industry (June 1978)--the informatics industry received the benefits of being named a "strategic industry" in Japan's policy scheme.[25]

The specific policy instruments accomplish four purposes. First, public and private collaborative R&D encourage the diffusion as well as the development of technology among domestic producers. Research and development funds from the government for selected technologies serve to reduce risk, initiate competition, and signal enduring government interest. While the pool of government funds is not in itself large enough to support corporate programs, it can serve to induce other investments and corporate

commitments. Such collaborative public and private R&D
efforts have also borne fruit for the Japanese. A
noteworthy instance of this was described above--the
Very-Large-Scale Integrated Circuit (VLSI) Project created
by MITI and the Nippon Telephone and Telegraph Company (NTT)
in 1976, which culminated in the success of Japanese semiconductor firms on world memory markets.

A series of new programs have been initiated in the
last few years. The program objectives are startlingly
ambitious and the funds involved are quite large both in
real terms and relative to past governmental commitments of
funds. Here we briefly highlight five of the most significant cooperative projects.[26] These are the Optoelectronics
Measurement and Control project, the New Function Elements
semiconductor project, the Superspeed Computer project, the
Fifth Generation Computer project, and NTT's Information
Network Systems project.

The Optoelectronics project was begun in 1979 by MITI's
Agency of Industrial Science and Technology (AIST), and will
culminate in 1987. Direct government funding has amounted
to approximately $80 million, with total costs of the pro-
ject approaching $200 million. Approximately one-third of
direct funding has been contract research to the
Optoelectronics Joint Research Laboratory, with non-
refundable government consignment payments ("itakuhi")
covering expenses. The Lab is focusing on integrating both
optical and electronic elements monolithically on an
integrated circuit. Most of Japan's major electronics companies have participated in the research. The project is
credited with advancing the state of Japan's optoelectronics
work, and with helping to ensure that Japanese producers are
competitive on world markets in optoelectronic components,
equipment and systems.

The New Function Elements project has three precise
semiconductor development aims. These are development of
extremely fine lattice-structure elements capable of very
high computation speeds at room temperature, development of
3-dimensional device technology, and development of devices
capable of functioning in hostile environments (e.g. nuclear
reactors, space, auto engines). MITI is spending
approximately $115 million during the decade of the 1980s to
advance these aims. Total costs are likely to approach one-
quarter of a billion dollars. Again, itakuhi payments are
the principal form of government sponsorship.

The Superspeed Computer project is aiming at
establishing Japanese superiority in superspeed components
and computing architecture. The project is funded directly

132

at about $105 million during the 1980s, with a real cost
approaching $250 million. Component work focuses on gallium
arsenide field effect transistors, high mobility electron
devices (HEMT), and josephsine junction elements.
Architectural work is focusing on parallel processing, vec-
tor and scalar processing and pipelining. The overall official goal is to produce a supercomputer capable of
performing one gigaflop--one billion floating point
operations--per second by 1989.

The much-publicized Fifth Generation Computer project
aims at producing commercially viable knowledge information
processing systems and symbolic inference machines with the
speeds of supercomputers and intelligent interfaces. The
project is being carried out under the auspices of the
Institute for New Generation Computing (ICOT), with funding
from MITI through AIST. Direct funding is in the range of
$200 million, with real costs estimated at close to one-half
billion dollars. The project's first stage, completed in
1985 defined and developed the basic hardware and software
technology. The second stage, running through 1989, will
attempt to develop an inference subsystem capable of
learning, associating and inferring, and a knowledge subsystem with large, relational data and knowledge bases
manipulated in parallel. A complete integrated system is
planned for the final phase, from 1989 to 1992.

The aim of NTT's ambitious Information Network System
project (INS), is to create by the year 2000 a fully
integrated, digital communications infrastructure for Japan,
linked by broadband fiber optic cable and microwave equipment.[27] INS is Japan's full-blown vision of ISDN. In
essence, INS aims to put a digital, broadband infrastructure
in place in anticipation of its uses, while simultaneously
developing those uses through model programs and pilot projects targetted at business and residential users. In order
to understand the planned evolution to INS, it is necessary
to realize that NTT operates four separate major networks
for communications services in Japan, each of which have
been developed independently. These include the PSTN
(wireline and radio), the telegraph (telegram and telex)
network, digital data networks (DDX) and a digital facsimile
network.

The INS network will evolve from the gradual unification
of these independent digital data and facsimile networks,
with the public switched telephone network (as it is
digitized). Most critically, aside from extending the
fiber-optic trunk network, NTT intends to move aggressively
to revamp the local loop network by installing fiber-optics

and digitizing it as part of the INS evolution. Several
parallel projects--some of them implemented in pilot form in
a model demonstration INS--are also underway to develop
equipment and services that can take advantage of the INS
infrastructure. These include interactive visual communications networks (NTT's Video Response system or VRS)
integrated voice-data and voice-video equipment, optical scan
document terminals and fast mini-faxes, and optical instrumentation and control systems for industrial and office
applications.

It is estimated that the entire INS project will require
between $80 to 120 billion in investment over the next 15
years. Estimates of the markets for INS-related private
investment and products (including terminal equipment and
software) approach $250 billion. Given the huge size of
these markets, INS offers enormous leverage for NTT to continue its developmental role to the advantage of Japanese
producers.

Aside from such cooperative projects, government procurement has also served to develop and to diffuse technology. In this regard, the role of NTT as "creative first
user"--much as the Department of Defense was in the early
history of the U. S. microelectronics industry--has already
been described above. (We briefly examine the changing role
of NTT below). Even in areas where government procurement
might have been insufficient to develop and diffuse technology, private procurement analogues have been created and
nurtured. Perhaps the best example is the Japan Electronic
Computer Company (JECC), which was organized by the government in 1961, with the participation of Japan's computer
industry producers who are the primary shareholders. Its
mandate was to purchase computer hardware and software from
Japan's manufacturers and lease the equipment to users at
preferential rates. This eliminated the financial burden on
each computer manufacturer of having to carry leasing inven-
tories, finance leases and engage in expensive equipment
buy-backs, and permitted a rapid diffusion of successive
generations of equipment to computer users.

Standards to structure and channel competition is a
second crucial but little explored instrument of policy.
For example, common operating standards in personal computers have been adopted by agreement and established in
machine tools by Fujitsu Fanuc's domination of the
controller market. Where such standards exist, competition
is channeled away from a struggle about basic operating
parameters and into products with different applications.
Indeed, if this is intentional promotion--and we cannot

judge clearly whether it is--it is an extremely clever use
of market forces. The fact that standards shape competition
is of international concern. The international issue is how
the standards are set. Product standards, often developed
within MITI structure councils, serve to define the lines of
an industry's evolution. American firms note that shortly
after the formal promulgation of standards, products flood
the market so quickly that they would seem to have been in
development during the processes of adopting standards.
Thus the Japanese decision to include foreigners in
structure-council deliberations is quite important.

The standard setting mechanisms raise a more general
problem troubling U. S.-Japanese relations. The
"transparency" issue has come to represent a thorn in the
side of U. S.-Japanese trade relations. Trade negotiators
from the United States have repeatedly charged that the
American policymaking system is much more "transparent" than
the Japanese system and that it is far easier for Japanese
officials to know what is going on in Washington and to
influence the course of events than it is for any foreigner
to have an impact on Japan's highly private, "opaque" processes of decision-making. For this reason, during January
of 1984, the U. S. Undersecretary of Commerce for
International Trade, Lionel Olmer, succeeded in extracting
concessions from the Japanese allowing American representatives access to and permission to address meetings of
MITI's Industrial Structural Council. It was, he suggested,
merely a matter of reciprocity, no different from the ease
with which Japanese and other foreigners can lobby the U. S.
government. While there has been some optimism expressed
over Olmer's achievement, it is by no means certain that it
will produce any worthwhile results. For instance, even if
American representatives are allowed to sit in on the
Council's deliberation sessions, they will have no means to
influence the decisions of MITI (its sponsoring ministry),
not to mention other ministries concerned with a particular
issue, or the trade associations of an industry affected by
a council recommendation. Thus, although the "transparency"
issue lies submerged, it may not be long forgotten.[28]

Subsidies and tax incentives are a third category of
promotional policies. Actually, the term "subsidy," as
applied to Japanese industrial policy is something of a
misnomer. More precisely, subsidies are usually either
grants that take the form of conditional loans (hojokin), or
government contracted work, that takes the form of con-
signemt payments (itakuhi).[29] Here the case of government
subsidies to Japan's machine-tool industry--a case that

gained notoriety in this country because of the petition for
relief filed by Houdaille Industries--provides an
interesting example.[30]

Also, certain measures within Japan's corporate tax
system are used to target specific industrial policy objectives. For example, the pattern of special depreciation
measures tends to be biased toward manufacturing in general,
and the measures are purposely geared to stimulate markets
for types of goods for which the government would like to
see greater domestic production.[31] Aircraft is the most
recent instance. The market failure of Japan's first entry
into the commercial aircraft business saw the government
writing off nearly $100 million in loans. Its second entry
will be jointly financed by the government and a group of
firms in a venture with Boeing. These loans lower and diffuse the risk of new ventures. Other special tax measures
have accomplished similar ends. For example, computer producers have received four specific tax breaks in addition to
vastly accelerated depreciation (for both producers and
purchasers). These include an incremental 25% R&D tax
credit, a deduction for 50% of 'software realized income'
which permits a tax free reserve to cover software
development costs, a deduction equivalent to 20% of training
expenses for software engineers, and a reserve contingency
loss fund equivalent to 2.5% of sales to cover the return of
older generation equipment via JECC.[32]

Finally, policies to promote industry rationalization
and to create cartels in designated industries represent a
fourth broad category of measures designed to nurture
promising new industries. In a 1973 policy statement issued
by the Economic Planning Agency, the importance of industry
rationalization in Japan's future growth industries is
clearly articulated:

> At the same time as all industries should be induced to
> become knowledge-intensive through (1) promoting a
> higher degree of processing and higher product quality,
> (2) even when the finished product remains the same,
> attempting to make the processes of its production and
> distribution information-intensive, labor-saving, and
> pollution-free, and (3) trying to systematize vertically
> several industries from material procurement to
> processing and distribution or to establish horizontal
> systems unifying diverse functions.[33]

In addition, the Japanese government has encouraged the
creation of cartels in designated industries--such as

136

machine tools--in order to avoid the pitfalls of excess competition. It is believed by many that the Japanese government aids its chosen cartels by its lax enforcement of
Japan's Law Concerning Prohibition of Private Monopoly and
Maintenance of Fair Trade (the Anti-Monopoly Law).34
    Issues of policy--that is, government intention--must be
separated from matters of market structure. In the
abstract, this looks simple, but in practice it is hard to
do. For example, the Japanese financial system is thought
to provide advantages to national firms in the form of low
interest rates and longer term financing. The two-tier
labor market with lifetime employment and temporary labor in
the same factories, to choose another example, is a product
of policy choices. Inter-firm arrangements within Keiretsu
(industrial conglomerates usually organized around a bank
and a trading company) often make foreign entry into the
market difficult. The inter-firm holdings, Okimoto and
Krasner note, increased--seemingly as a result of government
encouragement--as foreigners were given permission to
acquire Japanese firms.35 These market arrangements in
their view, could be seen as a constructed market alternative to direct policy.

Accounting for Japan's Pattern of Trade

    The general pattern of Japanese trade is not unusual or
hard to explain, in our view. What is unusual and requires
explanation is that the Japanese trade structure, as we have
discussed, is unique in one revealing aspect: relative to
its trade partners, Japan does not import goods in sectors
in which it exports them. Its pattern of trade with other
advanced countries is distinct in this regard. The trade
among the advanced countries is intra-sector; that is, these
countries export and import within the same sector.
    This particular form--Japan's tendency relative to its
trade partners not to import goods in sectors in which it
exports--can be explained as a product of the particular
form of conscious domestic development during the fifties
and sixties. The policy has been well-documented. As we
discussed above, there is no debate that during the 1950s
and 1960s the government protected domestic markets for
Japanese producers and acted to help those firms acquire
foreign technology. The government did so by denying
foreign companies open access for goods to the Japanese
market and denying entry for direct foreign investment. The
multinational package of technology, capital, and management
was broken up by government policies, which permitted

Japanese companies to recombine the pieces under their own
control. Second, a series of large, well-financed
industrial groups created the basis of internal competition
behind protected walls.

Intense domestic competition in a protected and rapidly
growing internal market among firms that had access to
international product and production technologies had predictable results. For instance, as long as the Japanese
were aggressive and systematic technology borrowers in a
rapidly expanding domestic market, they faced a fundamentally different economic situation than that of foreign companies. Put formally, Japanese firms faced long-run
declining cost curves, rather than concave cost curves.
Japanese firms faced rapidly expanding demand and a stream
of replacement production technologies available abroad.
Therefore the jump to new technology (and lower cost curve)
was easier. One consequence of such a situation is that
profit maximizing firms will attempt to maximize market
share in order to have the volumes to introduce new technologies.

The need to maximize market share drives a very intense
domestic competition that often leads to overinvestment.
Protected domestic markets, policies to promote an expansion
of demand, policies that provide financing to facilitate
that expansion all sustain the competition for market share.
A second consequence is that surges in domestic investment
in search of market share to continue down the production
cost curve lead to focused export booms. Excess domestic
production can be sold abroad.

The overall result is straightforward, and if correct,
matters a great deal. Japanese firms built up internationally competitive product and production positions
behind closed markets. Rapid growth with assured finance
and protected markets permitted this follower nation to make
the massive investments that embodied real innovation in
production. There is no doubt that Japanese companies have
achieved real innovation in the mass production of consumer
durables in particular, or that such innovation has created
real advantages in world markets, but such innovation must
be understood at least in part as a function of past government policies. By the time that domestic markets began to
open, final markets in Japan were firmly held by Japanese
producers. Entry by foreigners that would once have been
based on substantial product or production advantage became
difficult. Suddenly it would require displacing Japanese
producers from convoluted distribution channels often tied
to those producers. At the same time, Japanese manufacturers had begun to establish themselves in foreign markets.

138

Our interpretation accounts for the unique features of
Japanese trade and the general pattern. It suggests that
the unique features of Japanese trade--specifically its
failure to import in sectors in which it exports--is a function of a strategy of trade and development. Moreover, it
suggests that as sectors establish themselves as competitive
in international markets, the sectors may be liberalized
without producing a stream of imports. Our attention in
this discussion should not be focused on the aggregate pattern of trade--which is inevitable if Japan is to exist as
an industrial country and thus borders on tautology--but on
two other matters: the pattern of intersectoral trade in
which Japan is unique and the pattern of policy in advanced
sectors where development strategies are applied.

No government, it should be clear, can simply shape the
trade patterns to its will. Japan has long used market forces as instruments of policy. It has chosen to accelerate
and direct the market rather than try to blunt it or
override it. Despite the elimination of formal barriers,
what many foreign observers fear is that domestic policies
and practices continue to act as a barrier to entry and to
the establishment and development of long term market positions. Indeed, a pattern of promoting the development of
"sunrise" industries, while managing the re-adjustment of
more mature sectors faced with intense foreign competition,
suggests a pattern of selective protection as an instrument
of policy.

It should be clear from the above discussion, that even
though its powers of control and intervention have
diminished, the Japanese government continues to act purposely and effectively in promoting promising new
industries, particularly informatics. Indeed, we believe
that Japan's unique pattern of trade with the rest of the
world can only be accounted for via an understanding of the
role that policy has played and continues to play.

NOTES

*This material is drawn from Creating Advantage, Michael
Borrus, Steven Cohen, Laura Tyson and John Zysman (eds.),
forthcoming, 1986.
    1. Representative works that express the conflicting
viewpoints and from which this paper draws include: F.
Gerard Adams and Shinichi Ichimura, "Industrial Policy in

Japan," in Adams and Lawrence R. Klein (eds.), <u>Industrial Policies for Growth and Competitiveness: An Economic Perspective</u> (Lexington, MA: Lexington Books, D.C. Heath and Co., 1983), pp. 307-330; Richard E. Caves and Masu Ueksa, <u>Industrial Organization in Japan</u> (Washington, D.C.: Brookings Institution, 1976), pp. 141-154 and passim; Hugh Patrick and Henry Rosovsky (eds.), <u>Asia's New Giant: How the Japanese Economy Works</u> (Washington, D.C.: Brookings Institution, 1976); Gary Saxonhouse, "Industrial Restructuring in Japan," <u>The Journal of Japanese Studies 5</u> (Summer 1979), pp. 273-300; Jimmy W. Wheeler, Mrit E. Janow, and Thomas Peper, <u>Japanese Industrial Development Policies in the 1980s: Implications for U.S. Trade and Investment</u> (Croton-on-Hudson, NY: Hudson Institute, 1983); Yasusuke Murakami, "Toward a Sociocultural Explanation of Japan's Economic Performance," in Kozo Yamamura (ed.), <u>Policy and Trade Issues of the Japanese Economy: American and Japanese Perspectives</u> (Seattle: University of Washington Press. 1982), pp. 3-46; and Murakami and Yamamura, "A Technical Note on Japanese Firm Behavior and Economic Policy," ibid., pp. 113-121; Kozo Yamamura, "Success that Soured: Administrative Guidance and Cartels in Japan," in Yamamura (ed.), <u>Policy and Trade Issues of the Japanese Economy</u>, pp. 77-112; Chalmers Johnson, <u>MITI and the Japanese Miracle: The Growth of Industrial Policy, 1925-1975</u> (Stanford: Stanford University Press, 1982); Ira C. Magaziner and Thomas M. Hout, <u>Japanese Industrial Policy</u> (Berkeley: Institute of International Studies, University of California, Berkeley, 1980), pp. 1-44 and passim; Takafusa Nakamura, <u>The Postwar Japanese Economy: Its Development and Structure</u> (Tokyo: University of Tokyo Press, 1981), passim; T.J. Pempel, <u>Policy and Politics in Japan: Creative Conservatism</u> (Philadelphia: Temple University Press, 1982), pp. 3-68, and his "Japanese Foreign Economic Policy: The Domestic Bases for International Behavior," in Peter J. Katzenstein (ed.), <u>Between Power and Plenty</u> (Madison: University of Wisconsin Press, 1977), pp. 139-190.

2. Pempel, ibid., p. 161. For a discussion of the role of the Japanese developmental state in "unbundling" the package of control and new technology represented by multinational corporations, see John Zysman and Stephen Cohen, "Double or Nothing, Open Trade and Competitive Industry," <u>Foreign Affairs</u> (Summer 1983), p. 1120.

3. Johnson, op. cit., p. 17.

4. Based on discussions with U.S. government and industry officials.

140

5. For a description of how that system works, see John Zysman, Government, Markets and Growth: Financial Systems and the Politics of Industrial Change (Ithaca, NY: Cornell University Press, 1983).

6. Hiroya Ueno, "The Conception and Evaluation of Japanese Industrial Policy," in Kasuo Sato (ed.), Industry and BUsiness in Japan (New York: Sharpe, 1980), p. 382.

7. Zysman, op. cit.

8. Johnson, op. cit.,

9. Ibid.

10. Adams and Ichimura, op. cit., p. 307.

11. David R. Henderson, "The Myth of MITI," Fortune (8 August 1983), pp. 114-16.

12. Charles L. Schultze, "Industrial Policy: A Dissent," The Brookings Review (Fall 1983), pp. 3-12, and his "Industrial Policy: A Solution in Search of a Problem," California Management Review 25 (Summer 1983), pp. 12-13.

13. Philip Trezise, "Industrial Policy in Japan," in Margaret E. Dewar (ed.), Industry Vitalization: Toward a National Industrial Policy (New York: Pergamon Press, 1982), p. 177ff.

14. Hugh Patrick, prepared statement in the U.S. Congress, Joint Economic Committee, Industrial Policy, Economic Growth and the Competitiveness of U.S Industry (Washington, D.C.: U.S. Government Printing Office, 1984).

15. See discussions in Michael Borrus, James Millstein, and John Zysman, Responses to the Japanese Challenge in High Technology: Innovation, Maturity, and U.S.-Japanese Competition in Microelectronics (Berkeley: Berkeley Roundtable on the International Economy [BRIE] 1983), passim, and Borrus, Millstein, and Zysman, U.S.-Japanese Competition in the Semiconductor Industry (Berkeley: Institute of International Studies, University of California, Berkeley, 1982), passim.

16. This is drawn from Michael Borrus, et al., Telecommunications Development in Comparative Perspective: The New Telecommunications in Europe, Japan and the U.S. (Berkeley: BRIE, May 1985).

17. This is based on conversations with U.S. Department of Commerce officials.

18. Borrus, et al, Telecommunications, p. 19.

19. See Michael Borrus, Reversing Attrition: A Strategic Response to the Erosion of U.S. Leadership in Microelectronics (Berkeley: BRIE, March 1985 and updates).

20. See George E. Lindmood, "The Rise of the Japanese Computer Industry," Office of Naval Research Scientific Bulletin (October/December 1982), pp. 55-72. Also based on data supplied by sources at IBM.

21. From Borrus, et al., <u>Telecommunications</u>.
22. For a thorough discussion of Japan's past policies
for nurturing sunrise industries, see Johnson, op. cit.,
pp. 236-238 and passim. Several other treatments of this
matter include Wheeler, et al., op. cit., Chapter III;
Magaziner and Hout, op. cit., Chapter III; Nakamura, op.
cit., Chapter 3; and Miyohei Shinohara, <u>Industrial Growth,
Trade, and Dynamic Patterns in the Japanese Economy</u>,
Chapters 2 and 3. The view that these once successful policies have outlived their usefulness is developed in
Yamamura, "Success that Soured," passim.
23. For evidence of the Japanese government's decision
to restructure the economy from a heavy and chemical
industries orientation toward knowledge-intensification of
industry, see Japan, Economic Planning Agency, <u>Basic
Economic and Social Plan, 1973-1977</u> (Tokyo: EPA, 1973), pp.
84-85 and passim.
24. Wheeler et al., op. cit., Chapter III. A related
and important point is discussed by Imai, who notes:

On the software side, along with such efforts as
implanting in society the concept of the increasing importance of information in the economy and the idea of
an information society through reports by the Industrial
Structure Council (mainly the Information Industry
Section) and through publicity concerning such a concept, the government also arranged for the formation of
an infrastructure in the information industry through the
'promotion of education and training related to information processing' and the 'expansion and improvement
of information processing in government offices.'

(Ken-ichi Imai, "Japan's Industrial Policy for High
Technology Industries," paper presented for the
Conference on Japanese Industrial Policy in Comparative
Perspective, New York, March 17-19, 1984, p. 8.

25. Former MITI Vice-Minister Yoshihisa Ojimi listed the
criteria for determining which industries are to be nurtured as including: those "industries where income elasti-
city of demand is higher, technological progress is rapid,
and labor productivity rises fast." Organization for
Economic Cooperation and Development, <u>The Industrial Policy
of Japan</u> (Paris: OECD, 1972), p. 15. For a technical
discussion of these criteria, see Shinohara, op. cit., p. 25.

142

26. The project descriptions which follow are drawn from a briefing book prepared for a conference held by BRIE at U.C. Berkeley, Advanced Computing: The Commercial Impact of Japanese Programs on U.S. Competitiveness, June 27, 1984.

27. From Borrus et al., Telecommunications.

28. See Robert Manning, "High-Technology High Noon," Far Eastern Economic Review 123 (23 February 1984), pp. 78-79; "Japanese to Let Americans Join Councils that Advise Industries," New York Times, 12 March 1984; "U.S. Role in Advisory Councils Discussed," Japan Economic Survey 8 (April 1984), pp. 13-14.

29. Wheeler et al., op. cit., p. 143-144.

30. Houdaille Industries, a diversified American company that manufactures, among other products, numerically-controlled machining centers and punching machines, submitted a petition for relief in 1982 to the U.S. President. Among other things, that petition claimed (and this was later substantiated) that the Japanese government was funnelling hundreds of millions of dollars worth of yen generated by wagering on bicycle and motorcycle races in Japan into the country's machinery industry, including the machine-tool cartel. For further discussion of the Houdaille case, see Chalmers Johnson, "East Asia: Living Dangerously," Foreign Affairs 62 (1984), p. 727.

31. Wheeler et al., op. cit., p. 147. for some other discussions of Japan's policy for sunset industries, see Edward Boyer, "How Japan Manages Declining Industries," Fortune (10 January 1983), pp. 58-63; Brian Ike, "The Japanese Textile Industry: Structural Adjustment and Government Policy," Asian Survey 20 (May 1980), pp. 532-551; and Richard J. Samuels, "The Industrial Destructuring of the Japanese Aluminum Industry," Pacific Affairs 56 (Fall 1983), pp. 495-509.

32. Supra, n. 20.

33. Japan, Economic Planning Agency, Basic Economic and Social Plan 1973-1977, pp. 88-89.

34. For a detailed discussion of Japan's Anti-Monopoly Law, see Johnson, MITI and the Japanese Miracle, pp. 299-303.

35. Stephen Krasner and Dan Okomoto, Japan's Trade Posture: From Myopic Self-Interest to Liberal Accommodation? Unpublished manuscript, Stanford University, Department of Political Science, February 1985.

7

Korea

Joseph S. Chung
Illinois Institute of Technology

INTRODUCTION

With the successful domestic development of 64K DRAM
chips without a foreign license in 1983 and 256K DRAMs in
1984, the budding informatics industry of the Republic of
Korea (Korea for short) made a small but giant step into the
highly competitive world of semiconductors as a major
potential player. The stakes are high for Korea's future
course of informatics industry and for the other players.
The development of 64K DRAMs by Samsung Semiconductor and
Telecommunications, a subsidiary of one of Korea's four
giant conglomerates, was achieved indigenously with the only
exception of the mask design provided by Micron Technology,
Inc. of the United States.[1] Samsung, which also developed
256K DRAMs for the first time in Korea, started to market
the chips in May of 1985. Korea has thus become only the
third country outside the United States and Japan producing
these chips at this time. The remaining three rival conglomerates (Hyundai, Gold Star, Daewoo) are equally poised to
develop and market 16K SRAMs, electronically erasable
programmable read-only memory (EEPROM) chips, microprocessors, and other memory chips.
These feats in semiconductors represent determined
efforts by the government and private industry to forge
Korea's economy to one increasingly founded on high
technology and high-value-added products both for domestic
production and exports, and lay groundwork for a faster pace
in the development of Korean-made computers. (See Table 7.1.)
The emergence of Korea as a potential world-class
informatics producer has prompted some industry analysts to
characterize her variously as, to sample a few, "next
Japan,"[2] "a sleeping giant starts to stir,"[3] "Korea arms for

TABLE 7.1
Production, Exports, Imports and Composition
of Electronics Products
(in million U.S. dollars unless otherwise specified)

	1970	1971	1972	1973	1974	1975	1976	1977
1. Production								
in million US$	106	138	208	462	814	860	1,422	1,758
as % of GNP*		1.5	2.0	3.4	5.3	4.1	5.0	4.7
as % of total manufacturing		7.2	9.0	13.8	20.7	15.9	18.2	17.5
2. Exports	55	88	142	369	518	582	1,037	1,107
as % of total exports		8.3	8.7	11.4	11.6	11.5	13.4	11.0
3. Imports	70	111	170	326	446	445	699	847
4. Composition of production (%)								
Consumer electronics	28.3	23.9	26.4	29.2	31.8	31.4	38.7	38.6
Industrial electronics	16.0	13.8	12.0	9.1	9.3	10.9	8.9	10.5
Parts and components	55.7	62.3	61.5	61.7	58.8	57.7	52.4	50.9

*In current prices (won)

Source: Electronics Industries Association of Korea (EIAK), Statistics
Statistics of Electronic Products & Electrical Appliances (1984), May

	1978	1979	1980	1981	1982	1983	1984	Growth rate per annum		
								1971–79	1980–84	1971–84
	2,271	3,280	2,852	3,791	4,006	5,558	7,170	46.4%	21.6%	35.1%
	4.5	5.1	5.1	5.8	5.8	7.6				
	16.5	30.1	17.6	20.3	20.7	27.1				
	1,359	1,845	2,004	2,218	2,200	3,047	4,204	47.7%	22.9%	36.3%
	10.7	12.3	11.4	10.4	10.1	12.5				
	1,156	1,386	1,460	1,774	1,979	2,683	3,163	39.3%	22.9%	31.3%
	40.8	41.9	40.3	41.5	38.7	39.4	33.8			
	9.2	9.8	12.8	13.0	16.0	17.0	16.9			
	49.9	48.4	47.0	45.5	45.4	43.6	49.2			

of Electronic & Electrical Industries (1984), February 1985; EIAK, Import 1985; The Bank of Korea, Economic Statistics Yearbook, various issues.

export assault,"[4] and "lean, mean and hungry: here come the Koreans."[5]   Korea is considered by some analysts as the only one among the so-called Asia's four dragons that has the manufacturing base to produce high-value-added products sufficient to sustain high growth rates over the next decade.[6] In 1984 Korea's electronics output reached $7.2 billion with exports amounting to $4.2 billion (see Table 7.1). Of the total exports, shipments of semiconductors constituted $1.3 billion and computers and peripherals $285 million (see Table 7.2).

This paper attempts to trace the development and performance of the Korean informatics industry, selected aspects of government policies and institutions that have greatly shaped its growth, and the problems and difficulties as well as the future prospects facing the industry.

EVOLUTION OF KOREAN ELECTRONICS INDUSTRY

Korea's informatics industry is an outgrowth of, and founded in, the successful development in the indigenous production and exports of her electronics industry. Recent emphasis on informatics simply reflects Korea's perception of changing domestic and international economic parameters and her desire to restructure the electronics industry based on a higher technology intensity. For this reason a brief survey of the electronics industry as a whole will provide a helpful background for the main topic of the paper.

South Korea's electronics industry began in the early 1960s when she began to assemble vacuum tube radios with imported parts under the import-substitution strategy in effect at that time. The first electronics exports took place in 1962 when Korea exported $4,000 worth of radios to Hong Kong. In 1965 total electronics output by 40-odd firms was running as low as about $14 million. The industry dominated by domestic capital up to the middle of the 60s began to attract foreign investment starting from Komy Corporation from the United States in 1965. Other leading semiconductor makers such as Fairchild, Motorola and Signetics followed, attracted by an abundance of skilled labor and lower wage scales and government's active policy of inducing foreign investment. Combined with the export-expansion program of the new government, electronics industry began to grow rapidly. Since 1969 the electronics industry received its full-scale government sanction with the enactment of the Electronics Industry Promotion Law, which designated electronics as one of the priority industries for

TABLE 7.2

Production, Exports, Imports and Domestic Sales
of Semiconductors and Computer Hardware 1977–1984
(Million US dollars)

	1977	1978	1979	1980	1981	1982	1983	1984	Growth rate 1980–84
1. Semiconductors & devices									
Production	327	370	459	425	473	648	850	1,268	22.5%
% of total electronics	1.86	16.3	14.0	14.9	12.5	16.2	15.3	17.7	
Exports	306	329	420	440	482	624	812	1,297	25.3%
% of total electronics	27.6	24.2	22.8	22.0	21.7	28.3	26.7	30.9	
Indirect exports	12	19	25	25	30	26	47	51	15.5%
Domestic sales	5	14	15	8	9	26	24	37	20.3%
2. Computer hardware									
a. CPU									
Production			0.2	2	17	5	73	150	275.9%
% of total electronics			0.01	0.08	0.45	0.13	1.31	2.09	
Exports				1		1	36	84	*231.3%
% of total electronics				0.03	0.00	0.02	1.17	2.01	
Indirect export									
Domestic sales			0.1	1	6	4	33	52	249.3%
Imports				35	35	56	76		**29.5%
b. Peripherals									
Production				7	14	42	134	278	*153.8%
% of total electronics				0.23	0.36	1.05	2.42	3.88	
Exports				6	12	36	85	201	*145.9%
% of total electronics				0.27	0.53	1.63	2.79	4.78	
Indirect export						1	1	6	
Domestic sales			3	2	2	5	34	3	82.8%
Imports				52	75	103	128		*35.0%
c. Total (a + b)									
Production			0.2	9	31	47	207	428	363.6%
% of total electronics			0.01	0.32	0.81	1.18	3.73	5.97	
Exports				6	12	36	121	285	*161.9%
% of total electronics			0.00	0.31	0.53	1.65	3.96	6.79	
Indirect export						1	1	6	
Domestic sales			3	3	7	8	67	105	108.0%
Imports				87	110	159	204		**32.9%

Sources: Electronics Industries Association of Korea (EIAK), Chunja kongup
pyunram (The Handbook of the Electronics Industry), various issues;
EIAK, Statistics of Electronic & Electrical Appliances (1984),
February 1985; "Export expansion and problems of domestic computer
industry," Journal of Korean Electronics, February 1985, p. 33.

Notes: * 1981–84
** 1981–83

development, recognizing strategic potential for exports.
A comprehensive eight-year development program followed.
Inflow of foreign capital and technology since the mid-60s
played a cardinal role in absorbing the technology, managerial and other knowhow, thus starting the "foreign-led"
exports of the electronics industry.

In the early 1970s, manufactures of parts and components such as transistors, diodes, integrated circuits,
radio receivers, and black and white television parts dominated. Since 1974 color TVs began to be produced, fueling a
fast expansion in consumer electronics. By the end of the
1970s Korean-made products included electronic calculators,
electronic watches, and finally VCRs. Korea in 1979 became
only the fourth country in the world producing VCRs. Since
the 1980s the consumer electronics sector has been concentrating in such products as color TVs, VCRs, and newly
introduced micro-wave ovens. Computer and peripheral equipment production and exports began to grow rapidly as computer makers began to substitute imports for the domestic
markets. Though on the declining trend, the share of parts
and components still ranks the highest. In the past foreign
and joint venture firms have tended to concentrate in this
segment, while indigenous firms dominated in consumer
electronics. The trend has begun to change recently as
large domestic firms recently entered into production of,
and became self-reliant in LSI and VLSI.

Reaching a level of $7.2 billion in 1984, total
electronics output in 1984 was 67.6 times that in 1970 ($106
million), registering an annual average growth rate of
35.1 percent during 1971-1984 (see Table 7.1). Between
1971-1979, the industry grew at a whopping rate of 46.4 percent. The rate of growth in electronics exports has been
equally high. Electronics output grew faster than GNP and
the manufacturing sector as a whole. As a result, the share
of electronics output in GNP grew from 1.5 percent in 1971
to 7.6 percent in 1983 (in terms of current won). As a
share of total manufacturing output, electronics output
increased from 7.2 percent to 27.1 percent in the same
period. Electronics exports, too, grew faster than total
exports so that electronics share in total exports steadily
rose from 8.3 percent in 1971 to 12.5 percent in 1983. In
recent years there has been a shift in the composition of
the industry. The share of industrial equipment has been
on the rise at the expense primarily of consumer
electronics, reflecting Korea's move into computers and
peripheral equipment.

INFORMATICS INDUSTRY

Korea is a relative latecomer to the new information age. It was as late as in 1967 when the first computer in the country, an IBM, was installed for the Economic Planning Board.[7] Like the first one, early hardwares were large-frame computers used primarily for statistical compilation by non-private organizations. Only in the latter part of the 1970s did private business begin to utilize computers for their operations with imported medium- and small-frame computers. As computer use spread widely and the Korean economy grew, the domestic market for computers, their peripherals, and softwares began to grow rapidly. Realizing the growing potential of the domestic informatics market and of exports, many indigenous makers began to supply domestic hardware needs by producing components and establishing assembly plants under foreign licenses or technical cooperation. Until the very recent beginning of indigenization of semiconductor production, the parts sector was predominantly under a "bond" arrangement. In the semiconductor field, Korea simply supplied labor; the foreign firms (Fairchild, Motorola, Signetics, etc.) brought in processed wafers under a bond arrangement and the final products were shipped out of Korea. This explains the high export to output ratio in this sector.

Trend in Output and Trade Flows

Although Korea has had a longer involvement in semiconductors, her venture into computers and their peripherals began in earnest only in the late 70s and early 80s (see Table 7.2). Starting from a combined output of $200,000 for the entire computer hardware in 1979, the industry has experienced an explosive growth in the production and export of both computers and peripherals so that in 1984 the total output rose to $428 million (see Table 7.3). Exports which began only in 1980 with $6 million increased to $285 million in 1984. Total output of computers and peripherals increased at an annual rate of 363.6 percent during the five years between 1980-1984. Though the high rate reflects the low base from which the Korean industry started in 1979, the sustained pace of the growth can be seen from the fact that in 1984 production and export of both hardware and peripherals more than doubled. With less than a half billion dollars in 1984, the output of the informatics industry is still small but if the present trend continues

TABLE 7.3
Production, Exports and Domestic Sales of Informatics Industry:
A Breakdown   1983-1984

| | 1983 | | | (Thousand US dollars) |
	Production	Exports	Domestic	Production
I. Hardware	207,247	120,249	66,833	427,496
% of total	99.1	99.3	98.7	99.7
a. CPU	72,888	35,727	32,992	149,707
% of total				
hardware	35.2	29.7	49.4	35.0
Analogue				
machines				380
Medium-size				
computers				158
Minicomputers	8,148	145	8,294	11,896
Microcomputers	20,409	16,332	–	26,826
Personal				
computers	38,564	18,789	19,430	108,333
Word processor	5,767	461	5,268	2,652
b. Peripherals	134,359	84,522	33,841	277,789
% of total				
hardware	64.8	70.3	50.6	65.0
Auxiliary				
storage units	4,892	–	3,880	7,983
Printers	12,959	–	9,033	15,058
Terminals	112,980	84,521	18,072	248,651
Controllers,				
modems	3,528	1	2,856	6,097
II. Software	1,862	830	891	1,463
% of total	0.9	0.7	1.3	0.3
III. Total				
Informatics	209,109	121,079	67,724	428,959

Source: EIAK, Statistics of Electronic & Electric
Industries (1984), February, 1985.

1984 Exports	Domestic	Growth Rate (1984/1983)		
		Production	Exports	Domestic
285,224	105,154	106.3%	137.2%	57.3%
99.9	98.9			
84,255	52,201	105.4%	135.8%	58.2%
29.5	49.6			
-	374			
-	79			
-	12,084	46.0%		45.7%
16,554	6,969	31.4%	1.4%	
65,548	32,547	180.9%	248.9%	67.5%
2,153	601	-54.0%	367.0%	-88.6%
200,969	52,953	106.8%	137.8%	56.5%
70.5	50.4			
1,907	6,000	63.2%		54.6%
124	15,252	16.2%		68.8%
198,077	27,141	120.1%	134.4%	50.2%
861	4,560	72.8%	86000.0%	59.7%
266	1,215	-21.4%	-68.0%	36.4%
0.1	1.1			
285,490	106,369	105.1%	135.8%	57.1%

one can easily see the potential of Korea as a major producer country.

At the present Korea continues to be a net importer of
informatics hardwares. However, with the rate of growth in
imports far below that of exports, the trade gap has been
narrowing in relative terms (imports/exports). At this rate
it will not be surprising if in the near future Korea
becomes a net informatics exporter. Another indication of
the growing importance of domestic production of informatics
in Korea is the fact that domestic sales have been growing
much faster than imports; domestic output has begun
increasingly to meet the fast growing domestic informatics
market.

With the rapid growth in computer hardware, its relative share in the electronics industry has been increasing
steadily so that in 1984 it accounted for about 6 percent of
the total electronics output and slightly less than 7 percent of total electronics exports. Up to now, peripherals
have occupied a much larger share of both output and exports
than CPUs. Around 1983-1984, the division of the share in
output is roughly one-third and two-thirds between CPUs and
peripherals. The division is roughly 30 percent and 70 percent in the case of exports. (See Table 7.3).

Semiconductors play a major role in the total Korean
electronics picture (18 percent of output and 31 percent of
exports in 1984) with an annual growth rate of more than
22.5 percent and 25.3 percent between 1980-1984, respectively, for output and exports (See Table 7.2). It has
grown to be a $1.3 billion business in 1984. For Korea, the
growth and increased indigenization of semiconductors are
considered essential for gaining an internationally competitive position in high technology fields including informatics.

Informatics Firms

Informatics production in Korea is primarily by
electronic firms producing a wide variety of electronics
(and electrical appliances). Further, the field is dominated by the four domestic conglomerates whose activities
run from automobiles, construction, ship-building, telecommunications and general trading, just to name a few, as well
as the whole gamut of electronics and electrical equipment
and parts. This makes it difficult to separate manpower,
R&D, and other profiles of informatics activities per se
other than fragmentary data. However, data available for
the electronics industry as a whole provide an indirect picture of the informatics sector.

The number of firms engaged in electronics production has been increasing rapidly, from 231 to 1,026 in 1983 (see Table 7.4). Over the years there has been a definite shift in the distribution of firms according to the types of electronics products. While the percentage of those firms engaged in consumer electronics remained about the same, that of firms producing parts and components has risen significantly at the expense of the industrial equipment category. In 1983 there were 281,000 employees in the industry with a mean of 274 employees per firm. The mean was the highest for the components category, perhaps reflecting the more labor-intensive manufacturing process of the semiconductors and other electronics parts. In the same year, the mean size of the semiconductor sector was nearly 1,300. According to data showing the number of employees engaged specifically in computers (CPUs only), there were in 1983 about 5,000 employees with about 38 percent engaged in production work and 23 percent in R&D.

Needing foreign capital and technology, the electronics industry including informatics has from the beginning had the strong presence of foreign and joint-venture firms. This is indicated by the fact that in 1982, out of 858 electronics firms operating in Korea, there were 41 (7.0%) wholly-owned foreign subsidiaries and 105 (12.2%) joint venture firms. In that year these firms contributed 19.8 percent and 21.9 percent, respectively, of the total electronics output,[8] revealing that these firms were much larger on the average than purely locally-owned firms.

More detailed information available for 1983 and 1984 (see Table 7.5 on pp. 156-157) shows that wholly-owned foreign subsidiaries contributed about 17 percent of the total electronics output but they were responsible for nearly 20 percent of total Korean electronics exports. Their share of the domestic sales, which is dominated by local firms, is almost negli-gible. Consumer electronics is predominantly the domain of local firms while the share of foreign firms is larger in the components than in other sectors. About 30 percent each of the industrial and components sectors, respectively, is contributed by joint venture firms. In all three electronics categories, foreign firms contributed a larger share of the exports than their share of output. In the domestic sales of consumer electronics, the share of the local firms was nearly 100 percent while in both the industrial equipment and components categories, local firms and joint venture firms nearly equally divided the domestic sales.

In the semiconductor field, unlike the general trend in the electronics industry as a whole, foreign firms dominated

TABLE 7.4
No. of Enterprises and Employees of Informatics Industry

	No. of firms				No. of employees		Average size (No. of employees)
	1971	(%)	1983	(%)	1983	(%)	1983
1. Electronics Industry					(1000 persons)		
Total	231	100.0	1,026	100.0	281	100.0	274
Consumer	54	23.4	234	22.8	59	21.0	252
Industrial	90	30.0	207	20.2	44	15.7	213
Parts & Components	87	37.7	585	57.0	178	63.3	304
2. Computers (CPU only)					(persons)		
Total					4,916	100.0	
R&D					1,122	22.8	
Production					1,844	37.5	
Maintenance & others					1,950	39.7	
3. Semi-conductors					(persons)		
Total			24		31,147		1,298

Source: EIAK, Chunja kongup pyunram (1984-85)

both output and exports. In 1983, nine foreign firms
contributed 54 percent of total output and 55 percent of
exports while the equivalent figures for the nine local
firms were 41 percent and 43 percent, respectively. The six
joint ventures produced a very small share of both output
and exports. In the semiconductor field, as in other
electronics sectors, foreign firms tend to be larger in
terms of output than either local or joint venture firms.
However, judging from these figures, local semiconductor
firms tend to be much larger than local firms in other
electronics fields. This is explained by the fact that,
like Japan, informatics manufacturing, particularly
semiconductors, in Korea is dominated by the country's most
powerful multi-billion dollar conglomerates.

POLICIES, LEGISLATION AND STRATEGIES

     The role of government has been crucial in the economic
development of Korea, particularly since 1962 when the first
of the series of five-year economic plans was instituted.
Electronics industry, and recently the informatics industry
in particular, has been no exception. The government's
policies have been instrumented through various means:
economic plans, trade barriers, subsidies, special tax
breaks, R&D expenditures, research institutes, educational
and manpower policies, foreign capital and technology
inducements policies, and special legislation.

Overall Informatics Policies and Specific Legislation

     The priority Korea places on the development of high
technology industries requiring little resource base is
predicated on her fundamental strategy of maximum utilization of her perceived comparative advantage arising from
Korea's resource endowments: poor endowment in natural
resources on one hand, and the availability of a large pool
of skilled and disciplined labor on the other. High technology industries are energy- and resource-saving as well as
provide high returns for her relatively scarce capital (high
value addition). Additional factors for Korea's pursuance
of high technology industries are that such industries help
bring about a higher degree of independence in domestic
defense industries, have maximum effect on spreading modern
technologies, and have the least effect on industrial pollu-
tion.[9]

TABLE 7.5
Share of Electronics Production, Exports and Domestic Sales
by Domestic, Joint-Venture and Foreign Firms (1983-84)

(Million U.S. dollars)

	1983							
	Production	(%)	Exports	(%)	Domestic sales	(%)	Ind. exports	(%)
1. Electronics, total	5,558	100.00	3,047	100.00	1,674	100.00	596	100.00
Domestic firms	3,555	64.0	1,843	60.5	1,264	75.5	186	31.2
Joint ventures	1,061	19.1	306	10.0	406	24.3	363	60.9
Foreign firms	942	16.9	898	29.5	4	0.2	47	7.9
Consumer, total	2,189	100.00	1,161	100.00	788	100.00	2	100.00
Domestic	1,942	88.7	915	78.8	783	99.4	0.8	40.0
Joint ventures	68	3.1	63	5.4	5	0.6	1.6	80.0
Foreign	179	8.2	183	15.8		0.0	0.1	5.0
Industrial, total	943	100.00	441	100.00	481	100.00	6	100.00
Domestic	576	61.1	294	66.7	272	56.5	4	66.7
Joint ventures	289	30.6	68	15.4	209	43.5	2	33.3
Foreign	78	8.3	79	17.9		0.0		0.0
Components, total	2,426	100.00	1,446	100.00	405	100.00	587	100.00
Domestic	1,037	42.7	635	43.9	209	51.6	180	30.7
Joint ventures	704	29.0	174	12.0	192	47.4	359	61.2
Foreign	685	28.2	637	44.1	4	1.0	47	8.0
2. Semiconductors, total								
(# of firms in 83)	850	100.00	813	100.00				
Domestic (9)	348	40.9	350	43.1				
Joint ventures(6)	47	5.5	14	1.7				
Foreign (9)	456	53.6	449	55.2				

Sources: EIAK, Chunja kongup pyunram (1984-85); EIAK, Statistics of
Electronic and Electrical Industries (1984).

1984							
Production	(%)	Exports	(%)	Domestic sales	(%)	Ind. exports	(%)
7,170	100.00	4,204	100.00	2,026	100.00	781	100.00
4,522	63.1	2,573	61.2	1,583	78.1	238	30.5
1,403	19.6	445	10.6	439	21.7	495	63.4
1,245	17.4	1,186	28.2	4	0.2	48	6.1
2,426	100.00	1,523	100.00	956	100.00	2	100.00
2,121	87.4	1,231	80.8	950	99.4	1	50.0
101	4.2	97	6.4	5	0.5	1	50.0
203	8.4	195	12.8	1	0.1		0.0
1,213	100.00	552	100.00	565	100.00	12	100.00
740	61.0	297	53.8	388	68.7	7	58.3
325	26.8	106	19.2	177	31.3	5	41.7
148	12.2	148	26.8		0.0		0.0
3,531	100.00	2,129	100.00	504	100.00	767	100.00
1,662	47.1	1,045	49.1	245	48.6	230	30.0
976	27.6	242	11.4	257	51.0	489	63.8
893	25.3	843	39.6	2	0.4	48	6.3

158

This fundamental strategy was reiterated in the Korean
delegation's report at the Eighth General Assembly of the
Asia Electronics Union on October 21, 1983, held in Jakarta,
Indonesia, which stated:[10]

> The recent fundamental restructuring of the Korean
> industrial pattern is attributable mainly to its
> scanty natural resources, which leaves the country
> with no other alternative but to turn to
> technology-intensive industries represented by
> electronics. It remains the national concensus
> that, as a strategic industry designated for the
> fifth Five-Year Economic and Social Development
> Plan, the electronics industry should play the
> propellant role in accelerating the pace of economic
> growth of the nation to expedite achievement of a
> highly developed economy and a welfare state.

The rapid success in the electronics industry
particularly up to the mid-70s has been largely attributed
to several major factors, as seen by Korean industry
sources. First, a "superior" and abundant labor force which
enabled Korea to maintain a competitive position in the
international market. Second, the size of the domestic
market for electronics products expanded as national income
increased with growth. Third, expansion in foreign direct
investment through various incentives and the creation of
free trade zones played a crucial role in production and
exports. Fourth, the government's determination to help
develop the industry through establishing the Electronics
Industry Promotion Law and industrial estates contributed
greatly to promote both domestic and foreign investment and
to expand productive capacity. The fifth factor is the
successful raising of productivity in the industry.[11] The
rising wage level in Korea, along with economic development
and competition from other low-wage countries of Asia in
recent years, prompted Korea more resolutely to develop
high-value-added products within the electronics industry
based on modern facilities and newest technologies. Industrial electronics including informatics hardwares and semiconductors have been identified as industries with the
highest priority.
    In the Fifth Five-Year Plan which went into effect in
1982, the electronics industry was designated as one of the
country's ten major strategic industries, with the principal
targets being: (1) increasing the value added and the
international competitiveness of home electronic appliances,

(2) priority development of a brain-intensive, resource-saving electronics industry, (3) developing and achieving self-sufficiency in the production of industrial electronic equipment, and (4) domestic development of the principal electronics parts. These goals are translated specifically into encouraging the production of such electronics products as: computers and terminals and other peripherals, wire communication equipment and electronic measuring instruments in the industrial equipment segment; VCRs, audio equipment, and color TVs in the consumer electronics; and semiconductors, speakers, lead frames, switches and connectors, magnetic heads, tape transport mechanisms, cartridges, micromotors, color picture tubes, FBT and yokes and magnetic tapes in the parts and components sector.[12]

The broad development plan for the informatics industry has been translated into special legislation covering the electronics industry. The Electronics Industry Promotion Law, first enacted in 1969, was revised in 1981.[13] Under the law the Minister of Commerce and Industry is directed to establish and make public plans for the development of the industry. The legislation also provides for establishing the electronics industry promotion fund to assist the industry to promote overseas investment, technology imports, domestic and overseas industrial exhibitions, and other related activities. It provides measures for promoting indigenization of electronics equipment, creation of industrial estates, financial assistance of in-house research institutes, and the establishment of the Electronics Industries Association of Korea (EIAK). The main functions of the association, which receives financial assistance through government's budgetary process, are promotion of industry development plans, stimulation of indigenization of the industry, and promotion of electronics exports and international cooperation.

An example of the industry development plan is the Semiconductor Industry Fostering Plan adopted in 1983. Under the Plan domestic firms can borrow $346 million over the 1984-1986 period. In addition, in 1984 an additional $91 million was set aside for a VLIC project in order to develop a 1-Mb MOS DRAMs by 1989.

Foreign Capital and Technology Inducement

Korea has very aggressively sought foreign direct investment both as an effective way to attract needed capital for development and advanced technology by providing a wide array of special tax and other incentives. Successful infusion of large volumes of foreign investment and technology has been recognized as one of the major factors responsible for Korea's rapid economic growth.

The Foreign Capital Inducement Act, originally enacted on August 3, 1966, governs all aspects of foreign investment. The act has been amended twice since, once in 1973 and recently in December, 1983. The second revision went into effect on July 1, 1984. With each amendment, reflecting the changing economic climate of Korea, foreign investment has been streamlined and the existing restrictions have either been eliminated or relaxed. The most important aspect of the current amendment is the introduction of an automatic approval system and the shift from a system based on a positive to a negative list. Under the automatic approval system, investment projects meeting certain conditions are to be immediately and automatically approved by the Ministry of Finance which handles applications. Further, whereas previously investment was allowed only in specifically listed areas, under the new system all investment projects are allowed in all areas unless specifically prohibited or restricted in the negative list. Electronics and informatics manufacturing is not included in the current negative list.[14]

There is no upper limit to the equity share allowed under the revision. A foreign investment project with a ratio of less than 50 percent can be approved immediately and automatically, whereas when a case is with a ratio of 50 percent or more, approval is subject to review. Although foreign-invested enterprises and domestic firms come under the same laws governing incorporation, foreign-invested enterprises are required to register with the Ministry of Finance upon completion of the agreed investment and establishment of an enterprise. Except for cases specifically prescribed by law, foreign-investment enterprises enjoy the same legal protection and treatment as the Korean nationals.

The revised foreign investment law removed restrictions on repatriation of capital. Until the amendment, repatriation was possible only after two years of profit-making activities. Now the government guarantees the overseas remittance of dividends of profit accruing from the stock or shares acquired by a foreign investor, proceeds from the sale of stock or shares, principal, interest and fees to be paid under a loan contract or public loan agreement, and royalties to be paid under a technology contract in accordance with the contents of the government's approval.

As incentives to attract foreign investment and
technology, Korea has offered generous tax benefits to
foreign-invested firms. Previous to the current amendment,
they were given a five-year exemption from nearly all taxes
including corporation tax, property tax, acquisition tax and
dividend income tax as well as a 50 percent reduction
in taxes for the following three years. Capital goods
imported as part of the investment enjoyed exemption
from custom duties, special consumption tax, and value-
added tax. Under the current amended law, these tax exemp-
tions have been abolished with a view to bringing about more
equal and freer competition between local and foreign firms.
However, capital goods imported as foreign investment will
continue to receive exemption from customs duties, special
consumption tax and value-added tax, except when the goods
can be produced locally. In addition, where any foreign
invested project is deemed to greatly contribute to the
development of the national economy, a five-year tax exemption can be given, but a 50 percent reduction in the ensuing
three years is no longer available. Instead of tax exemp-
tions, the foreign-invested firms may choose a 100 percent
special depreciation, which might prove more attractive to
capital intensive investment projects.

With the first case in 1962 starting with $575,000,
foreign investment in Korea has grown rapidly. As of March
1984, there is a cumulative total of 974 projects with a
cumulative value of $1.753 billion. Japan and the United
States are by far the two principal contributors, with the
former contributing 68.8 percent of the projects and 48.6
percent of the value of total cumulative investment. The
equivalent figures for the United States are 18.5 percent
and 27.7 percent, respectively. Of the cumulative total,
20.1 percent (196 cases) of the projects and 15.8 percent of
the invested value ($277.6 million) was in the electric and
electronics industry. Of the cumulative total, 130 projects
(with the invested value of $591.5 million) are wholly-owned
foreign firms while 129 projects ($212.0 million) had an
equity share between 51 and 99 percent. Of the rest, the
number of projects with an equity ratio of 50 percent, between 25 and 49 percent, and below 25 percent are, respectively, 303 ($523.5 million), 361 ($329.4 million), and 51
($106.6 million). Of the 196 projects made in the electric
and electronics sector, the number for each investment-ratio
category in descending order are 49 ($166.7 million), 23
($22.0 million), 65 ($20.4 million), 49($41.0 million), and
10 ($27.5 million).[15]

162

Manpower Policy

In the Korean educational system formal education in
electronics starts at the technical high school, usually
through its electronics department. The majority of the
skilled labor force in manufacturing industries, including
electronics industry is made up of the graduates of these
technical high schools. The next step in the educational
ladder is the two-year junior technical college. Most
colleges of engineering through their departments of
electronics offer courses in research, laboratory work, and
field training in electronics. In order to lessen the
shortage of skilled personnel required to utilize and
support emerging electronic data-processing systems, many
universities have recently started to provide courses
in computer technology and theory. Middle and high schools
are also rapidly incorporating fundamental computer
technology as part of the regular curriculum.

Beyond the academic institutions there is the Korean
Advanced Institute of Science and Technology (KAIST) which
offers graduate work in a wide variety of subjects
including electronics. Academic theories are combined
with their practical applications at the KAIST. In addition,
electronics engineers have a ready access to other public
higher research/professional institutes like the Korea
Institute of Electronics Technology (KIET) and the Korea
Electrotechnology and Telecommunications Research Institute
(KETRI), as well as KAIST for research, studies and
laboratory work. Major electronics firms also operate their
own in-house research institutes mainly for the purpose of
product development, quality improvement, and assimilation
of advanced technology.

Under the Semiconductor Industry Fostering Plan,
training programs have been instituted to ensure a supply of
highly skilled labor for the VLSI and other related projects. During the 1980s, Korea plans to produce 1,360 semiconductor and 820 computer experts. In addition, the KIET,
through its liaison office in Sunnyvale, California, con-
ducts basic semiconductor research, then passes the results
to industry back in Korea.[16]

Research and Development

The government encourages private firms to conduct
research and development through various systems of incentives including tax write-offs (discussed later). The

three public research institutes (KEIT, KETRI, and KAIST), two of which specialize in electronics research, reinforce private R&D as well as fill the gap created by the inability of small electronics firms to do their own R&D. These institutes have concentrated on assimilation and application of imported technologies, and "in due course, the foregoing research institutes are expected to generate high technologies for integrated circuits, computer and telecommunications equipment, which in turn hopefully will lift the domestic level to international standards."[17]

R&D expenditures have been rising rapidly in recent years in both absolute terms and relative to the size of the economy. Rising from $224 million in 1977 to $611 million in 1982 (see Table 7.6), total Korean R&D expenditures reached nearly a 1 percent level of GNP in 1982 from 0.6 percent in 1977, the sharpest increase occurring in 1982, the last year for which such information is available. The share of research carried out by public research institutes has been steadily on the decline, while that by both private firms and universities is on the rise. Slightly less than 30 percent of the expenditures by the private firms in 1982 was allocated to R&D in the combined electrical and electronics category.

The rapidly increasing trend in R&D is indicated also by the trend in research personnel involved in R&D. The total number of researchers increased from about 13,000 in 1977 to more than 28,000 in 1982, of which 4,000 (14.2 percent) were engaged in R&D in the electrical, electronics and communications areas. The increase in R&D manpower outpaced that in total population, which raised the per capita manpower ratio.

The government in 1984 instituted a joint research project for the development of VLSI whose project cost (estimated at $91 million) will be shared between the government and Korean chip makers. The government also allocated $12 million out of a $100 million IBRD education sector loan as well as $10 million budgeted to the Korean Science and Engineering Foundation and to the KAIST, for research in such high technology areas as micro electronics, semiconductors, genetic engineering, new ceramics and the like.[18] A new strategy involving R&D as well as marketing activities adopted by Korean informatics makers in recent years consists of establishing subsidiaries in Silicon Valley in California, discussed below.

164

TABLE 7.6
R&D Expenditures and Personnel

	1977	1978	1979	1980	1981	1982
1. R&D Expenditures						
Total, million won	108,286	152,418	174,039	211,727	293,131	457,688
(million US dollars)	224	315	360	321	418	611
Research instit.	61,089	78,073	98,208	104,473	145,309	186,077
(%)	56.4	51.2	56.4	49.3	49.6	40.7
Universities	5,482	20,543	16,536	25,902	27,268	66,610
(%)	5.1	13.5	9.5	12.2	9.3	14.6
Private firms	41,715	53,802	59,295	81,352	120,654	205,002
(%)	38.5	35.3	34.1	38.4	41.2	44.8
of which in electrical & electronics research (% of private firms)						58,827 28.7
Total as % of GNP	0.64	0.67	0.60	0.62	0.69	0.95
2. R&D research personnel (persons)						
Total	12,771	14,849	15,711	18,434	20,718	28,448
Electrical, electronics & communications research (%)						4,029 14.2
Per 1,000 population	0.35	0.40	0.42	0.48	0.54	0.72

Note: Excludes defense related R&D expenditures and personnel.
Source: EIAK, Chunja kongup pyunram (1984-85).

Protection of Domestic Informatics Industry

Founded on the Presidential Order on the "Regulations Concerning the Imports and Utilization of Computers" issued on May 24, 1982, various specific government regulations by several agencies concerned (Ministry of Commerce, Ministry of Science and Technology, and EIAK) protecting the budding domestic personal computer industry have come into effect since August 1983. These regulations attempt to promote the indigenization of mini computers, micro computers and personal computers as well as such peripherals as magnetic disks and tapes (including floppy disks), terminals and printers. Parts, though unspecified, are included. All non-governmental imports of these items require government permits. The Minister of Science and Technology is empowered to require governmental agencies to purchase Korean-made computers and peripherals where appropriate.

Tariff is another means of protecting the infant informatics industry. According to Ministry of Commerce and Industry senior official Bom Hee Lee, "U.S. computers dominate the Korean market, gaining $200 million annual rental fees alone. As an emerging industry, Korean personal computers should be allowed a moratorium on the [tariff] liberalization until such time that it gains sustaining capabilities."[19]

According to government figures, the total Korean market for computers and peripherals was estimated to be at $112 million in 1982, and is projected to expand at an average annual rate of 27 percent for the next several years.[20] The size of the informatics market in 1982 was much larger than the $86.8 figure projected for 1983 by the U.S. Department of Commerce based on a 1979 study.[21] According to the study, the Korean market for computers and peripheral equipment was $18.79 million, $21.96 million, $34.72 million, and $31.1 million, respectively, in 1976, 1977, 1978, and 1979. The U.S. domination of the Korean market as Korea embarked on the development of its own domestic informatics industry can be seen in Table 7.7.

Technology Imports

In developing its electronics industry, particularly in the area of informatics, Korea has relied on foreign technology. Although they can take many forms, the following have been Korea's principal means of technology imports and absorption.

166

TABLE 7.7
Cumulative Number and Value of Installed Computers
by Major Suppliers, as of June 30, 1979

	Number of units	Value ($million)	Market Share (%)
IBM	60	64.58	45.5
Fujitsu	36	20.83	14.6
Univac	29	19.07	13.4
CDC	16	17.33	12.2
Hewlett-Packard	22	4.42	3.1
NCR	15	3.63	2.6
DEC	27	3.44	2.4
Data General	26	2.66	1.9
Nippon Minicomputer	10	1.55	1.1
Wang	28	1.34	0.9
Nippon Electric	1	0.94	0.7
Burroughs	11	0.50	0.4
ICL (U.K.)	3	0.04	---
Others	12	1.87	1.3
Total	296	142.20	100.0

Note: Value is based on original purchase price. Figures
      include leased equipment counted at its original list
      price as if sold outright.
Source: Computers and Peripheral Equipment: Korea, U.S.
        Department of Commerce, International Trade
        Administration, country

1. Direct foreign investment by multinational firms in the form of wholly-owned subsidiaries: As mentioned above, Korea has offered a wide variety of incentives to induce foreign investment, and there is no upper limit to the foreign equity ratio. The importance of these firms in production, exports and domestic sales in the electronics industry has already been discussed (Table 5). Technology transfer is initiated by the parent firm in this case.

2. Joint venture with capital participation by the foreign firm: Under this form, as in the case of licensing arrangements, the initiative for the transfer of technology is taken by the recipients. This is a more common form of direct investment in Korea. Her expanding domestic market and the government protection of the market from PC imports work to stimulate joint ventures as Korea intended. For example, Samsung entered the computer market in 1984 through a join venture deal with Hewlett-Packard Co. to manufacture the Unix-based HP3000 Series 44 minicomputer.

3. Licensing arrangements: This is done without any equity participation but with design and supply of equipment, and with technical assistance. Samsung, for example, produces 4-in. wafers at its new VLSI plant in Suwon under a technology agreement with ITT Corp. Its 64K DRAMs were developed after obtaining the design in an agreement with Micron Technology Inc., of Boise, Idaho, and Samsung has a tentative agreement to license a complete product line of microprocessors. Hyundai's technology agreements include one concluded with Britain's Inmos Ltd. to second-source its 256K DRAM, and with Western Design Center Inc., of Mesa, Arizona, to manufacture its 8- and 16-bit CMOS versions of the 6502 microprocessors.

Of a cumulative total of 27 cases of technology purchase in the area of computers and their peripherals between 1980 and 1984, 16 were from the U.S., the remaining 11 from Japan. Twelve cases were related to CPU technology, the remaining 15 to peripherals. In the semiconductor sector, there were a cumulative total of 23 cases of technology purchases between 1969-1983. The United States and Japan were chief suppliers with 12 and 8, respectively. West Germany supplied two, and Sweden supplied the remaining case.[22]

4. Establishing subsidiaries in Silicon Valley: All four Korean conglomerates have recently established facilities in Silicon Valley, California. Their main activities appear to lie in product design, development, testing and marketing of chips with the help of U.S. engineers and other talents hired locally. The prototypes are sent back to Korea for mass production. Hyundai,

Korea's largest conglomerate, spent $40 million for its
100,000 square foot facility, Hyundai Electronics America in
Santa Clara, California, which contains a plant to fabricate
5-in. wafers. Samsung opened a 38,000 square foot IC design
center and fabrication plant for 5-in. wafers in 1983 through
its Santa Clara subsidiary, Samsung Semiconductor Inc.
(formerly Tristar Semiconductor). The Lucky Goldstar Group
plans to spend $60 million in a design center in Sunnyvale,
California. The Daewoo Group, which originally established
its Santa Clara subsidiary, ID Focus, for the development of
64D and 256K DRAMs, temporarily postponed its semiconductor
operations to provide marketing support to its consumer and
telecommunications products divisions.[23]
     5. Hiring Korean engineers and scientists in the
U.S.: Another very important means of securing trained
manpower in electronics at the upper echelon has been hiring
Koreans educated and trained in the U.S. These returnees,
most of them with Ph.D.s in electronics or computer science
and substantial practical on-the-job experience at major
U.S. informatics firms such as IBM, have assumed important
managerial/development/research positions at the major Korean
informatics firms. The Ministry of Science and Technology
reportedly was planning to bring back some 300 Korean
overseas scientists in 1984.[24]

Government Subsidies

     Various government assistance programs benefit the
informatics industry. Most of these benefits deal with the
electronics industry as a whole. Some programs apply only
to certain informatics products. Some of the important
features of these programs are summarized below.[25]
     1. Favorable tax treatment: The informatics industry
is eligible to receive various forms of favorable tax
treatment such as special depreciation allowances, deductions
from investment tax, reduction in income and import taxes,
and establishment of reserves for investment and the
development of overseas markets.
          a. assistance to key industries: The electronics
             industry is identified as one of the 6 key
             industries considered playing leading roles in
             economic development.
          b. assistance to small and medium enterprises
          c. expenditures on technology and manpower development
          d. assistance to export and tourist development
          e. assistance to overseas investment

f. assistance to defense industries
g. royalty on imports of technology
h. investment on ventures utilizing new technology
i. expenditures on research laboratory equipment
j. reserves for R&D
k. imports of industrial equipment in
   technology-intensive industries
l. income of foreign technicians working for indigenous
   firms
m. in-house research institutes

2. _Financial:_ Financial assistance is provided to
informatics and other industries from funds established under
various provisions. Some of the important funds are:

a. fund for the development of the electronics industry
b. fund for national investment. The fund is used for
   stimulating the development and exports of key
   industries.
c. technology development fund
d. fund for the promotion of small and medium
   enterprises
e. assistance to export financing
f. financial assistance to small and medium
   communications enterprises

Besides tax subsidies and financial assistance programs,
there are other avenues for government provision of
incentives to industries. They include the establishment of
industrial estates and the favorable treatment extended to
plants locating in the estates.

CONCLUSION AND PROSPECTS

Korea's informatics is a continuum in the development
of her highly successful electronics industry. Her current
strategy of restructuring the electronics industry toward
informatics in both production and exports reflects her
evaluation of the changing domestic and international economic and technological parameters. Because of rising domestic wage levels and emergence of competition in labor cost
from Taiwan, Malaysia, the Philippines, and recently China,
Korea came to the conclusion that its labor-cost advantages
over developing countries are rapidly diminishing, which,
coupled with the expanding domestic market, made Korea's
need for high technology more pressing in recent years.

Though growing at a galloping rate since about 1980, the value of output and exports of the Korean informatics industry is still relatively small, being a newcomer. Conditions exist, however, which tend to foresee an emerging new challenger in the field: growing indigenization and technical sophistication in semiconductors; small but fast-growing PC and peripherals output and exports; increasing technology imports; growing domestic R&D expenditures and manpower to name a few. Coupled with the already existing solid technological and managerial base in electronics and the government's determined efforts to nurture high technology industries, the probability is high that Korea will continue her growth to become one of the few world's major producers and exporters of informatics.

In the process of developing the informatics industry, Korea relied heavily on foreign technology through wholly-owned foreign subsidiaries, forging joint ventures with leading firms, and purchase through licensing agreements. In so doing, Korea has to turn primarily to the U.S., mostly by default. As Wan Hee Kim, Chairman of the Electronics Industry Association of Korea, explained, "Japan is reluctant to give us technology."[26] Japanese investment projects, such as VCR production, are said to "call for technology that is no longer state of the art. Moreover, they [Japanese firms] are increasingly eyeing the nation's rapid progress as a threat and are resisting transferring their technology for fear of a boomerang effect, in which the commercial rival uses the company's own innovation to grab shares of its markets. This has pushed Korean conglomerates into the arms of U.S. companies, especially for the semiconductor technology to underpin their next export thrust."[27] It appears that at this stage many U.S. firms view selling technology to Korea as profitable, considering the competition as mostly a Japanese problem. According to Arthur J. Davie, an ATT executive who serves as chief officer of a Gold Star-ATT joint venture, for example, "we meet each other's needs. Gold Star is solving our objective of lowering production costs and building capacity, and we're meeting their objective of foreign marketing and broadening their product base."[28] Thomas Kurlak, a semiconductor analyst with Merrill Lynch, Pierce, Fenner & Smith, contends that licensing technology to Korea is a good business move for U.S. firms. In addition to an up-front licensing fee, U.S. firms receive a 1 to 2 percent royalty on future sales, rights to a certain percentage of Korean output, and access to low-cost labor markets.[29] One important explanation for the weak domestic technology base and

the continued need for foreign technology in the electronics
industry in general has been Korea's reliance on assembly
processes in the past, taking advantage of a cheap and abundant labor supply.

Besides acquisition of foreign technology, other Korean
strategies for developing informatics include designing and
developing new products in the U.S. for production in Korea,
protecting domestic latecomers, hiring Korean talent in the
U.S., hitting the world markets with their new products.

Problems, some of which may prove serious, becloud an
otherwise rosy picture of Korea's informatics development.
Growing protective sentiments in the U.S., Japan and
European countries against imports of semiconductors and
other informatics products is one. This is aggravated by
the fact that Korea's exports in general and of electronics
products in particular are highly concentrated in the U.S.,
Japan and Europe. For example, 60.5 percent of Korean
electronics exports were destined for the U.S. in 1983. The
increasing reluctance of advanced countries like Japan to
sell technology to Koreans is another. If, at some future
point, the U.S. firms become alarmed by Korea's competition,
Koreans will find it difficult to buy U.S. technology with a
severe adverse effect on the Korean industry. This is why
the indigenization of production and technology is so
important to them.

A high rate of reliance on foreign raw materials is
another problem area with which Koreans are concerned and
attempting to reduce. The sluggish development of domestic
software industry is another dampening factor which must be
addressed. The lack of name recognition is an additional
hurdle in Korea's efforts to market her products in
the global market, at least at the present time.

NOTES

1. Korea Trade and Business, (January, 1984), p. 4.
2. Electronics Week, (May 6, 1985), p. 48.
3. Electronic Business, (January, 1984), p. 90.
4. Electronics, (April 19, 1984), p. 106.
5. Electronic Business, (May 15, 1985), p. 44.
6. Electronic Week, (May 6, 1985), p. 48.
7. The Journal of Asian Electronics Union, (March, 1982), p. 58.
8. The Journal of Asian Electronics Union, (March, 1984), p. 108.

172

The Electronics Industries Association of Korea, _Chunja kongup pyunram, 1984-1985_ (The Handbook of the Electronics Industry), (Seoul, 1985), p. 37.

10.   _The Journal of Asian Electronics Union_, (February, 1984), p. 99.

11.   EIAK, _Chunja kongup pyunram (1984-1985)_, p. 42.

12.   "Recent Trends in Electronics Industries of Southeast Asian Countries-Korea/Taiwan" (Part 2), _The Journal of Asian Electronics Union_, (October, 1982), p. 45.

13.   For the complete text of the law, see EIAK, _Chunja kongup pyunram (1984-1985)_, pp. 411-415.

14.   Information on this and subsequent paragraphs on the foreign investment law is derived primarily from the following publications of the Ministry of Finance, Republic of Korea: _Investment Guide to Korea_, (July, 1984); _Foreign Capital Inducement Act: Enforcement Decree and Working Rules_, (July, 1984); _Guidelines for Foreign Investment - Negative List Attached_, (July 2, 1984); _Criteria for Permitting Foreign Investment on the Restricted Industries_, (February, 1985).

15.   _Investment Guide to Korea_, pp. 90-93.

16.   _Electronics Week_, (May 6, 1985), p. 49.

17.   A report made by the Korean delegation to the Eighth General Assembly of the Asia Electronics Union, on October 21, 1983 at Jakarta, Indonesia, _The Journal of Asian Electronics Union_, (March, 1984), pp. 108-109.

18.   _Idem_.

19.   As quoted in "Will Korea open its PC market to U.S. vendors," _Electronic Business_, (February, 1984), p. 98.

20.   _Electronic Business_, (February, 1984), p. 98.

21.   _Computers and Peripheral Equipment: Korea_, U.S. Department of Commerce, International Trade Administration, Country Market Survey, (March, 1981), pp. 2-5.

22.   EIAK, _Chunja kongup pyunram (1984-1985)_.

23.   "Lean, mean and hungry: Here come the Koreans," _Electronic Business_, (May 15, 1985), p. 48.

24.   _Korea Trade and Business_, (March, 1984), p. 9.

25.   Information for this section is based on Yu Won-yung, "A Proposal to the Government for the Development of Semiconductor Industry," _Journal of Korean Electronics_, (April, 1985), pp. 22-26; EIAK, _Chunja kongup pyunram_, various annual editions.

26.   _Electronics Business_, (January, 1982), p. 115.

27.   Karen Berney, "The Four Dragons Rush to Play Catch-up Game," _Electronics Week_, (May 6, 1985), p. 50.

28.   _Idem_.

29.   _Idem_.

8

Mexico

Debra Lynn Miller
Barnard College, Columbia University

INTRODUCTION

Mexico is the second largest producer and consumer
of computers in Latin America. In 1985, the Mexican market
for computers was approximately $450 million.[1] Although
the country has used data processing equipment since the
1960s, and has produced electronic components and telecommunications equipment since the 1970s, Mexico imported essentially all of its computers until 1981. That same year, the
government issued a formal sectoral decree on the manufacture and trade of computers and peripherals, and implementation of the policy began in 1983.[2] Although in effect
less than three years at the time of this writing, the
policy has already produced significant results. The
country now produces computers locally, using foreign technology and capital and has reduced its dependence on imports
of finished foreign computer systems and components. In the
long run, Mexico hopes to develop technological capability
and an R&D infrastructure in this sector with the assistance
of foreign firms and to become a major exporter of microcomputers.

This paper describes the size and shape of the
Mexican market, details the Mexican informatics policy and
analyzes to what extent it is enforced and why. The paper
assesses the policy's impact on the sector, using interviews
with firms operating in Mexico and with the Mexican government, and identifies obstacles to development in this sector
stemming both from problems with the informatics policy
itself and general problems in the Mexican economy.
Finally, future developments for both policy and the market
are forecast, and policy alterations are suggested.

This paper reports three main findings. First, Mexico's policy banning most imports of finished micro- and minicomputer systems has had the desired effect of attracting foreign capital and technology to the country for the purpose of manufacturing computers locally. Before the import ban, foreign firms exported computers to Mexico but did not produce there. Second, Mexico's strategy of building its technological infrastructure in this area by using foreign technology and fostering a cooperative triangular research relationship between government, private industry, and universities appears to be working well.

In contrast to the two previous, more positive assessments, this paper concludes thirdly that Mexico is somewhat at risk in this sector because of the country's general economic conditions and large foreign debt. Since the 1982 balance-of-payments crisis, Mexico has instituted foreign exchange controls, devalued the peso several times, and cut imports dramatically during 1982 and 1983.[3] These measures had the effect of contracting the economy. This situation has acted as a disincentive to foreign investment. Mexico is relying on foreign investment and continued growth in the economy to spur the production and use of computers; thus, there is a need for the economy to be stabilized and reactivated. Until it is, the sector will be at risk in two ways. New foreign investment may not grow as fast as the government hopes, and the Mexican market for computers may shrink in a contracting economy.

This paper makes two arguments. First, despite major exceptions and reports to the contrary, Mexico has developed a fairly coherent policy on computers which is enforced in a consistent manner. Second, now that the protectionist policy has been in effect for several years and the sector has begun to mature, the policy should be altered in the direction of allowing more foreign competition in the informatics sector.

THE MEXICAN INFORMATICS MARKET

Mexico has imported informatics equipment since the mid-1960s.[4] The country has produced sizable quantities of middle-level technology electronic componentry since the late 1960s. Building on this capability, Mexico began to produce televisions, stereos, radios, and other audio equipment in the mid-1970s, using foreign technology and capital, but with components almost entirely made in Mexico.[5] Mexico also produces telecommunications equipment and is currently

converting the country's phone lines to a digital system
from an analog one, is launching two satellites via U.S.
NASA, and is expanding its data transmission networks.[6]
Finally, Mexico began importing electronic data processing
equipment in the 1960s, and since 1981 has begun to produce
computers and peripherals locally.[7]

Except for electronic componentry, the production of
most informatics and electronics goods in Mexico relies
heavily on foreign capital and technology. In addition,
subsidiaries of foreign firms are usually the dominant companies in each of the informatics subsectors. Thus, for
the telecommunications sector, although there are over 100
firms producing such equipment, three foreign subsidiaries
have the largest market shares: ITT's Indetel, GTE, and
Swedish Teleindustria Ericsson. Siemens of West Germany
dominates the telex market. A similar situation exists for
televisions. U.S. investors, as well as some Japanese and
West European firms, dominate the market.[8] Lastly, as will
be discussed in greater detail below, the computer sector is
heavily dependent on foreign technology and capital.

Although other types of products are also considered
informatics goods, this paper will primarily focus on computers and peripherals. Thus, the remainder of this section analyzes the computer market.

In 1969, there were only 300 computers operating in
Mexico. Most of these were medium- and large-scale computers
and almost all were leased to users. Twenty-three percent
were used in the distribution and service sector, 22% in
manufacturing, 25% in government administration and government-owned industry, and 20% in financial institutions.
PEMEX, the Mexican government-owned oil company, was the
largest user of computers. In this early era, computers
were supplied to the Mexican market via Mexican sales subsidiaries of foreign (principally U.S.) firms. In 1969,
Burroughs, CDC, IBM, Bull/GE, NCR, Remington Rand, RCA, and
Honeywell all had sales subsidiaries in Mexico.[9]

There are no official or even completely reliable statistics concerning the production and sale of computers
systems and peripherals in Mexico today. However, using a
variety of sources, the following Table 8.1 has been
constructed to offer an approximation of the direction of
growth in the Mexican computer market since 1960.

TABLE 8.1
The Mexican Computer Market (in $US millions)

Year	Market size (Imports + local production)	% Imports
1960	1	100
1970	14.5	100
1975	89	100
1977	118	100
1981	600	100
1982	285	start-up year for local production
1984	450	70
1988	[666]*	[30]*

Source: See note 10.

*forecasted estimate

The Mexican market has grown at a very fast pace. It is now the second largest computer market in Latin America, roughly one-third to one-half the size of the Brazilian market, but still only one-twentieth the size of the U.S. market. Together, Mexico and Brazil account for 70% to 75% of the Latin American market. With Argentina added, the three comprise 85% of the market.[11] In the year 1984 alone, over 30,000 mini- and microcomputers were sold in Mexico,[12] 1000 times the total number of computers in use in 1969. The market's growth rate would have been linear (and exponential) were it not for the 1982 foreign exchange and balance-of-payments crisis and the ensuing recession which caused production and demand to drop across all sectors.

Nevertheless, since 1982 the market has grown and local production of computers has mushroomed from essentially nothing at the beginning of this decade to supplying 30% of the market's needs. There has also been significant growth in the export sector. Mexican government officials have estimated that for every dollar imported into this sector, 50 cents was exported in 1984, compared to two cents in

1981.[13] Imports of finished computer systems are forecast
to drop 1.9% a year through 1988 from a high of $174.5
million as local production grows (approximately 20% a year.)
Imports of peripherals will grow (forecasted at 39% a year)
during this period from $5.9 million in 1982.[14]

The type of computer equipment demanded and produced
over the past 15 years has also changed. As noted above, in
1969 almost all of the 300 computers installed in Mexico
were large and leased. Because of advances in computer and
miniaturization technology, today the growing demand is for
smaller, less expensive minicomputers and microcomputers
which are purchased outright. Many of these smaller
machines used for business (rather than recreational) purposes can do what only a larger machine could do in 1969.
Market shares for mainframes, minicomputers, and microcomputers are currently projected as follows:

TABLE 8.2
Market Shares for Mainframe, Microcomputers and
Minicomputers ($US millions)

	1982	1984	1986 (est.)	1988 (est.)
Mainframe	12	13	15	13
Minicomputers	91	102	122	114
Microcomputers	26	74	140	228

Source: Wallace y Associados, S.C. Profile of the Mini and
          Micro Computer Systems Market, Mexico, p. 15.

The highest growth rate projected is, as seen above, for
microcomputers.[15] Industry analysts and government sources
alike estimate that this subsector will grow at a rate of
between 30% and 35% a year through 1988.[16]

According to Mexican Department of Commerce data, in
1985, 70 companies were authorized to produce computers and
peripherals in Mexico and 100 may produce soft-ware.[17] Most
of these companies have been producing in Mexico less than
five years. For instance, in 1981, only one company was
authorized to produce microcomputers, and in 1984, twelve.
In 1984 there were about 20 companies authorized to produce
minicomputers, including IBM, Cromemco, Hewlett-Packard,
NCR, Burroughs and Digital.[18]

Producers which have the largest market share for micros are Apple, Commodore, Columbia, Corona, and Cromemco. Both IBM and Radio Shack made plans in 1985 to begin producing microcomputers in Mexico. In order to ensure the survival of other producers, IBM, an extremely competitive company, will be limited by the Mexican government to a 20% market share.[19] It is a general rule in both the micro and mini markets that those companies with the highest market shares have some foreign participation. In the micro subsector, only IBM has been allowed 100% equity in its Mexican counterpart. In the mini-subsector, IBM and Hewlett-Packard have wholly-owned subsidiaries. The remainder of the larger companies operating in Mexico are joint ventures between a foreign firm and local capital. None of the computer companies operating in Mexico is government-owned. It should be noted that although local production of computers began only in the early 1980s, many of the firms manufacturing computers today in Mexico have been in the country for some time, starting as sales subsidiaries in the 1960s.

Although there have been complaints of a shortage of skilled workers for this field, several Mexican educational institutions provide computer and informatics training. The Universidad Nacional Autonoma de Mexico (UNAM) offers computer education programs in both its Science and Commerce school and its Business Administration school. The Instituto Tecnologico de Estudios Superiores de Monterrey (ITESM) offers a formal degree in the computer field. The Instituto Politecnico Nacional (UPIICSA and ESIME) the Universidad de las Americas and the Universidad Autonoma de Guadalajara also offer programs.[20] These programs are aided by funds, equipment and instruction from many of the foreign firms which have subsidiaries or joint ventures in the informatics sector in Mexico. As will be discussed later, all foreign investors must invest 5% to 6% of sales receipts in computer research and development in Mexico, some of which can be spent at government-specified educational institutions such as those above.

Commercial and vocational schools for computer training also exist. They include ICM de Mexico and Academia Mexicana de Informatica. The skilled labor force employed in the electronic data processing sector in 1977 was estimated at 12,525 people and, at that date, it was projected that 26,649 people would be employed in the sector in 1982.[21] The US Department of Commerce projected in 1981 that 43,000 trained people would be employed in the computer sector in 1985, based on a market projection of $300 million.[22] Given that the actual market was 50% larger than this figure in 1985, it is probable that this is a low estimate.

The largest end-user of computers is the government itself, with 25% of all computer purchases going for government administration purposes. The second largest user is the financial and insurance sector which accounts for 21% of all computer purchases, followed by retailing and whole-saling with 20.4%. Manufacturing accounts for 17.4% and utilities 4.3%. Government consumption is actually under-stated by these figures; counting the entities it owns in other sectors, especially manufacturing and finance, the government actually accounts for between 50% and 60% of all purchases in Mexico.[23]

In summary, the computer industry is growing rapidly in Mexico. Consumption has gone up in this decade, and pro-duction has begun. Two critical variables will affect the extent to which Mexico is able to create a viable informatics sector: government informatics policy and macroeconomic conditions in Mexico, especially the management of Mexico's debt. These variables are considered below.

INFORMATICS POLICY

Mexico has a clearly articulated industrial policy governing informatics. Its main provisions are found in the Development Program for the Manufacturing of Electronic Com-puter Systems, their Main Modules and Peripheral Equipment, written in 1981 and implemented in 1983. Other policy instruments also affect it: the Law to Promote Mexican Investment and Regulate Foreign Investment passed in 1973,[24] the Law of Control of Transfers of Rights of Technology, effective in 1973 and modified in 1982,[25] and various directives of the Secretariat of Commerce and Industrial Development on trade policy such as licenses, quotas, tariffs, and currency allocations. In essence, the policy relies on direct foreign investment to spur development of the sector by supplying most of the capital and technology. The sector has been offered a very heavy measure of trade protection, with essentially all imports of finished com-puter systems to be phased out if similar products can be produced locally. In this section the policy is first placed in national and international political economic con-texts. Then, the provisions of the laws and policies are discussed. Finally, discrepancies and consistencies between law and enforcement are analyzed.

The Context

Mexico is the second largest market in Latin America.
Since World War II, its government has sought to promote
domestic industrial development. The policies and methods
used have varied, but for the most part, they have been
designed to protect the domestic economy from international
competition. Import substitution, tariffs, and import
licensing systems have limited trade inflows. Foreign
investment and licensing are permitted but have been regulated. Recently, sectoral planning has also been used as a
development tool.[26]

There have been periods of relative openness during the
past 40 years as well. The government, in the late 1970s,
lowered tariffs and abolished its system of import permits,
but these were reinstituted in 1982. In addition, Mexico
has at times relied more on import substitution as a means
of industrializing, and at other times, export-led growth
(the two strategies are not necessarily inconsistent, but
relative emphases on them have varied over time).[27] Since
1985, Mexico has been in a liberalizing phase, and has taken
steps to open its borders to more foreign competition.[28]

Mexico's policies to promote industrial development can
be contrasted with those of the newly industrializing Asian
countries such as Korea, Hong Kong, and Singapore, which
have chosen to keep their economies more consistently open
than Mexico, and other Latin American countries, such as
Brazil, which have closed their economies even more than
Mexico. The Mexican policy mix can be explained by its
relations with other more industrialized states, the ideology of its nationalist, "revolutionary" ruling coalition
party, the Institutional Revolutionary Party (the PRI) and
the country's lack of indigenous comparative advantage in
high-technology goods.[29]

Mexico was a Spanish colony for three hundred years,
during which time the Spanish controlled the most productive industries in the country and extracted what they
could to further Spanish mercantile goals. During the 19th
century, both France and the United States invaded Mexico,
the French ruled briefly, and the country lost one-third of
its territory to the United States. From 1876 to 1910, when
the country was ruled by Porfirio Diaz, foreigners controlled one-seventh of the country's land and one-half of
its total assests.[30] Although Mexico has been an independent, sovereign state since 1917, foreign interests continue
to play a significant role in Mexico today. American,
European, and Japanese firms have invested heavily in the

Mexican economy. During the last decade, Mexico has amassed a large foreign debt of almost $100 billion, and has outstanding loans from American, European and Japanese banks as well as the International Monetary Fund (IMF).

The involvement of foreign interests in Mexico has helped the country industrialize. Many of the sectors in which there is direct foreign investment have proven to be the most dynamic and advanced, even producing goods that are competitive on the world market. Continued development is dependent, however, on foreign sources of capital, managerial expertise, and technology. These sources may be hard to attract given the current state of the Mexican economy, which has been devastated by its large debt. The economic adjustment program implemented by President de la Madrid, in accordance with International Monetary Fund recommendations, has allowed the interest to be paid back on the debt, but has permitted almost no growth. GNP dropped 5% in 1983, grew 3.5% in 1984, and there was a recession in 1985. In addition, real wages have fallen 50% in three years, and imports are down from 1981 levels by 65%. The peso has been devalued several times and in 1985, the second devaluation was more than the inflation rate.[31] Unfortunately, the September 1985 earthquake will have effects on the economy as well. The current economic situation acts as a deterrent to foreign capital and growth in the informatics sector is dependent both on growth in the economy and on foreign capital.

Economic problems in Mexico also raise the spectre of political instability. The economic reforms which the government has instituted to pay back its loans have caused hardship and much discontentment among the people. This has been evidenced in mass demonstrations and diminishing electoral support for the governing political party, the PRI. The government has responded with repression, electoral fraud, and corruption at all levels. There is some speculation that the Presidential elections may not take place on time in 1988.[32] The threat of political instability also acts as a disincentive to further foreign economic involvement in Mexico.

Despite the benefits of certain of its foreign economic ties, the Mexican government's attitude has been ambivalent toward its links with the international political economy. Direct foreign investment has created a dual economy with the attendant problems of integrating the foreign and domestic sectors. In certain manufacturing sectors, local Mexican firms have been driven out of business because they have been unable to compete with foreign firms.[33] The country has become vulnerable to the vicissitudes of the international economy. If interest rates go up in the United States, the interest rates on Mexican loans rise as well. If the price of a barrel of oil falls, so, too, do Mexican export revenues (over 70% of which come from the sale of petroleum).

Some Mexicans diagnose Mexico's plight in terms of dependency theory, which at its extreme blames foreign interests for stunting indigenous Mexican growth or more mildly, suggests that involvement with the foreign economy has made Mexican development dependent on foreign resources and vulnerable to international economic events. These types of diagnoses, combined with the country's colonial heritage and having an economic and political giant as its closest Northern neighbor, have had the tendency to make Mexicans formulate nationalist economic policies.[34]

The last factor that should be considered in understanding the context of Mexican policy in informatics is the country's relationship to the United States. Two points are worth stressing here. First, the United States is Mexico's major trade and investment partner, and of course, an economic and political giant. This has given the United States considerable leverage in influencing Mexican domestic and foreign economic policy. For example, when the Computer Decree was published in 1981, the U.S. Office of the Special Trade Representative (STR) balked and the Decree was not incorporated into law at that time.[35] During 1985, the United States and Mexico have held a series of bilateral negotiations culminating in the decision of Mexico both to liberalize its national trade policy and to join the General Agreement on Trade and Tariffs (GATT). In the summer of 1985, Mexico liberalized its trade rules for over 2100 products and in the fall began to take steps necessary to join the GATT.[36] As will be discussed below, GATT membership may force Mexico to significantly alter its informatics policy. Thus, the United States has the ability to cause Mexico to make significant alterations in its economic policies.

The second point of relevance regarding the United States—Mexico relationship is that the United States has the comparative advantage in both high technology and technology-intensive goods. In Mexico, a country where 40% of the population is literate, success in the production of such goods has been based on heavy dependence on foreign technology from the United States. To reiterate, Mexico needs U.S. technology and the United States has continually pushed Mexico to open its borders to U.S. trade and investment, which has

influenced Mexico to choose policies that rely on U.S. technology transfer and usually capital as well. On the other
hand, despite U.S. pressure, the Mexicans have tried to protect these same high-technology sectors from import competition. We will see that the Mexicans have employed this
dual strategy in their sectoral policy on computers.

The Mexican Computer Decree

In 1981 the Undersecretary of Industrial Development
published the "Development Program for the Manufacturing of
Electronic Computer Systems, Their Main Modules [CPUs] and
Peripheral Equipment." The United States requested that
Mexico delay formal publication of the regulations in the
Official Gazette of Mexico in order to postpone the decree's
entry into law. Mexico complied, but the decree is now
considered official policy and is legally in effect because
it falls under the capital goods policy published in 1981 in
the Official Gazette.[37] Implementation of the decree began
in 1983. The decree contains regulations on both trade and
foreign investment. In order to export computers or related
equipment to Mexico, one must secure an import permit. To
invest in Mexico, the foreign firm needs the approval of
several government bureaus. Without government approval,
neither investing firms nor their partners or subsidiaries
have any legal rights in Mexico, nor are they eligible for
incentives or bonuses that the government has from time to
time bestowed upon foreign firms to encourage investment in
specific industries.

Although the provisions of the computer decree are very
detailed, they have not been implemented to the letter. In
practice, the decree is first a starting point for negotiations between the foreign firm, the Mexican government, and
the Mexican affiliate and secondly, a set of governmental
goals for the sector.[38] Exceptions have often been made to
rules. The government has changed, in a de facto sense,
several key provisions since enforcement began two years
ago, and is in the process of changing them again. Reasons
for changes in the enforcement of the decree and for incon-
sistencies in enforcement will be explored after we detail
the provisions.

The 1981 policy statement was motivated by several factors. First, the importation of finished computers into
Mexico had grown tremendously during the 1970s and the
government wanted to reduce its import bill. The government
estimated that the growth rate was 30% a year during most

of the 1970s and that between 1979 and 1980 demand grew by
179%.[39] Since Mexico manufactured essentially no computers
at this point, all computers were imported, using precious
foreign exchange. Given the country's balance-of-payments
problems, it was vital that this trend be stemmed. The
decree thus forbade the importation of finished mini- and
microcomputers. However, recognizing both the demand for
computers and the modernization and greater efficiency which
accrue through their use, the government sought to develop a
national capability to produce mini- and microcomputers. It
hoped to achieve this by encouraging import substitution, as
noted above, and concurrently by attracting and regulating
foreign investment and technology transfer in the area.
Ultimately, the government hoped to develop an export
potential in the area. The policy strategies for achieving
these goals are detailed below.

Incentives. To attract foreign investment and the technology to develop the national capacity for production,
Mexico originally offered incentives to firms which invested
in the sector, including several different types of tax credits and differential energy prices.[40] However, the incentives program was discontinued in 1985 in response to
discussions with the U.S. government.[41] The United States
argued that these incentives amounted to a subsidy under the
GATT subsidy code, and gave Mexican producers of informatics
goods an unfair edge in international trade. The chief
incentive which remains to manufacture computers in Mexico
is that since foreign firms are not allowed to export
computers to the country, they must manufacture the
computers in Mexico if they wish to penetrate the market.

National Integration. In order to reduce the import
bill and to horizontally integrate the national computer
sector and the foreign computer sector, Mexico requires that
all computer firms gradually decrease their reliance on
imported components to manufacture computers and peripherals
over a five-year period. Distributors, too, will have to
reduce their dependence on foreign goods during this period.
Substituted for foreign items will be domestically produced
goods. National integration is to be accomplished through
two policies. One is through import quotas; the other is
through the GIN or domestic content requirement. Each
manufacturer of computers will have an import quota which
will gradually be reduced over a five-year period so that
by 1988, local production will satisfy 70% of market demand
(up from 30% in 1983). The GIN requirement specifies the
percentages of weighted parts times cost integration base
for each type of good produced. Thus, for microcomputers,

the GIN for the first year should be between 35% and 45%;
by the third year it should be between 50% and 60%. For
minicomputers, the GIN for the first year should be between
25% and 30%; for the third year, it should be between 35%
and 50%.[42]

Exports. Mexico is interested in developing an export
capability in the computer sector. One reason for this is
to offset the price of imported components. Another more
general reason is that Mexico is interested in developing an
export capability in manufactured goods in order to pay debt
service costs and to reduce the impact that fluctuations in
the price of oil have on their economy. To achieve this
goal, the Mexican decree states that each company will have
a foreign currency budget for imports such that the company
must compensate the value of its imports with higher export-
import ratios every year. For microcomputers the ratios are
25% for the second year, 70% by the fifth; for minis the
figures are 30% for the first year, 100% by the fourth.[43]

Technology transfer. Mexico must develop a technological infrastructure in informatics in order to develop an
indigenous capability to produce computers rather than
merely remaining an offshore assembly facility for foreign
firms. To this end, the government has structured a
triangular relationship calling for cooperation among
foreign companies, computer research institutes in Mexico,
and the government. Foreign firms wishing to invest in
Mexico must abide by the Law on the Transfer of Technology.
They are also obligated to spend between 5% and 6% of the
value of sales on research and development (R&D) in Mexico.
Various activities qualify as R&D expenditures, from developing a new system or part of one at an approved Mexican
research center or at the Mexican plant, the development of
machinery and equipment for testing, to the adaptation of a
purchased system.[44] The government has approved several
facilities where firms can fund computer R&D, including the
Monterrey Institute of Technology, UNAM, and Unitech.

The type of R&D activity which the firm undertakes has
an effect in the calculation of the domestic content (GIN)
requirement for each good. The degree of national technology incorporated in the good (the 'T' factor) is used as a
multiplier in the GIN equation. The multiplier is of
greater value for activities that are undertaken at Mexican
research centers and for the development of new systems
rather than, for example, the training of personnel at the
local plant. A high 'T' factor can help offset low domestic
component content for a particular good and allow for the
satisfaction of the GIN requirement.[45]

The decree also suggests that the most advanced technology be transferred to Mexico and that the Mexican subsidiary or partner have access to the parent firm's R&D facilities in its home country.[46]

There are other policies which may have an impact on the behavior of foreign firms in the country. The two most significant ones are the Law to Promote Mexican Investment and Regulate Foreign Investment of February 16, 1973, in force since May 3, 1973 (hereinafter known as the Foreign Investment Law) and the Law on the Control and Recording of the Transfer of Technology and the Use and Exploitation of Patents and Trademarks (hereinafter known as the Technology Transfer Law) of December 29, 1981. The Foreign Investment Law limits investment to certain sectors and forbids foreign ownership greater than 49%. Equity restrictions are even stronger for some sectors. For the electronics sector, the computer decree has restricted foreign ownership in microcomputers to the usual 49% (although several notable exceptions to this have been allowed, as is discussed below). Any company which wishes to invest in Mexico must register with and have its contract approved by the National Commission on Foreign Investment (CNIE).

The Technology Transfer Law also applies to foreign firms, and firms in the informatics sector. That law prohibits 17 restrictive business practices, such as export restrictions, tie-in clauses, and free grantbacks of improvements of R&D, in contracts between the supplier and recipient of technology, and limits the royalties suppliers can collect on patents and know-how. Enforcement of this law has been less stringent in the 1980s than in the 1970s.[47]

The informatics industry encompasses not only computers and peripherals, but other types of equipment as well, such as copiers and duplicating machines, electronic typewriters, and other types of data producing, storage and retrieval systems. Not all of these fall under the jurisdiction of the computer decree. Nevertheless, the requirements for foreign participation are similar. Domestic content requirements, balance-of-payments and balance-of-trade stipulations, technology transfer provisos, and equity restrictions are all applicable to all informatics firms (and most foreign business which operates in Mexico).[48]

Other types of informatics firms do not receive as favorable treatment in their dealings with the government as do the manufacturers of micro and minicomputers. For instance, despite the Foreign Investment Law, and the provisions of the computer decree, the Mexican government

has allowed a few companies, such as IBM and Hewlett-
Packard, to create wholly-owned subsidiaries. Domestic content requirements for other informatics goods are often
higher than similar requirements for computers. For
example, the domestic content requirement for electronic
typewriters is 60%.[49] In addition, the Mexican government
has fully protected the market for mini- and microcomputers.
Other domestic informatics producers do not receive such
consistent and high protection. With the new trade
liberalization policy in July 1985, some producers may lose
all protection and yet continue to be required to abide by
domestic content legislation. This means that foreign
subsidiaries must utilize domestically produced components,
which sometimes are three to four times as expensive as
imports, and then compete with cheaper imports as well.
These firms may also be required to export their goods, made
with domestic components, to meet Mexican balance-of-
payments requirements.

Enforcement

As noted above, the Mexican computer decree is only a
starting point for negotiations between foreign firms and
the government. In addition, the enforcement of certain
provisions of the decree is more lax for this sector than
other sectors. During an interview with one executive of a
large US-based computer firm, when the discussion turned to
the Mexican policy on computers, he said, "What policy?"
although he was very familiar with the computer decree. He
clearly believed that the government's actions were
arbitrary and evidenced no consistent policy.

The overarching reason for incomplete enforcement of the
computer decree is that Mexico wishes to acquire technology
and capital to develop this sector, and they wish to com-
puterize the country in order to increase efficiency and
modernize. Thus, they wish to attract foreign investment,
not deter it. This does not mean that the Mexicans will
agree to any deal to obtain foreign investment, but they are
predisposed to accept capital and technology in this sector.

Interviews with several informatics firms as well as
Mexican and US government officials, however, indicate that
there is a rather consistent pattern of enforcement and
non-enforcement and rationales for behavior. The variance
in enforcement and explanations for such are discussed below.

Technology Transfer. The provisions in the computer
decree regarding the obligation of foreign firms to transfer

technology and to invest a percentage of their sales remittances in informatics development in Mexico are consistently enforced and most of the foreign firms in Mexico seem quite willing to assist the Mexicans with their development plans. The larger companies, such as IBM and Xerox, are quite proud of their efforts to aid Mexican technological development. For example, IBM is helping the Mexicans to produce multi-layer circuitized packaging, and to learn semi-conductor design, as well as demonstrating how to provide vendor support.

Exports. Mexico is also in the process of achieving its export goals for the sector. Mexico now exports 50 cents for every dollar imported, up from two cents in 1981.[50] In Mexico's recent deal with IBM, that firm has agreed to export over 90% of the microcomputers it makes locally.[51] Mexico exports computers to Canada and Latin America, with the exception of Brazil, Argentina and Colombia, which have protected informatics sectors.

Domestic Content. On the other hand, the government has found it impossible to enforce the domestic content requirement. This is largely because Mexican firms are not able to produce enough computer parts at a high enough quality to achieve the GIN targets.[52] The government has thus been lax in enforcing these provisions. Industry sources are mixed on whether or not Mexico will be able to upgrade its local capabilities so that foreign firms can meet the GIN requirements. One large computer firm suggested that the level of technology transfer to Mexico was so high and the government-sponsored programs were so good that within three years the country should have enough local computer firms producing high quality and competitively priced components. Another large informatics firm, which also has operations in Mexico, argued to the contrary. Nevertheless, the point is clear: the lack of enforcement of the GIN requirement is largely determined by the state of the country's capabilities. The length of time for upgrading these capabilities remains unknown.

Imports. The Mexican government has officially forbidden the importation of finished minis and micros to Mexico, thus affording Mexican producers of computers a very high degree of protection. Demand for minis and especially micros has been especially high in Mexico, however, and there is a sizable grey market whereby computers have been unofficially brought into Mexico and not registered as imports. It is estimated that, together, IBM and Radio Shack account for over 25% of the Mexican microcomputer market (by value), but that neither, as of yet, manufactures

micros in Mexico, nor does the government permit the legal
importation of the units (with very few exceptions). Yet,
in 1984, between 7500 and 15,000 IBM PCs and approximately
6000 Radio Shack micros were illegally brought into
Mexico.[53] It is expected that both of these companies will
be producing computers in Mexico shortly. The IBM deal will
be discussed below and Radio Shack is contemplating the
establishment of a Mexican subsidiary. If these plans go
through, the grey market may shrink considerably. There
does not appear to be a sizable grey market in minicomputers
since demand in this area is met by foreign firms with
operations in Mexico, such as IBM, Hewlett-Packard, NCR,
Burroughs, Digital, Control Data, as well as several smaller
Mexican firms.

Equity Requirements. As noted above, although the
Foreign Investment Law forbids greater than 49% foreign
equity participation, significant exceptions have been made
to this law. During the last two years, the Mexican government has indicated that it will allow certain foreign firms
to have wholly-owned subsidiaries, and this has been done for
three reasons.[54] First, because outstanding loans from
foreign banks to Mexico are so high, the debt burden has
become such that banks are wary about lending more money to
Mexico, and in the event, an increased debt service ratio
would be difficult to afford. Thus, Mexico has tried to
attract foreign investment to meet its capital needs, as
well as to produce manufactured goods for export to earn
needed foreign exchange. Second, the United States and IMF
have argued that the best long-term remedy for Mexico's economic problems is to open its market by liberalizing trade
and bringing in foreign investment. They have put pressure
on Mexico to these ends. This has caused Mexico to liberalize its trade policy, as noted above, and has also
influenced the easing of investment regulations. Third,
Harvard-educated President Miguel de la Madrid's own political and economic philosophies are more free-market than
'dependencia' in approach. De la Madrid's views are typical
of the new Latin American leaders of the 1980s. In contrast,
in the high-growth 1970s, many Latin American leaders,
including Echeverria of Mexico, challenged the Western free
market philosophy and liberal international economic system
and called for a New International Economic Order at the
United Nations that would restructure the market using political means to allocate more resources to the South.

Most foreign companies operating in the informatics
sector in Mexico must still adhere to the 51-49 rule.
Mexico has permitted a few exceptions, especially for mini-

computers. For instance, Hewlett-Packard produces its 3000
series minicomputer in Guadalajara at a wholly-owned subsidiary and IBM also produces minis in Mexico at a wholly-
owned subsidiary. However, H-P, Apple, and Commodore all
adhere to the 51-49 rule for the production of microcomputers.

Some companies argue that certain aspects of the 51-49
rule have not hurt them. One U.S.-based informatics company
said that most of the managers and employees of its Mexican
subsidiary were Mexican, and that all dealings with the
government were handled by these Mexican managers. The U.S.
managers believed that they were able to cut better deals
with the government this way since the Mexicans knew with
whom to deal in the bureaucracy and were skilled in doing
so, and that the government might be giving them better
treatment because it was dealing with nationals.[55]

On the other hand, one lawyer for American firms in this
area has suggested that high technology firms are loathe to
agree to 51-49 ownership and still transfer state-of-the-
art technology to the subsidiary. He argues that if the
foreign firm does not have direct and local managerial
control over the subsidiary, there is the danger of "conta-
mination" of the technology, and that the technology will be
leaked to other competitiors in the field.[56]

The IBM "exception". Of course, the newest and most
significant exception to the 51-49 rule has recently been
made to IBM in the microcomputer area. IBM refuses to
operate in a country if it cannot wholly own its subsidiary,
and has withdrawn from countries which do not permit it to
continue such ownership, such as India. The Mexican government was originally hesitant to allow IBM to come into the
country, and rejected IBM's proposal after a first round of
negotiations. A second round produced an agreement between
the government and the firm.[57] One reason the government
initially refused to grant IBM a wholly-owned subsidiary for
the manufacture of microcomputers is that it believed that
it would offend foreign firms that have adhered to the
equity rule and national firms that have had to make large
investments of their own. However, the main reason for the
initial refusal of the government to allow IBM to enter the
Mexican market was that local companies were afraid of
competing with "Big Blue." IBM has been in Mexico for some
time and has a base from which to build there. It has some
equipment, administrative and sales personnel and a sales
network. In contrast, most of the other microcomputer
companies are relatively new, being founded after 1982. IBM
has proposed to produce almost 80% more microcomputers than

all of the other producers combined, and at a cost to the
Mexican consumer of only 15% more than in the United States.
Presently, it costs Mexicans 50% more, on an average, to
purchase micros made in Mexico than in the United States.[58]
To assuage the fears of other local producers, IBM agreed
that it would have no more than a 20% share of the domestic
market, with the remainder of its production (over 90%) to
be exported.

The analysis offered above suggests that there is quite
a bit of consistency in Mexico's enforcement of the computer
decree. Balance-of-payments and export goal requirements are
regularly enforced by the government because Mexico needs
foreign exchange to pay off its debt and to ensure continued
development in the country. Domestic content requirements,
which would help achieve the same ends, are not enforced
because they cannot be enforced. Local Mexican producers do
not have the capacity or skills to meet the needs of foreign
investors in this area. To remedy this problem, the government insists that foreign firms abide by the technology
regulations so that the local computer infrastructure can be
built. The government has tried to protect the sector by
banning imports on finished micros and minis, but this
provision has proved difficult to enforce. The demand for
micros is higher than the country is now capable of
producing, so a sizable grey market has developed. This
situation should turn around within two to three years,
however, if IBM and Radio Shack go through with their plans
to produce micros in Mexico.

Finally, with the exception of IBM, microcomputer firms
have had to comply with the 49% limitation on foreign
equity, but some foreign firms which produce minicomputers
have been allowed wholly-owned subsidiaries. The non-
enforcement of this provision, like the non-enforcement of
the GIN requirement, stems from a deficiency in the local
market in terms of both a shortage in the capital market and
of Mexican personnel equipped to start up such joint
ventures. Thus, except with regard to IBM, equity restrictions have been enforced regarding the production of microcomputers.

Three factors can explain the extent to which there is
any variance in the above pattern of enforcement. First, a
firm which promises both to transfer technology not more
than six to 12 months old and to export large quantities of
computers from Mexico will probably get the best deal, since
these are Mexico's top priorities. This helps explain IBM's
eventual success in getting into the Mexican micro market
despite domestic opposition and an initial refusal by the

government to allow the company to build micros.

The second factor is the organization of the Mexican bureaucracy. Negotiation and approval of foreign investment contracts is handled by many agencies in a decentralized fashion. Foreign investors (or their national representatives) must negotiate their way through a maze of offices before they can get final approval of their venture by an interagency committee, consisting of representatives of the concerned offices.[59]

The main ministry involved is the Secretariat of Commerce and Industrial Development (or SECOFIN). Within this department, primary responsibility for the development of informatics policy belongs to the Deputy Director General of the Electronics Industry within the Underministry of Industrial Promotion. If direct foreign investment is involved, then so too is the Undersecretary for Foreign Investment and his office, the Committee on Foreign Investment (CNIE). The General Director of Control of Foreign Commerce is also a party in the discussion process because it has authority over issuing the import permits for parts, components and peripherals. The Ministry of Budget and Planning (SPP) also has a role in informatics policy. The General Director of Informatics Policy (SPP) is responsible for the use of computers within the public sector in Mexico. The General Director of Pricing in SPP reviews projects as well, because he controls public sector expenditures. Also, the Ministry of Budget and Planning reviews all informatics projects through the National Institute of Geography Statistics and Informatics.

Since technology transfer is involved in all informatics investment deals, two other bureaus are also involved. The technology transfer registry within SECOFIN is in charge of reviewing the terms of licensing agreements, and CONACYT, the science and technology ministry of Mexico is in charge of government-sponsored research and development efforts.

Given the large number of agencies involved, and the different agendas and goals of each, it is not surprising that it can take over a year before a deal is concluded. Complicating matters further for foreign firms is that some of the offices appear to be merely exercising their "functional" responsibility and are interested in attracting foreign investment while trying to achieve Mexican development objectives, while other bureaucrats are more "nationalistic" or ideological in their approach to approving foreign investment deals. Thus, the Director General of the Electronic Industry and several other officers in SECOFIN tend to be very nationalistic in their approach to dealing

with potential foreign investors and very attuned to domestic national producers' reactions to potential competitors.
The split in the ministries is in part because certain
commercial ministries have ties to domestic industry and
thus tend to be nationalistic. It is also a consequence of
the fact that the PRI tends to staff the bureaucracy with
elements from the left and the right in order to form a
coalition government. All of these factors complicate the
bureaucratic politics involved in negotiations between the
Mexican government and foreign informatics firms. They
produce long delays and increase the probability of some
variation in law enforcement.

The third factor that can have an effect on the nature
of the deal struck is high politics, or, more specifically,
the relationship between high officials in the Mexican government and the U.S. government. In 1985, the United States
and Mexico conducted several high level discussions on the
opening of the Mexican economy to greater trade and investment flows, and on the possibility of Mexico joining the
General Agreement on Trade and Tariffs, the international
treaty which promotes free and fair trade. These discussions resulted in Mexico's abolishing its incentive program
for foreign informatics firms, on the grounds that such incentives represented an export subsidy under the GATT, and
thus would be liable to countervailing duties in importing
countries. They also resulted in, as noted above, the
substantial trade liberalization policy Mexico announced in
July 1985.

Finally, some sources indicate that U.S. pressure had
much to do with getting the reversal of the Mexican decision
against IBM. It is suggested that one of the reasons for
the original rejection of the deal was that nationalists in
SECOFIN, reflecting the interests of the national computer
manufacturers, turned the deal down.[60] During the second
round of negotiations, however, the most nationalist of the
bureaucrats were isolated from the negotiating process, and
those who were included in the process were aware that the
President's office had given the word that the deal was to
go through. We can speculate that several factors had an
impact on that decision. It was impolitic to refuse IBM's
entry into the country because of the general U.S.-Mexican
relationship and refusal would directly contradict the spirit
of the U.S.-Mexican talks described above. Also, IBM's
entry into the Mexican microcomputer market, under the right
conditions, would ultimately help Mexico to attain its
export and development goals. Thus, the U.S.-Mexican

relationship helped reverse the government's original
decision, over Mexican domestic opposition.

CONCLUSIONS

   The informatics industry in Mexico is a high-growth
industry. Mexico has elected to be dependent on foreign
capital and technology to start up the sector but has
structured its sectoral plan so that there are incentives
for the development of local informatics firms and provisions for the development of a technological infrastructure
for the sector.
   It is probable that Mexico will follow its present path
throughout the rest of the 1980s in this sector, and enforce
the decree in a manner consistent with the approaches
described above. The IBM case is probably not a harbinger
of a relaxation of the equity restrictions on microcomputers.
It is difficult to foresee that any other company will be
able to offer Mexico as profitable an opportunity as IBM did.
Given its large debt, chronic foreign exchange shortages, and
emphasis on developing an export capability, Mexico is
likely to continue to enforce the balance-of-payments,
balance-of-trade and technology requirements in this sector.
If, as some believe, Mexico is able to develop more of a
local capability to produce computer components, we can
expect that they may also try to enforce the GIN provisions
as well.
   This paper noted earlier the necessity for Mexico to
rely on foreign capital and technology to develop this
sector. Mexico's situation is different from Brazil's in
that it recognizes a need to rely on foreign investment and
technology. Would it have been to Mexico's advantage to go
the other route, however, and keep its economy as open as
some of the newly industrializing Asian states? This would
imply fewer equity restrictions on foreign investors and the
abolition of balance-of-trade, balance-of-payments, and
domestic content laws, as well as permitting competition
from imported informatics goods.
   An open policy was probably not possible in 1981 because
of the state of the sector in Mexico and the need to
stimulate foreign investment rather than imports. A more
open policy may be possible today and may be advantageous.
First, Mexico may no longer have to protect this sector to
attract foreign investment. The crucial start-up capital
has been invested and foreign firms are making a profit. As
noted earlier, the government has been unable to control the

very large grey market for IBM and Radio Shack microcomputers, yet other foreign producers of microcomputers have invested in Mexico. Moreover, protection has high costs. A
Mexican microcomputer costs 50% more than its American
equivalent. This differential has been compounded by the
domestic content, balance-of-payments, and balance-of-trade
provisions of the policy. It may be that foreign investors
will not easily accept the latter provisions without a
promise of protection from foreign competition. In effect,
tinkering with the market in one area necessitates
interfering in another, producing further costs. In the
future, a less regulated trade environment should allow the
Mexicans to obtain their production and technological goals
as well as reduce the price of computers and increase
efficient production through the stimulus of foreign
competition.

Mexico may be forced to drop some of its trade restrictions in informatics if it becomes a full member of the
GATT. All of these regulations are in direct contradiction
to both the letter and spirit of the international trade
treaty. It is also possible that US pressure may result in
a relaxation of these restrictions. Using Section 301, the
retaliation section of the 1974 Trade Act, the United States
has aggressively attempted to open closed foreign markets
during the past two years. Currently it is pressuring
Brazil to open its informatics sector and Japan to promote
imports of semiconductors. It is likely that some of the
Mexican regulations may also be the target of Section 301
pressure.

Mexico's ability to develop an export capability is
dependent not only on a continuing stream of investment into
the country, but also on conditions in potential export
markets. Mexico exports primarily to Latin America and
Canada. Most of the larger Latin American markets are
plagued by debt, especially Peru and Venezuela. Demand for
computers must remain high there, and in Canada as well, or
Mexico will not have an outlet for her goods. Should Mexico
relax some of the protection offered to the informatics
sector, as suggested above, this policy change may well have
excellent repercussions on the international market. Mexican
exports would become cheaper and perhaps of higher quality
and thus more competitive abroad.

Mexico has made an impressive start in the development
of an informatics sector. To cope with the economic and
technological challenges facing the country in the late
1980s, Mexico must be prepared to alter its policy in
response to its growing abilities to manufacture computers

locally. A relaxation of some of its more protectionist
regulations may well lower substantially the price of
computers, stimulate more efficiency in the sector and make
Mexican goods more competitive on the international market.

NOTES

1. The Mexican government keeps no official records on
the size of the computer market, but this figure reflects the
estimate of Josef Warman Grig, Director de la Industria
Electronica y Coordinacion Industrial, SECOFIN. Personal
interview, Washington, D.C., September 1985.
2. Mexican Bureau of Industries, Development Program for
the Manufacturing of Electronic Computer Systems, Their Main
Modules and Peripheral Equipment, 2-VIII, Mexico, Fed.
Dist. (1981) (English translation available at the US
Department of Commerce, Washington, D.C.)
3. For an excellent discussion of current economic
problems in Mexico and the political consequences of the
situation, see Jorge J. Castañeda, "Mexico at the Brink,"
Foreign Affairs 64, 2, Winter 1985-6, pp. 287-303.
4. U.S. Department of Commerce International Marketing
Information Service (IMIS), Bureau of International Commerce,
World Markets for U.S. Exports, "Electronic Data Processing
Equipment-Mexico," June 1970, IMIS 70-212, p. 1.
5. Ventana Associates, Mexican Electronics Industry, an
independent consulting firm's assessment written in
1978-1979, pp. 3-5, unpublished, n.d., 24 pp.
6. U.S. Department of Commerce, CMP Industry Sector
Analysis, Mexico-Telecommunications Equipment, June 14,
1984, p. 12.
7. Wallace y Associados, S.C., Profile of the Mini and
Micro Computer Systems Market, prepared in Mexico, April
1985, under the International Market Research Program of the
U.S. Department of Commerce. This report estimates that
local production of mini and micro computers was $174.5
million, p. 2.
8. Ventana Associates, op. cit., pp. 2-4.
9. U.S. Department of Commerce, IMIS 70-212, op. cit.,
pp. 3-7.
10. Sources include the U.S. Department of Commerce, IMIS
70-212, op. cit.; U.S. Department of Commerce, IMIS, County
Marketing Survey, Computers and Peripheral Equipment,
Mexico, CMS 81-308, February 1981, and Business Equipment
and Systems, Mexico, CMS 76-030; U.S. Department of Commerce

incoming telegram from American Embassy Mexico, RO323162,
September 1981 on "Background Information on Computer Market
in Mexico;" and Wallace y Associados, op. cit.,

11. Estimates offered by Josef Warman Grig, personal
interview, op. cit.

12. Wallace y Associados, op. cit., p. 32.

13. Estimates offered by Josef Warman Grig, op. cit.

14. Wallace y Associados, op. cit., pp. 2-3.

15. Ibid., p. 18.

16. Wallace y Associados, op. cit., and Josef Warman Grig,
personal interview, as well as several managers from leading
American computer firms (background interviews) concur on
these figures.

17. Josef Warman Grig, personal interview, op. cit.

18. Wallace y Associados, op. cit., p. 46.

19. Based on interviews with Mexican government and IBM
personnel, Fall 1985.

20. C. R. Quick y Associados, S.C. (Consultants), Mexican
Market Survey for Computers and Related Equipment, prepared
for U.S. Department of Commerce, Bureau of International
Commerce, February 1979, pp. 28-30.

21. Ibid., p. 28.

22. U.S. Department of Commerce, incoming telegram from
Mexico City, September 1981, Tag RO323162.

23. Wallace y Associados, S.C., op. cit., pp. 56-57.

24. Law to Promote Mexican Investment and Regulate
Foreign Investment, Diario Oficial, D.O. March 9, 1973.

25. Law on the Registration of Transfer of Technology and
the Use and Exploitation of Patents and Trademarks, Diario
Oficial, D.O. December 30, 1972.

26. See U.S. International Trade Commission, Foreign
Industrial Targeting and its Effects on U.S. Industries, Phase
III, Brazil, Canada, The Republic of Korea, Mexico, and
Taiwan, USITC Publication 1632, January 1985; Comment, "The
Regulation of Foreign Business in Mexico: Recent Legisla-
tion in Historical Perspective," 7 North Carolina Inter-
national Law and Commercial Regulation, Summer 1982; Secre-
taria de Comercio y Fomento Industrial (Mexico), Program
Nacional de Fomento Industrial y Comercio Exterior 1984-1988
Poder Ejecutivo Federal, 1984.

27. For an interesting explanation of changes in Mexican
economic policy, see David Mares, "Explaining choice of
development strategies: Suggestions from Mexico,
1970-1982," International Organization 39, 4 (Autumn 1985).

28. "To Increase Exports, Mexico Intends to Let Industry
Raise Imports," Wall Street Journal, July 9, 1985, pp. 1, 20.

198

29. On this latter point, see Henry Nau's essay in this volume.

30. Comment, "The Regulation of Foreign Business in Mexico," op. cit., p. 384.

31. Castenada, op. cit., pp. 290, 294.

32. Ibid., pp. 288-294.

33. Epstein, "Business-Government Relations in Mexico: The Echeverria Challenge to the Existing Development Model," Case Western Reserve Journal of International Law, 12, pp. 525-526 (1980).

34. Debra L. Miller, "The Transformation of United States-Latin America technology transfer relations: The First Stage," in United States-Latin America Relations (Butterworths: London and Boston, 1982), pp. 173-176.

35. Note, "Mexico's Computer Decree: The Problem of Performance Requirements and a US Response," Law and Policy in International Business, 14, (1983), pp. 1172-1173.

36. "Mexico GATT Bid Called Bold Move," New York Times, December 9, 1985, p. D10.

37. Note, "Mexico's Computer Decree..." in Law and Policy in International Business, op. cit., p. 1172.

38. The same can be said for most Latin American regulation of direct foreign investment and technology transfer. See Miller, op. cit., pp. 188-190.

39. Bureau of Industries, Development Program for the manufacturing of electronic computer systems..., op. cit., p. 2

40. Ibid., pp. 10-11.

41. Interview with Josef Warman Grig, op. cit.

42. Computer decree, op. cit., p. 13, 23-25, 31-32, 34-35.

43. Ibid., pp. 32, 35.

44. Ibid., pp. 20-21 and "Addendum C," pp. 5-7.

45. Ibid.

46. Ibid., p. 20.

47. Miller, op. cit., p. 190.

48. Based on interviews with U.S. firm doing business in Mexico; see also "Symposium on Doing Business in Mexico: The Impact of its Financial Crisis," in International Lawyer, 18, 2 (Spring 1984).

49. Based on interviews with American managers of Xerox Corporation, November 1985.

50. Interview with Josef Warman Grig, op. cit.

51. "Mexico, in Reversal, to Let IBM Build and Own a Computer Plant," New York Times, July 24, 1985, pp. A1, D7.

52. Based on interviews with Josef Warman Grig, op. cit., and several U.S.-based computer firms.

53. Wallace y Associados, op. cit., p. 49.

54. "Mexico Eases Foreign Investment Rules but Investment Still May be Hard to Attract," Wall Street Journal, June 20, 1983, p. 31.

55. Based on interviews with one U.S.-based informatics firm in November 1985.

56. Based on interviews with Robert Radway, attorney, New York City, November 1985.

57. New York Times, July 24, 1985, op. cit., p. D7.

58. "IBM is Cleared to Build 100%-Owned Unit," Wall Street Journal, July 23, 1985.

59. Based on interviews with Mexican government officials, September 1985.

60. Based on interviews with industry sources, October 1985.

9

Taiwan

Denis Fred Simon
Massachusetts Institute of Technology
Chi Schive
National Taiwan University

INTRODUCTION

In 1979, Minister K.T. Li, the man considered to be the
principal architect of Taiwan's economic development, stated
that "the development of the information industry is a
worldwide trend, and Taiwan's economic future depends very
much on our ability to catch up with this trend."[1] One year
later, at a national conference on Taiwan's economy, a reso-
lution was passed calling for promotion of two so-called
"strategic industries," machinery and informatics. From
that time onward, the development of the informatics
industry has become a symbol for the island's economic
progress. As such, it has continued to occupy a central
position on the policy agenda of Taiwan's industrial and
technological leaders.[2]

The decision to emphasize development of an indigenous
informatics industry can be traced to two primary sources.
First, even though Taiwan has enjoyed a comfortable growth
rate of about 8.0 percent during the 1970s, the two oil crises (1973 and 1979) along with the two global recessions
have had a severe impact on the local economy. Strong
pressures for major cost reductions and greater production
efficiency were generated by both internal and external
sources. The increased application and integration of automation and information technologies in both manufacturing
facilities and the modern office have been viewed as one
effective means of responding to these pressures.

Second, by the end of the 1970s, Taiwan had reached a
point where more than half of its GNP was exported. Looking
into the future, however, it became clear that the world
market for some of the island's traditional products no
longer looked promising, particularly in such areas as

textiles and some segments of consumer electronics--where
increasing protectionism in the industrialized world and
growing competition made re-examination of the island's
development strategy a necessity. Additionally, some of
Taiwan's more immediate rivals, such as South Korea, seemed
poised to embark on a major move into new and more sophisticated product areas. Pressures for introducing similar
shifts in the focus of Taiwan industry began to emerge.
Newly emerging technologies such as informatics seemed to
hold great potential as a means of maintaining the island's
future competitive position in the global marketplace.[3]

This paper will examine the status and development of
the informatics industry in Taiwan. In section one we
discuss the characteristics of Taiwan's present development
strategy. We examine the broad economic and political context in which the development of informatics is taking
place. In section two, we focus on the current situation in
the industry with respect to overall output as well as product and market orientation. In section three we examine
the targets set by the industry and the efforts that are
underway to reach these targets. In section four, we focus
on the industrial policies put forth by the government to
facilitate the island's transition into higher technology
and higher value-added industries such as informatics. The
conclusion will then highlight some of the outstanding
issues that confront both business and government as they
attempt to stimulate expansion of this critical industry.

TAIWAN'S CURRENT DEVELOPMENT STRATEGY

Since the late 1970s, Taiwan has been embarked on a
development program designed to shift the economy away from
reliance on cheap, labor-intensive, low skill industries
towards development of both skill-intensive and knowledge-
intensive products and technologies.[4] A combination of
rising domestic labor costs and structural changes in the
world economy have necessitated this shift.[5] In particular,
Taiwan has been forced to expand exports of technology-
intensive goods as the Southeast Asian nations and China
have started to catch up with the island in the field of
light industrial products.

Government policy has been to use a variety of instruments to lay a foundation for the development of a series of
new critical industries. Depending on the circumstances,
the government has been willing to act as initiator, regula-
tor, strategic decision-maker, diffuser of technology and

entrepreneur--though in the last instance it has maintained a commitment to private sector predominance. Moreover, government officials of Taiwan have recognized that "policies to promote technological advance" can be just as important as the "technology policies" themselves. Their reliance on a broad mix of policy tools underlies their belief that activities in the technological sphere have as much to do with the nature of the economic environment and the structure of incentives and rewards.

In May 1978 a new "science and technology development plan" was formulated and passed by the Executive Yuan in May 1979. The plan laid out a development course for the island that entailed greater investment in research and development and education, industrial restructuring, and improved linkages between defense and civilian industries in high-technology fields. By 1982, a list of strategic industries was identified. These strategic industries were made eligible for a variety of tax incentives, preferential financing packages, and technological support.

The essential features of the island's new development strategy is its emphasis on these strategic industries (machinery and informatics), restraints on the expansion of energy-intensive industries, and program to modernize labor-intensive industries. This is to be accomplished through the acceleration of industrial technology development and application. The government has assumed a critical role by establishing a special commission to provide industrial guidance, expand funds for training and technological renovation, and implement a program of industrial consolidation and corporate mergers.[6]

In essence, the government has adopted a two-pronged strategy for meeting its technological needs. One major objective has been to expand and extend the island's interdependence with key actors in high-technology segments of the world economy. Through its use of various incentives designed to increase the attractiveness of the island as an investment site for advanced technology industries and as a source of high quality, sophisticated components, Taiwan is attempting to hurdle the technology gap that separates the advanced industrialized nations for most of the developing world.

The other major objective of the leadership is to strengthen the island's capacity for greater technological self-reliance. This is being accomplished by significant increases in R&D spending since the late 1970s as well as the government's willingness to absorb the financial costs of serving as the initial recipient of key priority tech-

nologies that must be purchased from abroad. As Simon has
noted, "imported technologies are to be used to break down
pockets of domestic technological stagnation and stimulate
development of indigenous science and technology
capabilities."[7]

The centerpiece of Taiwan's new development orientation
is the Hsinchu Science-Based Industry Park. The park was
created to act as a catalyst in Taiwan's efforts to move
into more technologically advanced industries. It was originally conceived in 1969 and developed with the assistance
of the National Science Council. The site of Hsinchu was
chosen because of its proximity to two of Taiwan's leading
science and engineering universities, National Chiao Tong
and Tsinghua. According to K.T. Li, the park should provide
the powerhouse for Taiwan's future development in much the
same way that the export processing zones created in the
mid-1960s helped spark the island's greatly successful
export-oriented phase of development.

Work on the park sparked a lively debate within
Taiwan's economic circles in the early 1970s as disagreement
arose over the initial orientation of the park. First,
there was a debate over basic versus applied research, with
the former giving way to the latter. Second, at that time,
many of Taiwan's economic leaders lumped "technology intensive" and "capital intensive" industries into one category.
The global energy crises, however, helped resolve the disagreement, allowing a clear distinction to be made between
these two sectors. With the onset of the 1980s, Taiwan
officials realized that their development objectives,
including employment and income distribution concerns, could
be better managed by focusing on skill-intensive industries.

By the end of 1984, 71 plants had been registered to
set up operations in the park, with 56 having operations
already underway. The key industries identified as investment priorities are information, communication, precision
instruments and machinery, special materials, and biotechnology.[8] The interesting aspect of the park is that it is
built around the presence of some of the world's leading
high technology firms in microelectronics, computers, etc.
On the other hand, the establishment of the park as well as
the broader commitment to high-technology development has
stimulated the return of large numbers of ethnic Chinese
scientific and technical personnel. By reversing the "brain
drain" problem of the past, Taiwan officials hope the influx
of returnees will serve as a pool of entrepreneurial as well
as engineering talent to support high technology industry.

Taiwan's decision is to rely mainly on imported tech-

nology to spearhead activities in the park. This approach
is viewed as part of a broader strategic consideration that
sees the island's comparative advantage not in basic R&D,
but in the ability to innovate, adapt, and improve
established technologies.[9] Overall, Taiwan's bargaining
position vis-a-vis technology transfer has steadily improved
as a result of several factors. First, the growing presence
of other high-technology firms reinforces the attractiveness
of the island as a site for manufacturing of specialized
components and final products. Second, there is an ample
supply of qualified technical personnel and engineers, some
of whom have been able to provide expert advice to the
government on a host of investment proposals and/or prospec-
tive licensing agreements. And third, the overall competence of the bureaucracy has improved due to its extensive
experience in interacting with foreign firms. The value of
this experience should not be underestimated since it goes a
long way toward explaining why Taiwan's counterparts on the
China mainland have had such difficulty in acquiring foreign
technology over the last several years.[10]

Generally speaking, the government sees the park as
bringing together foreign firms with local R&D organizations and the private sector. Several of the firms
operating in the park are 100% locally owned. The best
example of the coming together of these three actors is the
highly touted United Microelectronics Corporation (UMC).
The company, which received 25% of its initial start-up
capital from the Bank of Communications, a public bank for
industrial development, secured its know-how as a result of
a licensing agreement for integrated circuit technology that
was arranged between the government-sponsored Industrial
Technology Research Institute (ITRI) and RCA of the US.
Today, UMC, which presently manufactures ICs for use in
digital timepieces and calculators, is one of the largest IC
suppliers in Southeast Asia.[11] And, it recently has made
plans for a "reverse foreign investment" by signing an
agreement to establish a facility in northern California's
Silicon Valley.[12]

STATUS OF THE INFORMATION INDUSTRY IN TAIWAN

Roots of the Information Industry

In 1952, the first computer (IBM 650) was introduced in
Taiwan at National Chiao Tong University. This marked the
beginning of what in the 1980s would become one of the most

dynamic and progressive industries in Taiwan. In its for-
mative years, the industry amounted to no more than computer
software services, ranging from equipment rentals and maintenance to basic data processing. Even during the 1970s, in
spite of the fact that there were some locally-made monitors
being produced for export and there already was a domestic
electronics parts industry in place, the existing data, presented in Table 9.1, indicates that there was no local commercial production of computers and related products.

The big breakthrough in Taiwan's development of informatics came in 1980 when the production of minicomputers and
computer terminals began (See Table 9.2). Yet, the overall
output in terms of quantity and dollar value still remained
negligible. A year later, however, a local television manufacturer began to mass produce terminals, which achieved an
export value of US $4 million in that year. It also should
be noted that, during this same time period, production and
exports of other key products, such as minicomputers, disk
drives, and printers began as well. Thus, while a foundation may have been in place by the mid-1970s, Taiwan did
not actually move into the information industry until the
1980s--a fact that makes the present level of achievement
even more remarkable.

The market orientation of the information industry is
summarized in Table 9.3. In 1982, the industry had a total
output value of US $67.8 million, out of which 99.6% derived
from hardware sales. Ironically, while the production of
hardware was highly export-oriented, with an export ratio of
close to 94% and a dollar value of US $63.6 million, the
domestic market relied mainly on imports to meet demand.
Imports accounted for 97% of the market in 1982. The fact
that the industry was so export-oriented may seem quite surprising, but for those who have followed the development of
similar industries in Taiwan in the past, the results seem
quite consistent with previous experiences. In general, the
level of demand from local end-users remained small at this
time and did not offer much of an attraction from the perspective of those considering future investment.[13] On the
other hand, foreign firms saw Taiwan as a potential source
of low-cost components and specialized peripherals at an
early point in time, and thus the incentives for new entrants
to look outward were strong at the inception of the industry.

The growth rates of the information industry have been
quite impressive. In terms of exports, the average annual
growth rate between 1981-1984 was 278%. Obviously, part of
the reason for the tremendous rate of increase is due to the
small base from which it started. Yet, as Table 9.2 shows,

TABLE 9.1
Domestic Markets Sales, Production, and Exports
of the Informatics Industry

Unit: $ million (%)

	Domestic Market[1]	Local Supply (% of)	Domestic Production[2]	Exports[2]
1972	3.4	0	0	0
1979	19.7	0.0	0.1	0.1
1980	54.4	0.6	5.4	5.0
1981	65.8	0.6	14.3	13.9
1982	115.5	3	67.5	63.6

Source: Promotion of the Information Industry, the
First Stage Report
(Institute for the Information Industry, 1984)

Note: [1] Including software

[2] Excluding parts, including monitors

TABLE 9.2
Exports and Imports of Informatics Hardware 1980-1985
Unit: $ million (1,000 units)

Year	P.c. Exports	P.c. Imports	Terminals Exports	Terminals Imports	Disk Drives Exports	Disk Drives Imports	Printers Exports	Printers Imports	Total Exports	Monitors Exports	Parts Exports
1980	N.A.	N.A.	N.A.	8.2	N.A.	N.A.	N.A.	N.A.	N.A.		
1981	0.4	8.9	4.0	8.2	0.0	0.8	0.1	8.1	4.5	8.6	91.8
1982	2.0	13.1	12.8	11.7	0.4	2.7	4.6	11.2	19.8	33.6	95.6

Source: 1. Promotion of Information Industry, First Stage Report (Institute for the Information Industry, 1984).

2. United Daily News, April 19, 1985.

3. S.C. Ke, Technology and Administrative Control: A Case Study of Mini-Computer Industry (Draft)

Note: 1 For the first nine months only
2 For the first six months only
3 Estimated figures

TABLE 9.3
1989 Targets of the Informatics Industry
Unit: $ mil

Year	Domestic Production							Domestic Market (%)			
	Hardware			Software				Hardware		Software	
	Exports	Domestic Market	Total	Exports	Domestic Market	Total	Total	Imports	Total	Imports	Total
1982	63.6 (94.0)	3.9 (6.0)	67.5	0.3	0.0	0.3	67.8	112.0 (97.0)	115.5	7.0 (100.0)	7.0
1989	2,820.0 (72.0)	1,080.0 (28.0)	3,900.0	350.0 (50.0)	350.0	700.0	4,600.00	720.0 (40.0)	1,800.0	150.0 (30.0)	500.0
Annual Growth Rates (%)	72	123	78		55			30	48		84

Sources: Promotion of the Information Industry, the First Stage Report (III, 1984).

projections for 1985 are that total exports will reach
US $810 million, a considerable jump from the 1984 total of
US $326.8 million. In 1984, exports of information-related
equipment and components constituted 26.9% of total electronics exports. In this same year, electronics, for the first
time, replaced textiles as the island's leading export
industry. If present trends continue as projected, informatics will occupy an increasingly large portion of the
electronics industry as well as Taiwan's overall export mix.

The Commodity Structure of the Information Industry

The trade statistics shown in Table 9.2 present a clear
picture of the commodity structure of the informatics
industry on Taiwan. First, terminals have dominated the
industry's exports, accounting for two-thirds of the export
market until 1984. In 1985, however, it is projected that
the share of overall informatics exports accounted for by
terminals will drop to around 40%. The second major export
item is the personal computer, whose share of informatics
exports in 1985 is expected to be 35-40%. Two additional
items, disk drives and printers, are also expected to be
significant export earners, with projected export values of
US $100 million and US $80 million respectively.

While the relationship of the above products to the
information industry is quite clear, in some other areas
the distinction is much more cloudy. For example, in the
case of monitors and computer parts, it is difficult to
assess the dollar amounts of the output that are directly
associated with use in the information industry. Before
1982, these two items, which originally were developed in
the 1970s, accounted for a much larger quantity and value of
exports than the four above products. (See Table 9.2). In
1984, the total export value of monitors was US $318 million,
which was only slightly less than the total of export value
of terminals, personal computers, disk drives and printers,
combined--which amounted to US$326.8 million.

For 1985, the projected export target for monitors is
US$430 million. If one broadens the definition of the
information industry to include a larger range of related
electronics products and components, then the total export
value of informatics equalled US $1,005 million in 1984 and
will likely surpass US $1,700 million in 1985. By the first
quarter of 1985, informatics exports, broadly defined,
totalled US $322 million, an increase of 126% over last year,
suggesting that the target is well within reach.

The dominant position of monitors in the overall export mix of informatics products, especially in the 1980s, should not be a major surprise to those who have followed Taiwan's industrial and technological development over the last two decades. By the mid-1970s, Taiwan already had become a major producer of television sets. In 1979, exports of black & white TVs totalled 4.8 million units, while exports of color TVs reached 1.3 million sets. By 1984, total exports of color televisions was valued at US $400 million. In many respects, the monitor industry is, in fact, a part of the television industry. In a large number of cases, the monitors that are making inroads in foreign markets are being manufactured by current or former producers of television sets. As the market for black & white televisions began to shrink at home and abroad, producers looked to move quickly into feasible substitutes, of which the monitor was a readily available alternative.[14]

Product and Technology Development

Given the short history of the informatics industry in Taiwan, the general product and technology base has just begun to take shape. In addition, the nature of industrial organization has been mixed, with different roles being played by government, the private sector, and foreign-based actors. The experience of local firms entering the information industry reflects five different models of start-up and organization.

The first model is characterized by companies founded by people with first-hand experience in information technologies, who have taken the growing demand for informatics products as opportunity for starting their own businesses. For example, Multitech, a local computer based in the Hsinchu Science and Industry Park, was founded by a few university professors in 1976. The company's first products were not computers, but rather automation testing instruments for industrial use. In 1976, its first prototype computer was assembled; its main use was for educational purposes. Later on, after developing the sequential control language, the firm engaged in R&D related to computers and produced its first self-designed minicomputer for industrial use a few years later. In another case, when the government closed all television game playhouses in 1981, some television game manufacturers moved to assembling personal computers. This type of company is usually small and depends largely on the technical expertise of a few individuals.

Another group of companies became involved in the industry by marketing products for large foreign firms. After the company has been able to master some technical know-how, it has moved into product manufacturing. In some cases, a number of these firms were invited by their foreign partners to engage in such production. In most instances, these firms have maintained their links with foreign companies as a means to secure additional access to technology and market information.

A third group of companies was organized by large multi-national firms through foreign direct investment. Qume, for example, has terminated its production of disk drives in the US and moved its entire manufacturing line to Taiwan. Wang Laboratories also has a sizable venture in Taiwan both in manufacturing minicomputers and in local-based R&D. Generally, these foreign firms have preferred to retain 100% ownership in their investments. They see their business activities in Taiwan as a means to support their overall marketing and development activities for responding to changing demands and new technological opportunities.

A fourth category of companies got their start-up in response to initiatives on the part of the government. In an effort to encourage entry into particular product segments and technology areas, the government has been willing to absorb part of the start-up costs in terms of capital investment and, on occasion, by providing assistance in securing foreign technology and then diffusing it to local firms. In some cases, the government has been known to contribute as much as 50% of the paid-in capital. And, it has been satisfied with allowing these firms to maintain their status of privately-owned ventures. Such instances where these types of public-private interface take place usually involve large-scale efforts focused on the development of new, specialized technologies.

The last category of firms has been organized directly by large domestic firms who are anxious to expand their own product lines. Most of the technology has been acquired through licensing or other cooperation agreements with foreign firms. In some cases, these firms also have engaged in outward foreign direct investment in their dominant product areas--which may or may not have been outside of informatics. For example, a few years ago, a local cable and wire producer, the largest one in Taiwan, decided to set up an R&D laboratory in Silicon Valley in California. In early 1985, this same firm also established an integrated circuit plant, of which 15% of the capital was provided by the subsidiary in the form of specialized technical know-how.

Each of these different categories, however, is not
mutually exclusive. In 1984, three new "local" firms began
operations in the Hsinchu Park. One of the firms, the New
Development Corporation (NDC), which is a joint venture with
the China Development Corporation and ITRI, signed a five-
year contract with IBM to design and develop products for
that company. IBM will send out technical personnel to NDC
to assist with product research; it also agrees to purchase
all the products NDC turns out in both the microcomputer and
software areas. By engaging in such a venture, NDC hopes to
acquire new software development methodology while obtaining
the marketing channels of a large, highly successful multinational firm. In return, IBM hopes to be able to develop
hardware and software packages of satisfactory quality at a
fraction of the development cost in the US.

The level of technological advance in the informatics
industry has been appreciable, particularly in view of the
fact that just a few years ago, this industry did not even
exist on the island. Several major technological break-
throughs were made during 1984. For example, a 3.5 micrometer 64K CMOS D-RAM was developed in November 1984. Less
than 6 months later, the technology for a 1.5 micrometer
256K CMOS D-RAM was mastered. Only two other firms in the
world, Hitachi (Japan) and Intel (US) have been able to
develop this technology. In 1985 the government announced a
ten million Taiwan dollar program to enter the VLSI market
through the establishment of an advanced manufacturing
facility that will use foreign integrated circuits designs.
The next step is aimed at 1.0 micrometer 1024K chips. Also
in 1984, the first 16-bit personal computer was marketed.
Recently, Phillips Taiwan proposed production of 0.29 m.m.
high analytical color picture tubes in the future. The
significance of this announcement, however, was somewhat
tempered by the fact that a locally-based firm had already
been working on a similar product for some time.

Along with hardware development, Taiwan firms also have
paid close attention to software development. They recognize that without development of standardized software packages foreign firms will continue to have advantages in the
local market and Taiwan-made machines will not be able to
gain widespread acceptance in foreign markets. In this
regard, development of a new software package called "the
big five," including a Chinese language word processing
system, an electronic calculation sheet, a file management
system, a graphics system, and a communication system, has
been given support by the government and is scheduled to be
introduced into the local market by June 1985. The ability

to develop Chinese language software is a main attraction
for the growing foreign investments by foreign firms. Some
of the large multinationals such as HP and IBM wish to
further strengthen their competitive position in Asia by
gaining access to such specialized software packages.[15]

INDUSTRY TARGETS AND EFFORTS

In order to promote the development of the informatics
industry in Taiwan, the government has set up a series of
production and marketing targets over a ten-year period.
More specifically, the Council for Economic Planning and
Development under the Executive Yuan has worked with several
other organizations to develop a ten-year plan for the
industry. The current plan calls for the accomplishment of
five major tasks: 1) to increase the use of computers at all
levels of government organization; 2) to develop and manufacture minicomputer systems and selected peripherals; 3) to
establish software engineering capabilities; 4) to develop
an expanded base of trained personnel; and 5) to build an
electronics/information science and technology exhibition
center to serve as a central headquarters for the informatics and electronics industries.[16] The government hopes
to achieve these goals through several primary means:

a) popularization of the benefits of computers and
their applications in business and government;

b) identification of government-supported domestic
markets for informatics products to attract domestic
and foreign investments and to accelerate the accumulation of technical experience and managerial skills;

c) encouragement of more participation by foreign firms
in the overall development of the informatics industry;

d) improvement of organizational coordination and
planning.

By 1989, total output in the information industry is
projected to reach US $4.6 billion, of which US $3.9 billion
will be from hardware and US $0.7 million from software.
Total exports of hardware and software are slated to be
US $2,820 million and US $350 million respectively. Given
present rates of growth in information industry product output in other countries, Taiwan-made products should occupy

about 2.0% of the world market. To achieve these goals, the industry will have to attain an average annual growth rate between 1982-1989 of 78% (see Table 9.3).

These targets, however, will be difficult to achieve. There are both technological constraints and market barriers that will limit Taiwan's ability to obtain 2.0% of the world market. Nonetheless, one cannot discount the industry's potential. Output of informatics products on the hardware side has been increasing at a tremendous rate: 241% in 1983, 382% in 1984, and 148% in 1985. Thus, it is not inconceivable that the above projections could actually be achieved. The possibilities are also enhanced by the fact that Taiwan producers are often able to overcome their own limits in assessing exports markets by tying themselves closely to the needs of foreign firms from the US and Japan.[17]

In February 1982, a special government-sponsored task force under the Executive Yuan was set up to promote the growth of the informatics industry. Under the jurisdiction of the special task force are three government organizations at the ministry level and two non-profit ones (See Chart 9.1). It is the function of the task force to ensure that activities among these five units are well-coordinated and focused on the priority areas selected for the industry in the ten-year plan. In July of that same year, an implementation plan was announced, laying out 22 tasks in seven categories: manpower development, technology development, market development, government assistance, promotion of the public interest, encouragement of foreign investments, and modification of government procurement practices.

In terms of specific responsibilities, the two non-profit organizations play a critical role in research and development. The first organization, the Institute for the Information Industry (III), concentrates on software development. For example, the "big-five" project mentioned earlier was sponsored by the III. Founded in July 1979, the III is jointly supported by government, academic institutions, and private organizations. (There are 43 members on the Board of Trustees, 6 from government, 7 from academia, and 31 from the private sector.) Its main mission is software development, including providing advice and guidance to government and private organizations.

The other organization is the Industrial Technology and Research Institute (ITRI). As noted, ITRI is the largest R&D organization on the island. Within ITRI are several specialized institutes; the key one in the information industry is the Electronics Research and Service Organization

216

CHART 9.1
Organizations Promoting the Information Industry
Promotion Team for Information Industry

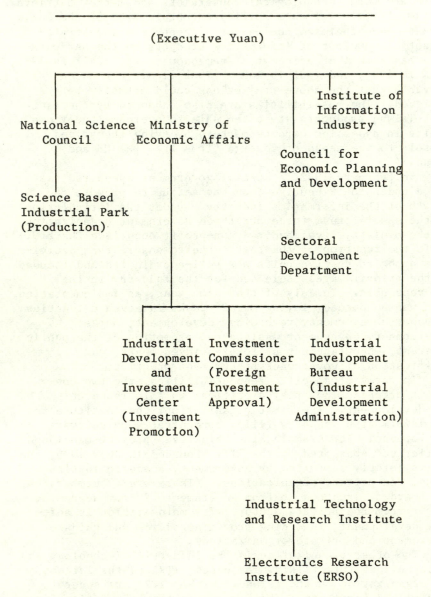

(Executive Yuan)

National Science   Ministry of   Institute of
   Council   Economic Affairs   Information
                                             Industry

                                          Council for
                                          Economic Planning
                                          and Development
Science Based
Industrial Park
(Production)
                                          Sectoral
                                          Development
                                          Department

              Industrial   Investment   Industrial
              Development   Commissioner   Development
              and   (Foreign   Bureau
              Investment   Investment   (Industrial
              Center   Approval)   Development
              (Investment   Administration)
              Promotion)

                            Industrial Technology
                            and Research Institute

                            Electronics Research
                            Institute (ERSO)

(ERSO). ERSO operates its own integrated circuit facility and a related subsidiary in the Hsinchu Science-Based Industry Park. Several of the critical innovations that have spearheaded the emergence of Taiwan's integrated circuit industry have come from within the ERSO laboratory.

As a knowledge-intensive industry, research and development play an important role vis-a-vis the development of new technology and products.[18] Total R&D expenditures for the information industry in 1979 were US $4.1 million, or 3.1% of Taiwan's total R&D expenditures during that year (See Table 9.4). By 1982, that amount increased to US $37.4 million, or 11.0% of the island's overall R&D spending (excluding defense). During 1982, the electronics industry spent approximately 1.10% of the industry's sales on R&D. Based on a recent sample of 26 firms in the informatics industry, however, spending on R&D averaged 3.3% of sales, reflecting the high degree of R&D intensity within that rapidly growing sector.[19] At the same time, Korean electronics firms spent 2.44% of sales on R&D in 1982, American firms spent 7.6% (1980), and Japanese firms spent 4.06% (1981).[20]

The pattern of growth in R&D spending in the information industry is consistent with the general increases in R&D expenditures over the last several years. In 1979, total R&D spending in Taiwan was US $133 million, or 0.42% of GNP, as shown in Table 9.5 By 1982, this amount increased to US $321 million, or 0.7% of GNP. The R&D/GNP ratio was aimed at 1.0% in 1984, and is expected to climb to 1.2% in 1985 and 2.0% in 1989. Given this trend, it is probbable that projections for R&D spending in the informatics industry will be met and that the informatics industry will continue to be the island's leading R&D industrial and technological target.

As a result of its designation as a "strategic industry," companies active in the informatics field are eligible for a special low-interest loans. If the firm's proposal includes one of the 150 selected priority projects chosen by the information industry task force, it can obtain funds at 2% below the regular long-term loan rates. So far, a total of US $3.75 million has been made available to domestic firms to support product development. Among the applicants, the electronics parts producers took the lion's share--25.73%--of the total funds. Informatics firms, including software producers, took another 10.5% from the pool. It is the government's intention to increase the size of this pool in order to encourage substantial increases in R&D and investment in both product and process technology.

218

TABLE 9.4
R&D of the Information Industry
$ million (%)

	1979	1982
Government	3.4 (83.9)	n.a.
Private	0.6 (16.1)	n.a.
Total	4.1 (100.0)	37.4
% of country total	3.1	11.0

Sources: 1. Development Planning of the Information Industry (CEPD, 1982).

2. Survey of Science and Technology Republic of China, 1982 (National Science Council, 1984).

TABLE 9.5
R&D of Republic of China
Unit: %

	1978	1979	1980	1981	1982	1984[1]	1985[1]	1989[1]
% of GNP	0.30	0.42	0.55	0.76	0.70	1.00	1.20	2.00
% from Private Sector	27.3	35.4	52.4	55.6	54.3	n.a.	n.a.	n.a.

Sources: 1. Survey of Science and Technology, Republic of China, 1982
              (National Science Council, 1984)

          2. Council for Economic Planning and Development

Note: 1 Target figures

Industrial Policies in the Information Industry

Along with the previously mentioned special organizations to promote the information industry and the availability of low-interest loans, there have been several other incentive packages that have been introduced to stimulate technological advances and new product development.

Tax Incentives. The latest revision of the Investment Encouragement Law, which was promulgated in December 1984, provides a very generous tax deduction for R&D spending. Under the prevailing statute, R&D expenses are totally deductible for the year in which they occurred, accelerated depreciation can be applied to instruments and equipment purchased for R&D, and machinery and equipment imported for R&D are exempt from import duties. Also, any firm may request a deduction in corporate income tax equivalent to 20% of the company's additional R&D spending above the previous 5-year peak—but no more than 50% of the total corporate income tax liability. Another tax incentive that is soon to be introduced is that no foreign firm will have to pay income tax on royalties paid by companies in selected industries, one of which is informatics.

Direct Foreign Investment (DFI). Direct foreign investment has made a significant contribution to Taiwan's export growth as well as the transfer of technology.[21] By the end of 1984, almost every major multinational firm involved in the electronics industry had a venture in Taiwan. US firms have been the dominant participants with some recent increase in activities occurring among companies from West Europe and Japan. Most of these firms have come to Taiwan in response to the quality of the skilled labor force as well as the cost of skilled labor. This stands in sharp contrast to the past when the cost and availability of unskilled labor for simple assembly operations was the principal attraction of Taiwan.

Within the context of the move towards more technology-intensive industries, Taiwan's policies towards foreign investment have undergone significant changes in emphasis since the mid-1970s. In general, while becoming more selective, the government has also attempted to remove much of the red-tape that was a frequent source of complaints among foreign businesses in the past. Taiwan officials have let it be known that even in sites such as the export processing zones, they no longer encourage labor-intensive investment projects, preferring instead investment proposals that bring new technology or products to the island. Improved capabilities in screening and evaluating foreign investment projects have gone a long way toward helping to ensure a better match between Taiwan's development needs and the objectives of the foreign firms.

In an effort to attract more foreign firms to come into Taiwan, a variety of policy changes have been introduced in the investment regulations governing foreign investment. First, the previous requirements regarding export commitments are gradually being dropped, with the expectation that they will be largely eliminated over the next few years. Second, foreign firms, along with domestic firms, will soon be eligible for the special low-interest loans mentioned previously in the paper. Given the fact that the interest rate on "preferential" long-term financing in Taiwan has generally been lower than that in most of the OECD countries, except for Japan and West Germany, the availability of these monies might prove to be a major investment incentive.

Other Related Policies. The Hsinchu Science-Based Industry Park offers an ideal set of incentives for potential investors in the informatics industry. A five-year tax holiday is offered--but under the present circumstances, the investor can choose to begin the holiday period at any time during the investment's first nine years of operation. Moreover, the park acts as a "technological hothouse," where high-tech firms can be situated in one strategic location. Thus, from the perspective of those in the informatics industry, the growth in the park and its facilities is viewed as a continued benefit, especially in terms of attracting competent personnel and receiving government support.

Relatedly, a venture capital market was set up a year ago in order to help capitalize entrepreneurs looking to start operations in high-technology fields. Three firms have been established so far. In addition, the domestic stock market was opened up to foreigners in 1984, thereby further strengthening the opportunities for progressive ventures to get underway. The government has also taken strong steps to respond to the problems of industrial counterfeiting, a problem which has discouraged some firms from bringing advanced portions of their production and R&D activities to the island.[22] Severe penalties have been introduced for those who violate the proprietary rights of other firms. An island-wide inspection agency for the information industry has been established in order to better ensure the sanctity of technology and know-how.

The government has also retreated from its generally protective stance regarding the development of new, emerging

222

industries. As a result of the encouragement of several
progressive government officials, a decision was made over
the last several years to relax some of the previous
restrictions and heavy duties on imports. Government officials hope that the growing presence of foreign products
will help generate sufficient competition for overly
complacent local firms, thus stimulating them to pay more
attention to R&D, product design, marketing, cost, etc.

PROSPECTS AND CONCLUSIONS

      Recognizing that the informatics industry represents
the technological wave of the future, Taiwan authorities
have made a concerted effort to establish both a technological and manufacturing base for the industry on the
island. In order to accomplish this goal, they have
designated the information industry as one of the island's
strategic sectors and have provided a host of incentives to
present and potential entrants. In addition, through the
establishment of organizations such as the III, the government has created an institutional framework for better coordinating the activities of both public and private actors.
These actions all serve to reinforce the critical role
played by the state in developing this high-priority
industry.
      At the same time, it must also be recognized that the
government on Taiwan has not chosen to establish a public
enterprise in this field, though the public sector plays a
dominant role in the energy and several other heavy
industries, e.g. steel, shipbuilding, etc. Instead, its ongoing strategy has been to absorb some of the start-up costs
for the industry as a whole, thereby reducing, and in some
cases alleviating, the investment risks for the private
sector. The government has provided substantial amounts of
capital to facilitate the emergence of new enterprises in a
number of key product lines, but it has always remained
careful to leave the management to the private sector. Past
experience has taught Taiwan officials that in order to
develop a globally competitive industry, the quality and
standards of the products as well as their overall cost
structure must be judged first and foremost by the requirements of the market.
      The ability of the industry to produce computer-related
equipment has improved over the last few years, largely in
the medium-technology end of the spectrum. Moreover, Taiwan
has moved into the development of some frontier technologies

and products. Yet, mass production of these items has been carefully considered before moving forward. Instead of seeking to compete head on with firms from the industrialized nations, Taiwan has pursued a market niche strategy, seeking out specialized segments of the informatics market where it can develop a secure but competitive advantage. This has meant that producers have concentrated on specialized peripherals and related items as well as serving as OEMs for some of the leading multinationals from Japan, the US, and Western Europe. In this regard, the state also has played a critical role in structuring the relationships between the local economy and the large foreign firms, minimizing potential "damage" to local industry and facilitating the transfer and diffusion of technology.

The current success of the industry can be attributed, in large part, to the strong televison and electronics parts industries that were created during the late 1960s and 1970s. Production of monitors, terminals, and components such as semiconductors share many of the same technological skills and manufacturing requirements that had been mastered earlier. In addition, once established as reliable producers and plugged into active market channels, some firms found it easy to make the transition into these other product lines, especially since they were supported in their efforts by foreign firms.

Also, this paper has focused on the civilian dimensions of the information industry, ignoring the important role played by the military in providing funds for R&D and stimulating technological advance. In Taiwan, the military has become a major user of advanced informatics products and components. And, in the future, demands for such advanced products will likely increase, especially since there is a strong effort underway to promote stronger links between the civilian and defense industry. Software development appears to be the primary area where activity will increase at the fastest rate. As such, in addition to responding to foreign market demands and internal demands of a civilian nature, we may also see defense needs playing an even larger role in pushing out the existing technological capabilities of the industry.

Of course, the development of the informatics industry has not proceeded without problems. In spite of the rapid growth of the industry, in some respects, the strong technological and economic base that is needed to support the industry has not evolved to the extent desired by top government leaders. The implementation of the Statute for the Encouragement of Investment has not always been well-

coordinated with the development of the informatics industry,
at times hindering broad scale computer development and
applications. Also, private sector investments in R&D continue to lag--a pattern that has been typical of many Taiwan
companies in other industries in the past. There also have
been difficulties interpreting the various aspects of the
tax incentives for R&D-related activities, especially since
it is hard to define R&D and to make accurate determinations
about the end-use of imported equipment. And, on several
occasions, financial assistance for various projects has
been slow to materialize because in R&D-intensive sectors,
calculating precise returns on investment is frequently
problematic.

This litany of problems might lead one to suggest that
the difficulties have out-weighed the level of progress, but
this is not the case. The movement into high-tech industries
such as informatics represents a great challenge to both the
government and private business due to the complexity of the
problems, the broad scope of the sub-sectors and technologies involved, and the need for a high degree of coordination, cooperation, and competition. And, in spite of
the problems with "pirating," the current shift towards
skill-intensive and knowledge-intensive industries has continued to receive strong support from the foreign business
community. Informatics has become Taiwan's industry of the
future--as Minister K.T. Li suggested it should. The
challenges ahead will be to ensure more consistent implementation of government policies and to maintain the momentum
that has appeared since 1980. These will not be easy tasks,
particularly as the informatics industry becomes more competitive on a global basis. Nonetheless, the prospects
appear bright as Taiwan officials have tried to give each of
the key actors--governnment organizations, private sector
companies, and foreign firms--a vested interest in the success of the effort.

NOTES

1. K.T. Li, "Targets and Strategies for Developing the
Information Industry in the Republic of China," December 17,
1979.
2. For an overview of the key dimensions of the
information industry in general see Michael Dertouzos and
Joel Moses, eds., The Computer Age: A Twenty Year View
(Cambridge: MIT Press, 1980).

3. This theme is developed in Denis Fred Simon, Taiwan, Technology Transfer and Transnationalism: The Political Management of Dependency (Boulder: Westview Press, forthcoming).

4. Japan Economic Journal, November 15, 1983, p.5.

5. Chao Yao-tung, former Minister of Economic Affairs, attributed Taiwan's economic problems and inefficiencies in the 1970s to a) subsidization of domestic oil prices during the 1973 oil crisis, b) the low level of indigenous technological development, c) deficiencies in modern management, d) outdated government regulations, and e) lack of proper entrepreneurial spirit. China Post, March 23, 1983, p.10.

6. The reasons for the emphasis placed on industrial consolidation were: 1) Taiwan economic planners and administrators viewed the large number of small and medium size enterprises as a disadvantage as the island attempted to improve productivity and generate greater efficiency through economies of scale; and 2) after Taiwan had gone through two recessions in the 1970s, a smooth process for corporate mergers was viewed as a vital ingredient for facilitating needed economic adjustments. However, at the time, the existing tax laws actually discouraged corporate mergers. The current program, to a large extent, is designed to relax such unfavorable factors.

7. Denis Fred Simon, "Chinese-Style S&T Modernization: A Comparison of PRC and Taiwan Approaches," Studies in Comparative Communism, Volume 17, Number 2, Summer 1984, p. 91.

8. Of the 56 firms already in the park, 38 are involved in electronics and informatics, 9 in precision instruments, 6 in special materials, 2 in biotechnology, and one in computer services.

9. Science Bulletin, National Science Council, Taipei, Volume 16, Number 4, April 1984.

10. Taiwan's overall success regarding the acquisition of foreign technology is best exemplified by the performance of its petrochemicals industry, e.g. Formosa Plastics, as well as the achievements of such firms as Tatung and Sampo in the electronics industry. Of course, there have been exceptions due to poor planning or inadequate evaluation, resulting in very little actual technology transfer. Most observers within and outside Taiwan would agree, however, that these cases are in the minority.

11. Free China Review, December 1982.

12. Taiwan Industrial Panorama, Volume 12, Number 1, November 1, 1984.

13. It also must be recognized that, in many cases, local producers could not produce the type of sophisticated

equipment that was desired.

14. Taiwan's ability to expand exports of monitors can be attributed to several factors: a) increases in local content from 40-60%; b) sharp competition between Japan and the U.S. that has driven American firms to switch their CRT production sites to Taiwan; and c) growing technological capabilities. In addition, demand for CRT terminals is expected to grow over the next several years.

15. Science Bulletin, National Science Council, Taipei, Volume 16, Number 6, June 1984.

16. The Current Development of the Software Industry in Taiwan, ROC, Institute for Information Industry, Taipei, November 1982.

17. One of the critical weaknesses of the Taiwan economy has been its dependence on foreign firms, especially trading companies from Japan, for discovering emerging market opportunities. Government efforts have been underway to establish several large trading firms, similar in structure and orientation to those from Japan, in order to gain more autonomy in dealing with the marketing of locally-produced items.

18. "The Republic of China's 4-Year Plan: R&D in Science and Technology," Industry of Free China, Volume LIX, Number 5, May 1983, pp. 21-36.

19. S.C. Ke, Technology and Administrative Control: A Case Study of the Minicomputer Industry (Draft).

20. For Taiwan, the next three major areas of high R&D expenditure (1982) are automation--U.S.$26.3 million, special materials--U.S.$21.1 million, and energy--U.S.$14.2 million.

21. Gustav Ranis and Chi Schive, "Foreign Investment and Taiwan's Economic Development," in Walter Galenson, ed., Trade and Investment in Asian Countries (Madison: University of Wisconsin Press, forthcoming).

22. IBM is one firm that has experienced severe problems with respect to alleged counterfeiting of its products and technology by Taiwan firms. Asian Wall Street Journal Weekly, October 22, 1984.

10

U.S. National Policies for High Technology Industries: Some Lessons Learned

Aaron Gellman
Gellman Research Associates

All nations -- developed and developing -- have a body of programs and goals which combine to produce, implicitly or explicitly, an "industrial policy." In some nations (e.g., Japan), industrial policies are explicit (though less today than historically); in other countries (e.g., the United States) it is frequently denied that there is a "national industrial policy." In these cases, industrial policy is a montage of those laws, practices, mandates and restrictions through which governments influence industries and industrial development. In these circumstances, scholars and politicians find it difficult to agree on what actually constitutes national "industrial policy." But this often-emotional debate will not be considered in this paper. Rather the concept of "industrial policy" will be the focus, and some of the "lessons learned" by the United States, historically and currently, will be discussed.

First, industrial policy, one way or another, always includes the "picking of winners"; implicitly, this designates losers as well. It is seldom pointed out that such an exercise -- especially the "picking of losers" -- has sometimes become self-fulfilling prophesy, especially if the government puts enough chips on the winners and few or none on the losers.

A second attribute of most industrial policies is to emphasize the critical importance of economies of scale in manufacturing and distribution. Consequently, they invariably stress export markets for those industries the policy is intended to favor. (Sometimes there is even a statement that those industries which are not to be advanced have too few export opportunities to enable them to reach or maintain satisfactory scale.)

   With regard to these aspects of industrial policy, poli-
ticization of the process becomes an important consideration. In a government system such as that of the
United States, the political forces playing upon the scene
at any given time can induce untended and even wrong
results. Politics is people-intensive and while the
creation of jobs during times of less than "full" employment
is both highly desirable and politically attractive, the
abolition of jobs is never good politics. Yet, far-seeing
industrial policy sometimes requires restructuring of a
nation's industry if such a policy is to produce the desired
results.

   Partially because it is a political process, the
establishment, revision and execution of national industrial
policy inevitably invites a pork barrel approach. That is,
politicians tend to trade off what is beneficial to each
other in a narrow sense so that they can show something to
the home folks. This inevitably leads to the selection of
too many winners (either explicitly or implicitly) and the
failure to designate sufficient losers. One result can be
industrial development stagnation, often manifest in
regional, if not national, terms.

   Explicit industrial policy in a nation such as the
United States almost certainly must end in excessive
boosting of losers. Most often losers will be subsidized by
federal taxpayers, either directly or indirectly, so that
the losers appear not to be losers -- at least in the short
run. Misallocation of resources is the inevitable result.
These are the unavoidable costs of explicit industrial
policy in a country with a substantial quantum of politically democratic institutions.

   In the long run, then, a nation insistent upon adopting
and carrying out an explicit industrial policy can suffer a
slowing of its technological advance manifest both in the
production of science outcomes and in diminished innovation
propensities. This is especially the case in the United
States where the effect upon small business must be negative. Even if the selected winner-industries provide opportunities for small business establishment and development,
the preservation of losers rarely favors them. U.S. small
business is generally not well organized in a political
sense and, for a given industry that is not likely to
display dramatic growth, small entrepreneurial units may not
represent very large employment, even in the aggregate.

   Many "industrial policy" debates in the political arena
focus upon "high-technology." In the context of public
policy, the term "high-technology" generally refers to those
activities which are to be supported and prized in contrast

to those activities which are not. Put another way, the
phrase is loaded with political meaning even while it has
little precision in terms of the scientific or technical
content of the output of those firms and industries to which
the description is applied. The description "high-
technology" is loaded with implications far beyond the words
themselves.

For example, should an industry or a firm described as
"high-tech" today still be referred to in the same way if it
continues to run out substantially the same product or service in substantially the same way 20 years later? Most
agree that technical advance is a necessary condition for
the designation "high-tech," but if all sorts of benefits
attend the designation, the firm or industry so described at
one time will resist its subsequent "removal," especially by
the government in the context of its "industrial policy."
Such benefits typically include:

- a higher multiple on common stock;
- capital rationing in favor of such firms and
  industries;
- favorable treatment in export finance,
  especially by government agencies (e.g., the
  U.S. Export-Import Bank);
- a relatively large labor supply and pool of
  management talent (e.g., MBA graduates);
- other explicit benefits growing out of any
  generally pro-high-tech public policy (e.g.,
  R&D tax credits).

Partially because of these connotations, a preferable
concept is the technology-intensity of a firm or industry
rather than the "high-ness" of its technology base.
Further, the gauge of the intensity of technology of an
industry or company can be found in the marketplace. That
is, if the market is for automobiles, the firm or industry
or nation which produces automobiles employing technology in
the most productive way in that market has a greater technological intensity than firms and industries and nations
where automobiles are manufactured in other ways. It is the
marketplace that determines the value of the technological
processes and content of a given product or service. For
public policy formulation and monitoring, no other yardstick
has proven as valid and useful as that provided by the
marketplace.

The United States has probably suffered considerable
costs from a general misunderstanding of the concepts of
high and low technology for several decades. For example,
in about 1950, automobile manufacture in the United States

was designated as "high technology" even though there were
firms both in Europe and Japan beginning to outdistance the
United States in both process and product-embodied innovation. At the same time, the U.S. government (primarily the
Department of Commerce) designated agriculture in the United
States as "low technology" despite the fact that the agri-
cultural sector of the United States was producing with far
greater technological intensity than that of any other
nation in the world. Some of the public policies towards
industry that have ill-served the United States can be
traced directly to this inappropriate way in which technology has been viewed by the U.S. government since about
1950.

Another concept useful in formulating public and
national policies towards industry is "wide technology".
Technologically "wide" industries (and firms) are those
which take a relatively high proportion of their inputs from
technology-intensive sources. The ultimate wide-technology
activity today may well be the assembly of spacecraft. A
more ubiquitous example is manufacture of large transport
aircraft such as the Boeing 757 and 767, the just-launched
McDonnell-Douglas MD-11, and the Airbus A-320.

National policies towards technology-intensive
industries emerge in various ways. In Japan, for example,
one current policy of the government is to discourage long-
term investment in those industries that, to survive and
prosper, must bear heavy costs related to the logistics of
imported raw materials and components and to exported final
products. For example, shipbuilding and steelmaking in
Japan are being reduced dramatically and it will not be long
before it is clear that the Japanese do not expect to export
substantial numbers of automobiles much beyond the turn of
the century.

Fundamentally, this suggests other places for the
deployment of resources have to be found if the country is
to continue to prosper. This means increased emphasis on
such technology-intensive products as computers, phar-
maceuticals, biologicals, and electronics. But not
exclusively, for other industries will also be favored that
are not "high-technology." One of the latter is the
cosmetics industry which, in Japan, requires few imported
raw materials and needs little transportation to distribute
its products throughout the world.

A more direct policy towards technology-intensive
industries is manifest in the provision of test facilities
by the public sector to the private sector -- often at an
explicit cost to the latter. In the United States, the
National Aeronautics and Space Administration (NASA) serves

as an excellent case in point. Among other things, this agency has made facilities available to U.S. aviation and aerospace industries which, in many cases, could not have been justified by any single firm or even small groups of them.

Failures also tell much about the effectiveness of this kind of public policy towards industry. The U.S. Federal Railroad Administration committed substantial public funds to the establishment and operation of a railroad test track in Colorado to promote railroad transportation in the United States. Unfortunately, there was virtually no demand by industry for use of the facility. Industrial policy incorporating the provision of test facilities is only effective if the private sector responds.

Government sponsorship of basic research and even of development is sometimes explicit and at other times implicit. For example, Industrial Research and Development (IR&D) funding accompanies many government procurement contracts as a matter of policy. In this way, and others, the U.S. government manifests its general program of encouraging the founding, growth and development of industrial activities which are technology-intensive.

A step -- but a large step -- removed from government performance or sponsorship of research or development is government action to encourage cooperative research among private firms. This is a policy issue presently of the first magnitude. Again contrasting Japan and the United States, Japanese firms which otherwise compete in final-product markets are encouraged -- some say required -- to cooperate in applied research and often development. The firms which resist the Japanese government in this respect stand out as exceptions. Sony for its first several decades was a case in point and Honda continues to be. But the rarity of the exceptions underscores the power of the policy. Such governmentally encouraged efforts on behalf of the computer industry in Japan -- the Fifth Generation Computer Development Program -- sparked the formation of the first broad scale post-war industrial cooperative R&D activity in the United States, the Microelectronics and Computer Technology Corporation (MCC). Enthusiasts for MCC, and those recognizing the threat that Japanese policy towards industrial cooperation represented, pressed for the development and passage of the National Cooperative Research Act of 1984, a more explicit element of U.S. industrial policy than commonly thought.

The public policy rationale for both government research support and cooperative research ventures (CRVs) are

232

strikingly similar: both promote competition rather than
thwart it.   Each supports competitiveness in domestic and
world markets.   Such activities also recognize the
appropriability problem with regard to research and development.   Usually there is some positive contribution to
national defense although this may not be the explicit
thrust of the activities permitted or promoted.   Finally,
all such research and development efforts are carried out
under the assumption that the social benefits outweigh the
social costs incurred.

Public policy towards technology-intensive industries
and firms is also manifested in the manner in which governments themselves purchase products and services.   In too
many instances, government policy reflected in this way is
not very effective.   For example, with rare exceptions,
those agencies of the U.S. government which most routinely
require state-of-the-art technology and techniques often
approach procurement in ways that bias the system strongly
in favor of larger enterprises.   This is so, despite the
fact that it is smaller firms that have demonstrated
greatest ability to be innovative and to produce path-
breaking scientific and technological achievements.

A principal way in which government fails to support
technological innovation is through its heavy reliance on
design specifications rather than performance specifications
as a basis for purchasing goods and services.   Performance
specifications provide far more options from which to
choose.   They also heighten competition among firms of all
sizes.   By providing the government with more for its money
while also serving national interests in promoting competitiveness in foreign markets, this technique has much to
recommend it.

Government also plays an important role with regard to
the standardization of products and processes.   In the
United States, the National Bureau of Standards was
established in recognition of this role.   But current
government policy seems to deny the importance of standardization in encouraging the advance of science and technology in various fields.   The principal points to be
recognized are: standardization should support and promote
technological advance and market competition.   Among other
things, this means that standards must be reviewed at
appropriate intervals to make sure they are not frozen for
long periods.   "Out-of-date" standards discourage innovation
and subvert a standardization process intended to promote
innovative activity.

Second, there needs to be recognition of the difference
between de facto and de jure standards.   The computer field

is a case in point. IBM has been so dominant in the world
marketplace that, without a formal standardization process,
it has been able to establish standards to which others in
the industry adhere for the sake of their own business
growth and development. While this has negative connotations, it also has positive ones. For example, IBM's
ability to make standards stick on a de facto basis has
helped the U.S. computer industry overall, especially in
international markets. One of the concerns of public policy
in the United States, therefore, ought to be the extent to
which IBM's ability to set de facto standards is jeopardized
by the growing aggregate participation of Japanese firms in
markets which IBM previously dominated. Such areas as plug
design and component compatibility are important examples.
To lose such de facto standard-setting power to the
Japanese would be a grave blow for the U.S. computer
industry, which U.S. government policy clearly does not
acknowledge.

Another important area of government involvement relates
to data and information, scientific and technical information (STI) as well as industrial analyses. The value of
timely dissemination of data and information is extremely
high and considerable public resources should be devoted to
such activities. There should also be government recognition that industrial and economic data are important to
efficient and timely allocation of resources to and within
industries and that favorable benefit-cost relationships
justify devoting considerable efforts to assuring that such
data and information are readily available to all.

In the related issue of international flows of data and
information, the United States would be well-advised to take
strong positions to assure that international flows of STI
and other relevant data are unimpaired. Persuasive arguments can be mounted as to the benefits of unrestricted
international flows of data and information to all countries
and to the world as a whole. Failure to recognize the value
of these benefits is the basis for undue restrictions on
international flows of information in many cases.

Education, as related to technology-intensive industry
is another important consideration. Scientists and engineers would gain from more education about the uses of
science and engineering outcomes than is currently
available. The process of innovation, for example, is only
infrequently considered in engineering undergraduate and
graduate schools. This is a severe handicap on the ability
of a nation to perform at the level of its potential with
respect to the exploitation of science and technological

possibilities. Further, secondary school education about
the process of innovation and what constitutes efficient
applications of science and technology to economic development and welfare should be seriously considered, as well as
relevant courses for all students at university and graduate
levels.

Increasingly, and regretably, decisions about the applications of science and technology have become political ones
in almost all nations. Informed citizens are increasingly
the important determinants of national views on the value of
science and technology and of national policies towards the
application of these resources.

Government-industry-university cooperation is a final
important consideration. The Strategic Defense Initiative
(SDI) now being proposed by the United States represents
very wide technology, and, as such, should encourage a great
deal of useful cross-institutional cooperation at the
national level. Attempts to make the initiative an international cooperative venture also have the potential of
generating substantial benefits. For one reason, it represents international cooperation on a scale far larger than
any that has gone before.

Cooperative initiatives are also emerging in the United
States with regard to technological and industrial development at other than the national or international level.
Through the recently formed Midwest Technology Development
Institute (MTDI), a group of states and their industrial
leaders are seeking to use technological advance and
exploitation as a means of meeting regional economic growth
and employment goals.

Cooperation among institutions -- large and small,
public and private, domestic and international -- today
holds enormous promise for advancing the long-run economic
fortunes of the United States and many other nations. Of
course, effective public policy should encourage cooperation
only up to the point where further joint activities produce
anticompetitive effects. But most U.S. industries today are
far from restraint-on-competition limits. Cooperative
undertakings in science and technology therefore represent a
relatively "new" element of "industrial policy" with high
potential.

In conclusion, political institutions, industry structure, public awareness of the value of science and technology, relationships among national, regional, and local
authorities, information flows, and procurement regulations
all play roles in the design, implementation, and effects of
national policy to advance industrial development. The

United States is not unique in this regard, and these
"lessons learned" are, at the least, worth exploration by
other countries throughout the world.

Appendix A:
Agenda

"National Policies for Developing High Technology
    Industries: International Comparisons"

September 12, 1985
    Morning Session - 9:30-12:15

    Welcoming Remarks:
        Carole Ganz Brown   9:30 AM
            Division of International Programs
            National Science Foundation
        Francis W. Rushing
            SRI International
            Georgia State University

    Symposium Moderator:
        Henry Nau
            George Washington University

Country Studies: Findings and Discussion   10:00-12:15

    Studies Analyze:

    1. size and shape of informatics industry in
        these countries

    2. government policy to influence indigenous
        technology development

    3. impact of government policies on the infor-
        matics industry in particular, and more
        generally on the growth potential of the
        country

    Brazil Claudio Frischtak   Gil Coutinho
            The World Bank   Catholic University

    Mexico Debra Lynn Miller
            Barnard College
            Columbia University

    India   Amar Gupta
            Massachusetts Institute of Technology

Discussion of Developing Country Findings in the Context
of Industrialized Countries

    Japan   Michael Borrus and
                   John Zysman
                   University of California at Berkeley

    France   Ronald Brickman
                   Vanderbilt University

Lunch - 12:15-1:00

Session II - 1:00-5:00

Country Studies: Findings and Discussion

    Korea   Joseph S. Chung
                   Illinois Institute of Technology

    Taiwan   Denis Fred Simon
                   Massachusetts Institute of Technology
                       and
                   Chi Schive
                   National Taiwan University

Discussion of Developing Country Findings in the Context
of Industrialized Countries

    United States Aaron Gellman
                   Gellman Research Associates

Open Discussion on Cases, Authors and Symposium
Attendees

Reception for Symposium Participants and Invitees
    5:00-7:00

September 13, 1985

Session III — 9:00–12:00

Round Table Discussion

What are the major policy issues and conclusions we have learned from these case studies?

What are the possible modes and programs of cooperation in which these countries can work together to resolve outstanding issues and problems?

What are future research objectives in this area?

Adjourn — 12:00 noon

Appendix B:
Symposium Attendees,
September 12-13, 1985

Catherine P. Ailes
SRI International
Arlington, Virginia 22209

Albey Alpern
Chamber of Commerce of the
     United States
Washington, D.C. 20062

Julia Bender
CBEMA
Washington, D.C. 20001

Michael Borrus
BRIE/IIS
University of California/
     Berkeley
Berkeley, California 94720

Ronald Brickman
Vanderbilt University
Nashville, Tennessee 37203

Carole Ganz Brown
National Science Foundation
Washington, D.C. 20550

Wolfe Bruckemann
Chamber of Commerce of the
     United States
Washington, D.C. 20062

Judith Bruckman
AT&T International
Basking Ridge, NJ 07920

Sushil Chatterji
National Computer Board of
     Singapore
Cambridge, MA 02138

Dimas Chavez
National Science
     Foundation
Washington, D.C. 20550

Joseph S. Chung
Illinois Institute of
     Technology
Chicago, IL 60616

Gil Costillo Branco
     Coutinho
Catholic University
Rio de Janeiro, Brazil

Sheila Devi
Department of Commerce
Washington, D.C. 20230

Claudio Frischtak
The World Bank
Washington, D.C. 20433

Arnold Frutkin
Burroughs Corporation
Detroit, Michigan 48232

Aaron Gellman
Gellman Research Associates
Jenkintown, PA 19046

Arthur Gerstenfeld
Worchester Polytechnic Institute
Worchester, MA 01609

Amar Gupta
Massachusetts Institute of
    Technology
Cambridge, MA 02139

Patricia Hanigan
Department of Commerce
Washington, D.C. 22030

Peter Hanley
Hewlett Packard Company
Palo Alto, CA 94304

Eduardo M. Hosannah
Embassy of Brazil
Washington, D.C. 20008

Kaname Ikeda
Embassy of Japan
Washington, D.C. 20008

Peggy Kehshishian
Department of Commerce
Washington, D.C. 20230

Sheila Kern
Motorola, Inc.
Washington, D.C. 20006

Kyung-Ki Kim
The World Bank
Washington, D.C. 20433

Alison Lippa
Chamber of Commerce of the
    United States
Washington, D.C. 20062

George K. C. Liu
Coordination Council for
    North American
    Affairs Office in
    U.S.A.
Washington, D.C. 20008

General Walter Lotz
SRI International
Arlington, VA 22209

Keith L. Miceli
Chamber of Commerce of the
    United States
Washington, D.C. 20062

Debra Lynn Miller
Barnard College
Columbia University
New York, NY 10027

Henry Nau
George Washington
    University
Washington, D.C. 20052

Charles Puttkammer
India International
Washington, D.C. 20006

John Rist
IBM World Trade Americas/
    Far East Corporation
North Tarrytown, NY 10591

Francis W. Rushing
Georgia State University
Atlanta, GA 30303
    and
SRI International
Arlington, VA 22209

William C. Salmon
Department of State
Washington, D.C. 20520

Ricardo A. C. Saur
Asociacao Brasileira da
    Industria dos Componentes
    Perifericos
Rio de Janeiro, Brazil

Duane Shelton
NSF/PRA
Washington, D.C. 20550

Denis Fred Simon
Massachusetts Institute of
    Technology
Cambridge, MA 02139

Francisco Sousa
CACI-Federal
Arlington, VA 22209

Ronald A. Spinek
Digital Equipment Corp.
Acton, MA   01720

Charles Wallace
National Science
    Foundation
Washington, D.C. 20550

Josef Warman Grig
SECOFIN
06700 Mexico, D.F.

Deborah Wince
Office of Science and
    Technology Policy
Washington, D.C. 20506

Pamela Young
Honeywell, Inc.
Washington, D.C. 20036

John Zysman
BRIE/IIS
University of California/
    Berkeley
Berkeley, CA 94720

About the Contributors

RONALD J. BRICKMAN is Associate Professor in the Owen
Graduate School of Management at Vanderbilt University.
Dr. Brickman was a fellow at the Hoover Institution and the
American Enterprise Institute for Public Policy Research.
His research includes science and technology policy in both
the United States and Europe, particularly France.
Dr. Brickman has coauthored a forthcoming book Controlling
Chemicals; The Politics of Regulation in Europe and the
United States.

CAROLE GANZ BROWN is Senior Program Manager for Studies and
Assessments at the Division of International Programs,
National Science Foundation. Dr. Brown's responsibilities
center on assessments of world-wide S & T capabilities, analyses of international S & T policy issues, and comparisons
between U.S. and foreign research systems. In 1983-84, on
loan from the National Science Foundation to the Science
Office, U.S. Embassy, Brasilia, she consulted on U.S.-
Brazil technology-trade issues. Recent publications
include, "Setting Research Priorities: The Intellectual
Structure of the Discipline," "The Technological Relevance
of Basic Research," and "Manufacturing Technology:
Perspectives in the United States and Abroad."

MICHAEL GLEN BORRUS holds a J.D. with honors from Harvard
University and masters degree in Political Science. Dr.
Borrus is currently the Deputy Director of the Berkeley
Roundtable on International Economy (BRIE) at the University
of California, Berkeley, and has served as consultant to the
U.S. Congress, U.S. Department of Commerce, and several private high-technology firms. He has written on high-
technology industries including computers and
telecommunications.

JOSEPH S. CHUNG is Professor of Economics at the Illinois
Institute of Technology where he has served as chairman of
the Department of Economics and Finance. Dr. Chung has been

a consultant to the Hoover Institution, Rand Corporation,
and federal government agencies. He was a Fulbright lec-
turer in Korea and has written on economic development in
Korea and technology transfer.

CLAUDIO R. FRISCHTAK completed his Ph.D. in Economics at
Stanford University. He is currently an Industrial
Economist in the Industrial Strategy and Policy Division at
the World Bank. He has taught at both U.S. and Brazilian
institutions. Dr. Frischtak has co-edited a book with
Nathan Rosenberg entitled The International Technology
Transfer: Concepts, Measures and Comparisons.

AARON J. GELLMAN, a Ph.D. in Economics, is President of
Gellman Research Associates and Adjunct Professor of
Transportation and Regional Science at the University of
Pennsylvania. He has served as consultant to both private
firms and federal government agencies on a broad range of
issues including technology development and transfer, and
transportation planning and regulation.

AMAR GUPTA is currently Principal Research Scientist at the
Massachusetts Institute of Technology, a position he assumed
after serving in the Indian government and in private firms
in India. Dr. Gupta is an engineer and computer scientist
by education and experience and has written numerous books
and articles on computers. His latest book is Insights into
Personal Computers, which was published in 1985 as part of
the centennial celebration of the Institute of Electrical
and Electronic Engineers.

DEBRA L. MILLER received her Ph.D. from Harvard University
and is Assistant Professor of Political Science at Barnard
College, Columbia University. Dr. Miller has authored
papers on science and technology transfer in Latin America.
She has served as a consultant to the U.S. Department of
State and is currently authoring a book on technology
transfer and international politics.

HENRY NAU is Professor of Political Science and
International Affairs and a faculty member of the Graduate
Program of Science, Technology and Public Policy, George
Washington University. Dr. Nau served as a senior staff
member of the National Security Council from 1981-83 and was
responsible for international economic issues including the
annual economic summits. He previously taught at Williams
College, Stanford University, and Columbia University. His

numerous writings focus on international political economy issues.

FRANCIS W. RUSHING is Chairman of the Department of Economics and Director, The International Center for Entrepreneurship, at Georgia State University and Senior Economic Consultant, Science Policy Program, International Policy Center, SRI International. Dr. Rushing has published comparative studies on scientific and technical manpower training and utilization in the Soviet Union and the Peoples' Republic of China. In addition, he has authored papers on technology transfer, international science policy, international trade, and competition in high technology.

CHI SCHIVE is Professor of Economics at the National Taiwan University. Dr. Schive served as Visiting Scholar at the Harvard-Yenching Institute, 1984-85. His publications on the Taiwan economy include such topics as direct foreign investment, technology transfer, technological change, foreign trade, and economic growth and development.

DENIS FRED SIMON is the Ford International Assistant Professor of Management at the Sloan School of Management, Massachusetts Institute of Technology. Dr. Simon has been a research analyst at the National Foreign Assessment Center and the East-West Center, and served as a consultant to the Office of Technology Assessment and the Subcommittee on Trade with China, United States Congress. Dr. Simon's publications focus on science and technology and economic development in the People's Republic of China and Taiwan.

JOHN ZYSMAN is Associate Professor of Political Science and co-director of the Berkeley Roundtable on the International Economy (BRIE) at the University of California, Berkeley. Dr. Zysman has published both books and articles on the role of government in shaping industrial development and trade in Japan, the United States, and France. Dr. Zysman has served as advisor and consultant to the President's Commission on Industrial Competitiveness, the U.S.-Japan Trade Advisory Commission and Board of Examiners, National Policy Review, OECD, Science and Technology Division.